Jesus - The Greatest Life in History:

a background to the Gospels

Jonathan Couper

GILEAD
B O O K S
PUBLISHING

www.GileadBooksPublishing.com

First published in Great Britain, September2018

2 4 6 8 10 9 7 5 3 1

Copyright © Jonathan Couper 2018

British Library Cataloguing-in-Publication Data:

A catalogue record for this book is available from the British Library.

ISBN: 978-1-9997224-7-0

Unless otherwise stated scripture quotations are from the New King James Version®. Copyright © 1982 by Thomas Nelson. Used by permission. All rights reserved.

The publisher makes every effort to ensure that the papers used in our books are made from trees that have been legally sourced from well-managed and credibly certified forests by using a printer awarded FSC & PEFC chain of custody certification.

Cover design: Jeremy Couper

Contents

Introduction   11

SECTION 1: The Birth of Jesus   **12**

Chapter 1
Background. The Roman Empire   13
Mary (Luke 1:26-38)   14
Gabriel (Luke 1:26ff)   15
Visit to Elizabeth in Judea (Luke 1:39-57)   17
The Conception of Jesus (Luke 1:41-35)   18

Chapter 2
Mary tells Joseph (Matthew 1:19-24)   20
Departure from Nazareth (Luke 2:1- 4)   22

Chapter 3
The journey to Bethlehem (Luke 2:4-7, Matthew 2:1)   26
The birth of Jesus and the shepherds (Luke 2:8-20)   29

Chapter 4
The immediate aftermath of Jesus' birth
(Luke 2:21-38; Matthew 2:1-12)   32
Herod the Great King of Israel (Matthew 2:18ff)   34
Wise men from the East (Matthew 2:1-12)   37

SECTION 2 Jesus' Growing Years
From Bethlehem to Nazareth (Matthew 1:14-23, Luke 2:30)   **42**

Chapter 5
Flight to Egypt (Matthew 1:14)   43

Chapter 6
Roman taxation under Caesar Augustus (Luke 2:1,2)   46
Herod's death   47
Archelaus (Matthew 2:22)   48

Chapter 7
Jesus returns to Nazareth   51

Chapter 8
Jesus aged 12 (Luke 2:40ff)   56

Chapter 9
Politics when Jesus was in his twenties   63
Pontius Pilate (Luke 3:1)   64

SECTION 3 The start of Jesus' ministry   **66**
Chapter 10   67

John the Baptist
(Matthew 3:1-12, Mark 1:1-8, Luke 3:1-17, John 1:6,19ff)   67
The Baptism of Jesus Autumn 30AD
(Matthew 3:13-17, Mark 1:9-11, Luke 3:21-22, John 1:28ff)   68

Chapter 11
Jesus meets John the Baptist   71

Chapter 12
The temptations November 30AD (Matthew 4:1-11 Luke 4:1-13)   74

Chapter 13
John the Baptist v The Royal Family
(Luke 3:19, Mark 6:17,18, John 3:23,24)   78

Chapter 14
The first of Jesus' disciples (John 1:35-51)   83

SECTION 4 Jesus' Pre-Galilee Ministry   **86**
Chapter 15
Cana December 30AD- first week of January 31AD (John 2:1-11)   87
Family visit to Capernaum (John 2:12)   89

Chapter 16
The Passover Wednesday April 25th 31AD Feast of Unleavened
bread 26th April – May 2nd 31AD (John 2:13)   91
Chapter 17
At the Jordan May 3rd (John 3:22-35)   99

Chapter 18
The move to Galilee May 31AD
(Matthew 4:12, Mark 1:14, Luke 4:14, John 4:1-3)   102
The woman of Samaria May 31AD (John 4:4-42)   102

SECTION 5 The start of Jesus' ministry in Galilee   **107**
Chapter 19
The nobleman's son June 31AD (John 4:43-54)   108
Nazareth June 31AD (Luke 4:16-30)   110

Chapter 20
The move to Capernaum June 31AD (Matthew 4:13, Luke 4:31)   114

SECTION 6 Jesus' Galilee Ministry from Capernaum   **118**
Introduction   119

Chapter 21
Calling of the first disciples June 31AD (Matthew 4:18-22)   121
Galilean Ministry June 31AD (Matthew 4:23)   124

Chapter 22
The First Teaching Gathering in Capernaum June 31AD

(Matthew 5:1-7:29)   127
The Sermon on the Mount June 31AD (Matthew 5-7)   128
Capernaum synagogue June 31AD (Mark 1:21)   129
Healing of Simon Peter's mother -in-law June 31AD
(Matthew 8:14, Mark 1:29-31 Luke 4:38ff)   132

Chapter 23
Wider Galilean Ministry June/July 31AD (Mark 1:39, Luke 4:44)   135

Chapter 24
The Second Teaching Gathering July 31AD (Luke 5:1-12)   139

Chapter 25
The healing of the leper 4 July 31AD
(Mark 1:39-40; Luke 5:12ff, Matthew 8:1)   142
Back in Capernaum (Mark 1:39-40; Luke 5:12ff, Matthew 8:1,4)   143

Chapter 26
Centurion's servant July 31AD (Matthew 8:5-13, Luke 7:2-10)   145

Chapter 27
Healing of the paralytic (Mark 2:1-13; Matthew 9:1- Luke 5:18ff)   147
Call of Matthew (Matthew 9: 9-13 Mark 2:14, Luke 5:27ff)   149

Chapter 28
The Third Teaching Gathering July 31AD (Luke 6:17-19, Mark 2:13)   151
The sermon on the plain July 31AD
(Luke 6:20-49 Mark 3:13 Matthew 10:1)   152
The twelve chosen July 31AD
(Mark 3:16-19, Luke 6:12-16, Matthew 10:2)   154

Chapter 29
Controversy with the Scribes and Pharisees July 31AD
(Mark 2:15, Matthew 9:1ff)   157
The fast of Tammuz July 26th 31AD (Mark 2:18-22)   158
More Controversy with the Scribes and Pharisees July 31AD
(Mark 2: 23, Matthew 9:1ff)   158

SECTION 7 Jesus' Galilee ministry from Gennesaret   **160**
Chapter 30
The healing of a man with a withered hand August 31AD
(Mark 3:1-6 , Luke 6:6-11)   161
Jesus withdrew to the sea from Capernaum August 31AD
(Matthew 13:1 Mark 3:7)   161

Chapter 31   **163**
Nain October 31AD (Luke 7:11-14)   164
John the Baptist sends disciples to find Jesus October 31AD
(Luke 7:17 Matthew 11)   165
Bethany October 31AD (Luke 7:36-50)   166

Chapter 32
Jesus in Jerusalem for the Festival of Tabernacles October 20th to
26th and the Eighth day 28th 31AD (John 5:1-45)   170

Chapter 33
The Fourth Teaching Gathering December/January 32AD
(Matthew 13:2; Mark 3:20)   173

Chapter 34
Opposition December 31AD (Mark 3:22, 31, Matthew 12:24ff)   175

Chapter 35
Fourth Gathering continued: Teaching at Sower's Cove
December 31AD (Matthew 13:1, Mark 4:1ff; Luke 8:1-22)   179

Chapter 36
The storm at sea January 32AD
(Matthew 8:23-24 Mark 4:39ff; Luke 8:22-25)   182

Chapter 37
Gadarene demoniac January 32AD
(Matthew 8:28-34; Mark 5:1-20 Luke 8:26ff)   184

Chapter 38
Fourth Gathering continued– Sending out of the 12 January 32AD
(Matthew 13:53; Mark 5:21)   190

Chapter 39
Raising of Jairus' daughter January 32AD
(Matthew 9:18ff, Mark 5:21ff Luke 8:41)   192

Chapter 40
2 Blind Men. January 32AD (Matthew 9:27)   195
Healing of someone with a mute spirit January 32AD
(Matthew 9:32)   196

SECTION 8 From the "Twelve" to the "Seventy"
Jesus preaching the Gospel of the Kingdom in cities and villages
around (Matthew 9:35, Mark 6:56)   198

Chapter 41
Jesus visits Nazareth, January 32AD (Mark 6:1-6 Matthew 13:54)   199
The 12 anointed and sent out (Matthew 10:1, Mark 6:7ff)   199

Chapter 42
Return of Twelve April 32AD (Luke 9:10)   203

Chapter 43
Herod executes John the Baptist Spring 32AD
(Matthew 14: 1-12 Mark 6: 16-29 Luke 9:9)   205

Chapter 44
Jesus to Bethsaida (Mathew 14:13ff)   209
Feeding of 5,000 April 32AD (John 6, Luke 9:10, Matthew 14:14-21)   210

Chapter 45
Jesus walking on water April 32AD
(Matthew 14: 24ff Mark 6:45-53, John 6:16-21)   214

Chapter 46
Jesus at Gennesaret and Capernaum April 32AD
(Matthew 14:34, Mark 6:53-56, John 6 :41ff)   218

Chapter 47
Controversy at Capernaum (with the Pharisees from Jerusalem)
April 32AD (Matthew 15:1, John 6)   221

Chapter 48
Jesus no longer goes openly to Jerusalem and Judea (John 7:1)
Based in Galilee (John 7:9)   224
Mission to Upper Galilee May 32AD   224

Chapter 49
Jesus meets a Syro-Phoenician woman June 32AD
(Matthew 15:21-29 Mark 7:25-30)   227

Chapter 50
Ministry in Decapolis June 32AD (Mark 7:31ff)   229
Decapolis healing of deaf and dumb July 32AD (Mark 7:31)   231
Feeding of 4000 July 32AD (Matthew 15:29ff Mark 8:1-9)   233

Chapter 51
Magdala July 32AD (Matthew 15:39 Mark 8:10)   235
Controversy in Magdala from The Pharisees and Sadducees
July 32AD (Matthew 16 :1-6; Mark 8:11)   236
Bethsaida healing of blind man July 32AD (Mark 8:22)   237

Chapter 52
Caesarea Philippi July 32AD (Matthew 16 Luke 9:18 Mark 8:27)   239
Transfiguration July 32AD (Luke 9:28 Matthew 17:1 Mark 9 1)   242
Healing of a demonized boy July 32AD (Luke 9:37)   244

Chapter 53
To Galilee Matthew 17:22 (see Matthew 19:1) August 32AD
(Mark 9:30)   248

Chapter 54
Jesus' family in Capernaum September 32AD
(Matthew 17:24-27)   251
Travel to Jerusalem for the Feast of Tabernacles October 32AD
(Luke 9)   252

Chapter 55

Jesus in Jerusalem for the Feast of Tabernacles
October 9-15 32AD (John 7:2ff)   257
Woman caught in adultery brought to Jesus
October 17th 32AD (John 8:1-12)   261

Chapter 56

The Sending out of the "Seventy"
(Luke 10:1-24 [72 Luke 10:1NU text])   267
Feast of Hanukkah December Thursday 17-24 32AD
(John 10:22-40)   269
Return of the "Seventy" December 32AD (Luke 10:17-22)   271

SECTION 9 Jesus' itinerant ministry to all Israel   **272**
Chapter 57

Jesus Ministry to the rest of Israel January 33AD
(Luke 10:38-18:43)   273
Bethany (Luke 10:38-42)   273
From the Judean Hills to the west coast January 33AD   274
From the west coast to the south January 33AD   276
Judea February 33AD (Luke 12)   279
Woman healed in synagogue February 33AD (Luke 13:10ff)   281
Perea February 33AD Luke 13:23ff (see Luke 13:31)   281

Chapter 58

The Gathering East of the Jordan river February 33AD
(Matthew 19:1,2; Mark 10:1, Luke 16:18)   283
Ephraim February 33AD (John 11:53)   289
Samaria March 33AD   290
Healing of 10 lepers March 33AD (Luke 17:12)   290
Rich Young Ruler March 33AD
(Matthew 19:16ff Mark 10:17 Luke 18:18-30)   291

SECTION 10 The final journey to the cross   **292**
Chapter 59

Jesus foretells his death March 33AD
(Luke 18:31, Mark 10:32-34, Matthew 20:17-19)   293
James and John make a bid for leadership recognition
(Mark 10:32-45)   293
Bartimaeus March 33AD (Luke 18 :35-43)   294
Zacchaeus March 33AD (Luke 19:1-10)   296

Chapter 60

The onward journey to Jerusalem March 33AD   298
Palm Sunday (Mark 11; Matthew 21:1-11; John 12:1)   298

Chapter 61

Return to Bethany—Sunday

(John 12:1ff Mark 11:11, Matthew 26:2, Mark 14:3-11) 301
Return to Jerusalem—Monday
(Mark 11:11, Matthew21:12-14, John 12:12) 303

Chapter 62
Teaching in the temple
(Luke 20:1-38, Matthew 21:23-26:3, Mark 12:1-44) 307

Chapter 63
The Betrayal begins—Wednesday
(Matthew 26:2 Mark 14:3-11, John 12:2-11) 313
The Last Supper—Thursday (The first day of Unleavened Bread
6pm Thursday until 6pm Friday) (Luke 22:1-39) 316

Chapter 64
The arrest of Jesus Thursday (Luke 22:39-53) 318
Trial before the chief priests Friday (Mark 14: 53-15:20
John 18-19:13 Luke 22:1-23:25, Matthew 27:1-31) 320

Chapter 65
The end of Judas—Friday (Matthew 27:3-10) 326
The trial before Pilate Friday April 3rd (John 18:28-9:16;
Matthew 27:11-31; Mark 15:2-20; Luke 23:1-25) 327

SECTION 11 The death and Resurrection of Jesus
Chapter 66
Crucifixion—Friday April 3rd (Matthew 27: 33-50
Mark 15:21-41 John 19:23-30 Luke 23:32-48) 334

Chapter 67
Jesus' body taken down from the cross (Matthew27:57-61) 340

Chapter 68
The Resurrection of Jesus Sunday April 5th 33AD
(Matthew 28, Mark 16, Luke 24, John 20) 343
Magdala (John 21:1ff) 347

Chapter 69
Meeting in Galilee at Mount Tabor 350
The Ascension 350

Appendix 352
Bibliography 360

"He has done excellent things;
This is known in all the earth"

Isaiah 12:5

"We have beheld His glory, the glory as of the only
begotten of the Father, full of grace and truth"

John 1:14

Introduction

The life of Jesus is the most important there has ever been. Details of the events surrounding Jesus are written by two of his disciples who shared the journey with him – Matthew and John. These accounts are supplemented by the gospel of Mark, who was a young man growing up in Jerusalem at the time of Jesus and the gospel of Luke who wrote down the first-hand accounts he heard. These gospels in the New Testament are our primary source of information. This book also draws from the writings of Josephus – a Jew born in 37AD as well as recent archaeological finds to add detail and clarity. The events in Jesus' life have been pieced together to provide a 3D view of the gospels brought together in one coherent narrative.

I hope that you, the reader, will enjoy reading the life of Jesus, and that this book will provide a useful contribution to understanding something more about the greatest life in history.

I wish to thank Chris Hayes for his work to get the book ready for publishing, Jeremy Couper for the cover design, and Anne Couper for her helpful suggestions which helped in the formation of this book.

Jonathan

SECTION 1

The Birth of Jesus

Chapter 1

Background. The Roman Empire

History has within it the rise and fall of empires. Like the waves of the sea, empires rise and then fall, but the purpose of God continues as time unfolds. Over fifty years before Jesus was born, before Rome was an empire, Pompey, an important Roman general annexed Judea into Roman rule. The rise of Pompey in the east followed by Julius Caesar in the west brought Roman military might to most parts of the known world and provided the means through which the Roman republic would emerge as an empire. By the time Jesus was born, Pompey had died, and Julius Caesar had been assassinated. The Roman Emperor Augustus Caesar succeeded them, coming to power in 27BC He increased Rome's power and authority throughout the known world. He built major military roads to increase the speed and capability of the army to reach every part of the empire. He changed military base camps into cities like Rome establishing places of influence to promote her influence and authority. Even in Israel where Jews fiercely opposed pagan cultures and values, cities were built affirming the Graeco Roman values and although Augustus respected the Jewish religious sensibilities to keep Roman influence on a minimum in Israel, there was a military garrison in Jerusalem and Rome exercised its power and authority everywhere in Israel.

The stability the Roman empire gave benefited ordinary life. Rome did not interfere too much if its rule was not questioned, and trade was able to flow. The development of the Roman empire required money. Augustus was a successful general, a keen strategist and the adopted son of Julius Caesar; but his biological father was a banker. This gave Augustus a thorough working knowledge of the legal structure of Rome. He reformed the tax system of Rome introducing extra taxes to pay for military rule and the extension of Roman culture in all the empire. After successfully reforming the taxes in Rome, he delayed introducing new taxation rules to the rest of the empire until he was strong enough throughout his realms. By the time that Jesus was born, Augustus had ruled over twenty years. Just before Jesus was born he decided to start the preliminary moves towards introducing the taxation system on the whole empire. (Luke 2:1,2).[1] He decided to initiate an audit, so that he could get an accurate figure of tax revenue. This audit required people to register the lands on which Caesar's tax would be based.

Mary (Luke 1:26-38)

Far away, 70 miles north of Jerusalem was a village in the mountainous terrain of central Lower Galilee called Nazareth. One of the girls growing up in that village would become famous throughout the world. Her name was Mary daughter of Eli[2] Her family had lived in Galilee ever since they had moved from Judea a generation or so before her birth.[3] (Luke 1:36,39)

Mary's older sister of only one year or so [4]had recently married a local businessman in Capernaum, and Mary was looking forward to the day when she too would be married and have a home and family of her own. Mary was betrothed to be married to a builder from Bethlehem called Joseph. He was a craftsman – travelling to different towns

---

[1] For more information about the census see the appendix

[2] The genealogy of Jesus' line in Matthew 1 is of Joseph. The one in Luke 3 differs from this though Joseph is still at the end of it. The reason proposed by Ironside in 1930 is that Joseph is the son in law of Heli (Eli) the father of Mary – it being unusual for a woman's name to appear.

[3] Pompey encouraged those from Judea to move to Galilee and many thousands did. Since then Galilee had become an ordered place with farms and agriculture replacing thorns and briers.

[4] Salome the sister of Mary the mother of Jesus married Zebedee and had two children James and John. It is likely that Jesus was of a similar age to them – possibly James slightly older and John slightly younger than Jesus. Salome is the sister of Mary (compare John 19:25 with Matthew 27:56 and with Mark 16:1 – [note Mary mother of James and/or mother of Joses refers to Jesus' mother -Mark6:6])

wherever work took him. In recent years he had been working in the nearby town of Sepphoris and its immediate area. He knew the family and had asked Eli if he could marry his daughter. They had agreed and so in a formal ceremony and celebration Joseph and Mary had been betrothed. There was the usual time lapse between betrothal and the wedding day. Joseph was in his early twenties, but Mary was still young, and Joseph needed time to get everything ready, after which he would come to the family home amidst week long wedding celebrations to take Mary as his wife to his home in Bethlehem. Joseph had lived away from his home to earn a living for some time. He was used to building sites and was good at his job.

Gabriel (Luke 1:26ff)

In the winter of 7BC God sent a messenger – an angel – to her. In fact, this was no ordinary angel. As the archangel, he was a prince amongst angels sharing the same status in creation as Michael or Lucifer. This archangel's name was Gabriel. Four hundred years before he had talked with Daniel (Daniel 8:16). His power and standing in the heavenlies lay in his unique position of being able to stand and operate in the close intense glorious presence of God (Luke 1:19). Because of this, he exercised great authority. Gabriel although an angel had the form of a man (Daniel 8:15; 9:21) and it was as a man that Mary first met him. He came into the courtyard of her home. Workers with the family would often come into the courtyard during the day to pick things up or to drink the water from the pots that Mary or one of the others had filled earlier in the day and which were always there. She as a young girl did not know the business of grown men in the village and so never questioned any who came. She rarely had any conversation with them. Mary was engaged with her usual domestic tasks – tasks which had grown as she had grown. She had from her earliest years she could remember, been involved in some tasks around the home, and this day was no different to any other normal day. She was on her own as

Gabriel turned towards her and started to speak to her. She did not even notice he was there until he spoke (Luke 1:29a). She looked up. Seeing him there did not disturb her. There was nothing unusual about his appearance. it was what he said that troubled her (Luke 1:28,29). He addressed her as "highly favoured","the Lord is with you" and "Blessed are you amongst women". This man was stating with authority words which said she had specific favour in her relationship with God as a human being and favour in her relationship with mankind as a woman. Mary did not understand why he should say such a thing "out of the blue" and anxiety filled her heart as she wondered what his motive might be or what news there was to follow.

Her mind was soon put at rest when the "man" started to explain the nature of the favour from God. "Behold you will conceive in your womb and bring forth a son and shall call his name Jesus. He will be great and will be called the Son of the Highest; and the Lord God will give him the throne of his father David. And he will reign over the house of Jacob forever and of His kingdom there will be no end." Mary's reply questioned not the content of what she was hearing but the how it can happen "Since I do not know a man" Luke 1:34. Gabriel explained the conception would be through the Holy Spirit overshadowing her. He continued "God can do this" and then as a sign that what he said was true, he gave her the news that Elizabeth, one of her close relatives she knew who lived in Judea. Mary also knew she had not been able to have children and that she was of an age where it was unlikely. The angel told her that she who was past child bearing was now six months pregnant – news which had been kept hidden by Elizabeth and Zechariah from everyone and which therefore the family far off in Galilee had not heard.

Visit to Elizabeth in Judea (Luke 1:39-57)

When Gabriel went, Mary determined to make the trip to Judea to find out for herself. She went indoors and started to discuss her visit to Elizabeth with her parents. Eventually they gave her consent to go and made arrangements for her to visit Elizabeth. She as a woman – especially a young woman- would never travel alone. Some from Nazareth were going for the Feast of Dedication that year which ran from December 16th to 23rd was approaching[5]. So, Mary set off early on Sunday 12th December[6] with the family as they made their journey to Jerusalem.

On Tuesday afternoon 15th December Mary arrived at the village outside Jerusalem where Elizabeth lived. It was about the middle of the day when she said goodbye to her relatives, so they could go on to Jerusalem. Sunset was at 4:30pm and they had five miles to go to complete their journey.

Mary was in the hill country of Judah not far from west Jerusalem in a village called En Kerem.[7] She walked up the steep dirt tracks past olive groves and narrow terraced fields towards where her Elizabeth lived. There was nothing distinctive about the house. It was like the others.

---

[5] Elizabeth had conceived in June/ July. Zechariah, the husband of Elizabeth first heard about the future conception of his son from Gabriel when in the temple during his priestly duty there. Zechariah is of the division of Abijah (Luke 1:5) which meant he and his team performed their priestly duties eighth on the rota.(I Chronicles 24:1-7) in a year divided into 24 – so each duty lasted 2 weeks. His duty was thus 16 weeks from the beginning of the year (Nisan) and his meeting with Gabriel in the month of Tammuz (June July). John the Baptist conceived in July. December was her sixth month of pregnancy. Luke 1:36

[6] The journey to Jerusalem could take anything from three days to five days. Setting off as soon after the Sabbath would be the best. Sunday December 12th would allow the pilgrims travelling with Mary to get to Hanukkah which started in 7BC on Thursday 16th December (see Appendix re dates)

[7] The traditional birthplace of John the Baptist. There are 5 churches and monasteries built in the village because of this.

The Conception of Jesus (Luke 1:41-35)

As soon as she went through the front door, Mary called out to say she had arrived as she had done when a little girl. Elizabeth heard her and recognized the voice. Surprise to them both was that almost immediately Elizabeth prophesied. At the sound of Mary's voice her baby moved in the womb and Elizabeth was filled with the Holy Spirit. Mary entered the room to find Elizabeth sitting down obviously pregnant. She was alone as usual at this time of day. Zachariah her husband was out. All was so normal yet in the midst of that God was speaking. Before Elizabeth knew anything in the natural in response to the inspiration of God within her, she talked about the fruit of Mary's womb and how she was the "mother of my Lord". Later her child would be known as someone who was filled with the spirit from the womb. It was on this very day that it happened. All this took a few seconds, and there was a contagious effect on Mary. For her as she heard the prophetic words of Elizabeth she began to experience the overshadowing of the Holy Spirit prophesied by Gabriel as the way she would conceive Jesus in the womb. God came on her as the Spirit of God had come on mighty men and women in the old testament before her changing their lives and destinies. Now in this humble house, the Holy Spirit was overshadowing Mary and starting the unique moment in history where God became man. From this day Jesus started his journey of formation in the womb. Mary now began a hymn of praise. "Magnificat" expanded some of the revelation she had already received from Gabriel, but there was fresh revelation within its hymn-like words. There was no doubting that God was there in this meeting between them.

Far away in the east, Magi from the ancient civilizations of Persia and Babylon noticed the conjunctions between Saturn Jupiter and Venus that had been occurring on a regular basis since April that year (7 BC[8]). It occurred three times – an event that happens every 800 years. The wise men who had been watching them decided to travel to Judea as the conjunctions had been in the segment of the sky which indicated to them it was Israel. They set off in 6BC to meet the new king. They would arrive in Jerusalem two years after their first sight of the star at the end of 5BC

---

[8] See footnote 9 on page 20

Chapter 2

Mary tells Joseph (Matthew 1:19-24)

Mary stayed for three months with Elizabeth until the child was born helping wherever she could. In March 6 BC the child (John the Baptist) was born. And after the Passover[9] on Sunday April 11th (as April 10th that year was a Sabbath day) a few weeks after the birth Mary began the journey back to Nazareth. [10] During her stay in Judea, her body was already experiencing the changes of early pregnancy. Mary arrived back to Nazareth before the Sabbath at the end of April, and she knew her condition and the conversation she would need to have with her betrothed.

Joseph (not surprisingly) was bewildered to find out Mary was pregnant and whilst he calmly listened to her account, he did not believe the story she told. Joseph had not been there when Gabriel first came and now her delay in coming back from Judea was making sense. She must have met someone. Ne reasoned there was no on-going relationship, or she would not have returned home. He concluded she was taken advantage of – after all she is young. But he also knew this put their relationship in jeopardy. He as an upstanding Jew could not marry an immoral woman. He knew he would have to divorce Mary. It was the only way to break the betrothal. Such things he decided quickly. What troubled him was how to do this in such a way it was done quietly, to minimize any further problems for Mary. Such was his dilemma as he lay down to sleep that night He was in turmoil. He did

---

[9] Passover that year was April 2nd followed by feast of unleavened bread 3-9th

[10] Mary must have travelled at one major Jewish festival and then probably returned with other members of the family at another festival 3 months later. If this is the case, she either came in September when the feast of tabernacles was held and returned in December after Hanukkah or arrived in December for Hanukkah and went back with the family returning from the Passover.

not want to make matters worse for Mary by publicly breaking the betrothal. He had decided to make clear the ending of the betrothal to the family (who knew already she was pregnant) and quietly leave Nazareth behind. The locals would not be concerned about Joseph's absence at first because he was always away on building jobs. By the time they discovered he was not coming back, Mary and the family could have sorted out their life. The child after all was not his.

This was the problem of resolution that filled his thoughts as he went to sleep. Then Joseph had a dream in which God gave him revelation as to why the child was to be called Jesus. Mary had told him the conversation with Gabriel so the name of the child being Jesus was no surprise news, but angel in the dream said, "You shall call his name Jesus for he will save His people from their sins" (Matthew 1:21). This was a pun from God. Jesus was a common name - the Greek form of the Hebrew name Joshua – but its Hebrew meaning was "God saves". The name suddenly made sense and the penny dropped for Joseph. He recognized God was in this it when he saw the meaning behind the name. Moreover, In the dream God gave Joseph the role to name the child as a father should. Joseph got up and went to see Mary and the family. He suggested that instead of waiting to get married as they had originally planned, they should get married immediately. The house was not yet built in Bethlehem and Mary would value the support of her family through her pregnancy. This seemed the sensible thing to do, and to Mary's relief all agreed.

Joseph's suggestion was the best way forward for all, but it meant that amongst those who knew Jesus was conceived out of wedlock, it would look like Joseph was the father who was now trying to do the right thing after immorality. From now on both Joseph and Mary (as well as Jesus) would bear the stigma of this. Even when Jesus was in his thirties what he said would be despised because it was known he was conceived out of wedlock (John 8:41). The months that followed were not comfortable for either Joseph or Mary. The marriage did not remove the disgrace from the family of pregnancy outside wedlock, and there were days when this was especially difficult for Mary and family. For the time being Mary had to stay in Nazareth. This made the pregnancy of Mary become public knowledge in the village. The family had hoped that the job Joseph had would have given adequate reason for Mary still staying at home, but they could not disguise her pregnancy and for a while she was a celebrity for all the wrong reasons.

Never before (or since) has a virgin conceived. This unique fact of history was God entering the world and the Word becoming flesh: 1 Timothy 1:15 John 1:14. It was no mean feat that both Joseph and Mary were able to adjust to such a unique event. Joseph married Mary, but they had no sexual intercourse until after the birth of Jesus (Matthew 1:25). Only they knew that – to everyone else they were a married couple. Joseph continued to be away from Nazareth for periods of time. He was a builder[11] and would go where the jobs took him. Joseph was from Bethlehem and intended to take Mary back to his home town -the important final stage marking their marriage. Normal procedure was for Joseph to take Mary to his home, but events had overtaken him. The house he planned to build was still not built. He was earning the money he needed so he could start to build. He knew once he had the money to buy what he needed, with his skill building the house it would take just weeks. With regards to building there was nothing he could not do.

Departure from Nazareth (Luke 2:1- 4)

Mary was still young and in the early months of pregnancy needed the support and help of her family, so Joseph continued to stay at Mary's home in a room set aside for them. They planned to move to Bethlehem

[11] Matthew 13:55, Mark 6:3 the word translated "carpenter" is more accurately "builder". The word means a person who had mastered his trade – the English word architect is from this same Greek word. He was a skilled craftsman both as a carpenter and as a builder

after the child was born by which time Joseph would have accumulated enough money to build a house on family land he owned This plan was unexpectedly brought forward because of a decree by Augustus Caesar who required Joseph to register in Bethlehem. The same taxation rules of Rome were now to be applied to all regions of the empire, even though it strengthened the narrative to these foreign countries of their subjugation by Rome. Judea with its strong religious identity was one of the most potential hotspots for revolt. Whilst the people were content with Roman rule, it was only a pragmatic acceptance. Underneath amongst much of the population there was adherence to obey God and any proposal to introduce a tax to Caesar risked playing into the hands of the religious extremists who wanted to rebel against Rome. Augustus Caesar did not want to have any trouble, but he also could not make an exception. Tax revenue should come to him from every part of the empire. Unknown to Caesar, this policy was to be the vehicle by which the old testament prophecies about the birth of the Messiah in Bethlehem – the city where David the first king had come from – would be fulfilled.

Bethlehem was the town where Joseph was from, and so as a necessary preliminary to obtain the information necessary to assess an area for tax (Luke 2:1), he was required to register there (Luke 2:4,5). Joseph had some family land and business interests in the city, so he had to register these in case someone else claimed them.

Augustus' fears of negative reactions to his tax proposals were soon realized. In Acts 5:37 Gamaliel states how at the time of this census Judas the Galilean arose against the Romans. The census stirred up a rebellion led by Judas a Galilean which dragged on for over ten years. The city of Sepphoris – a city near Nazareth - was at the rebellion's core, and so was burnt down by the Romans in 4BC after the death of Herod the Great, and its population sold into slavery. Despite this, pockets of rebellion still existed in the land. After his death, Herod's successor

23

Archelaus failed to process the introduction of the taxes or deal finally with the rebellion. Josephus states Judas the Galilean was only finally defeated by the Romans in 6a. d after Archelaus had been exiled. From that year Judea became a sub province of the Roman military province of Syria with its capital in Antioch. However, during Jesus' lifetime Israel was still definitely Jewish with a minimal Roman interference in Jewish culture or way of life.

Joseph set off with his pregnant wife for Bethlehem without a celebration or good wishes of the local community. Their "wedding" had been less than six months before. Joseph and Mary did not take long to get ready. Mary had little beyond what she stood up in. In one of the bags were some cooking vessels, cups, oil lamps and plenty of oil in jars sealed around the top with wax. They were all strapped on a donkey together with Joseph's precious carpenter tools and a few other useful odds and ends. Mary's family provided plenty of food for the journey with wine, oil and yeast – a sort of starter pack for newly married life. Mary's family bid farewell to her. No-one knew whether they would meet again, but any emotion felt was contained. They all had a job to do and they watched as Mary departed out of the village from where they descended the steep hills towards the level fields of the Jezreel valley below and then the dome shaped Tabor mountain which pointed the way to the Jordan. As they went Mary was aware of the difference between the reality of their leaving and the hope a year before that she had had of their marriage send-off back to Bethlehem. They both knew the subdued departure was because of Mary's pregnancy, but Mary had no regrets. God had a plan and they had plenty of other things to fill their thoughts. Joseph intended to work as a carpenter and builder in Bethlehem. He would build the house and look for a job. They both knew this was the time to go. He had to register in his home town where his family had always owned land, and

Bethlehem was where he had always intended to live. It all seemed clear enough.

Chapter 3

The journey to Bethlehem (Luke 2:4-7, Matthew 2:1)

It was nearly nine months since Mary had gone southwards in December to see Elizabeth. It was late summer. The weather was now being better than it had been then.

At the beginning of September, the daytime temperature was a welcome 70F degrees during the day – (a few weeks before it had been in the eighties)- and a pleasant 61 degrees Fahrenheit at night with no likelihood of rain, so the journey was going to be as good as it could be. The route was a familiar one to her. Throughout her life she had travelled with her family this way to Jerusalem. This time it would take them about a week to get to Bethlehem. (It was not far short of one hundred miles), and a Sabbath day on the journey would mean they would lose a day travelling. The roads were less busy than the times before when she had travelled, and so they anticipated the journey would be fine. It was some weeks before the crowds would go up to Jerusalem for the Feast of Tabernacles at the end of September (September 27- October 3rd)

Joseph and Mary soon left the Galilean hills far behind as they descended into the Jordan rift valley. Here they went through rural villages, olive fields and en route there were plenty of hospitable people to help them as they went towards Jerusalem. Nazareth was on the same range of hills as Jerusalem and Bethlehem, but any direct route over the mountains through Samaria though less miles could take longer and be more dangerous. They made steady progress turning westwards through Jericho before ascending through the dry desert hills towards Jerusalem. Last time Mary had been the hills around Jerusalem had been green, but now in the heat of summer they appeared yellow and dry.

When they got to Jerusalem, they went five miles south of Jerusalem on the road as it climbed up into the southern part of the Judean hills. Bethlehem was set on top of a high limestone cliff. As they approached the town they were nearly 100 feet higher than when they had set out from Jerusalem.

Joseph was now back in his home town after some years of absence. Jacob his father was dead otherwise he would have been the one to do this as the head of the family. Joseph had to register the family lands. Like others from Bethlehem he had relatives there, but none of them especially close. Joseph and Mary arrived unnoticed in the crowd. Bethlehem though relatively small in size, was a major town in Judea, and not far away the King had built his palace on an imposing hill he had created from a mound, and so the royal entourage would come into town periodically on their way from Jerusalem.

Many of its residents were returning to their home town because of Caesar's census registration as Joseph was. Work opportunities in Bethlehem were limited so many had moved away for work.,

It was not long before Joseph realized there was nowhere to stay in the town. Any relatives he knew had no room. Houses were small and families large, and those that might have had space already had other relatives staying with them. Joseph's absence whilst in Galilee meant he may have not been completely unknown, but less of a priority than others. Time and again their request for hospitality was turned down. No-one said anything, but Joseph suspected that others had an interest in the land for which Joseph had come to register[12]. There would be no dispute over the land for he had the right to put his name to it, but there was equally no-one willing to go the extra mile and welcome him and his wife into their home.

[12] The census was on ownership of assets (see appendix)

If they had only had more time to plan but they could not. Caesar's decree had changed all that. The birth of their son would now be without the support of her family, and it looked like also without the support from any of Joseph's family as well. There was much to concern them, but there was also an unflappable strength to both Joseph and Mary. They began to try to stay in guest houses. These were always less desirable places to stay. Most Jews stayed with other Jews as family, but when occasions demanded it, they also used more public places. Workman from afar had come to build the Solomon's pools above Bethlehem as part of the aqueduct complex which carried water from the hills of Hebron far to the south of Bethlehem right into the temple at Jerusalem. Others had come to help build the palace and associated buildings. The main workforce was not local as many of these "high Tec" projects relied on specialist labour. There was income for those who were willing to open their homes for guests.[13] Many had done so, but even these were full. There was nowhere in the whole town to stay.

Joseph had no wish to sleep out in the streets. He would have done so as a single man, but he had a pregnant wife to consider as well as the money he had brought with him to develop the new life they planned in Bethlehem. Sleeping on the streets was not an option. They kept walking through the town towards the south. When they were at the edge of the town they did find someone, who had room for the donkey though not for them.[14] Joseph in desperation asked him if he was willing to make the stable available for them too. He agreed. He took their rent for the donkey plus what had been agreed and showed them one of the stables used to keep the animals. He explained that no-one was using

---

[13] strangers could find hospitality in first century Israel as is referenced in the parable of the Good Samaritan (Luke 10:25-37)
[14] Luke 2:7 implies the stable was linked to the inn where there was no room. The Inn was a place to stay if you had no-one to stay with. It was a similar business to the inn mentioned at the end of the Good Samaritan parable.

that stable on that night so provided they did not mind the cold and rather primitive conditions, as they were willing to pay the asking price for the night, they were welcome. Mary and Joseph took their donkey into the stable. It was a cave in the cliff though used for animals could have been long ago someone's dwelling. As they entered although away from the entrance it was pitch black, it was a safe and a welcome place to sleep. Joseph got out the oil lamps from the saddle bags as well as the oil. He lit one whilst there was sufficient light outside to do so and placed it in the cave. Mary sat and looked around the walls of the stable by the light cast from the oil as it burnt while Joseph fed and watered the donkey. They then put the light out and lay down on the straw near the entrance, grateful for a roof over their head and a chance to sleep away from the dark streets of the town with any dangers that might lurk there.[15]

The birth of Jesus and the shepherds (Luke 2:8-20)

Joseph and Mary both fell asleep quickly, weary from their journey. It was, however only a few hours later that Mary awoke – her waters had broken. She told Joseph, who was quick to stir. He relit the oil lamps and started a fire just outside the entrance for heat and to heat water if necessary. The baby was on its way. Both Mary and Joseph had known the baby would arrive soon, but they had hoped the arrival of Jesus would be once they had got everything ready. Now they had to respond. The pains of labour had started. These continued into the night until the baby was safely born. By the light of the lamps Mary cradled the child.

[15] Justin said (in his Dialogue with Trypho Ch. 70 written 2nd century AD quoted by later sources) Jesus was born in a cave just outside Bethlehem (now the site of the church of the Holy nativity). Because he linked it to prophecy in Isaiah (33:16), many dispute this as historical fact. I take the opposite view. Why should Justin attach an obscure reference to a cave in Isaiah which is otherwise not directly linked to Messiah prophecy passages if the cave was untrue. Jerome in 4th century cast doubt on Jesus born in the cave as it was before Constantine a religious site for pagan worship. But at the end of the first century after the Jewish revolt many Christian sites were paganised alongside Jewish ones (e.g. temple site in Jerusalem became temple to Jupiter).

Following the usual practice of the day Mary & Joseph wrapped the new born child in swaddling clothes. On that night it was essential for the baby to be kept warm and for Mary to sleep. Joseph placed him into the manger he had first packed with fresh straw.

Just outside Bethlehem shepherds were guarding their sheep as they did each night preventing any thefts in the night hours by man or beast. They lived out on the open hillside with the sheep (Luke 2:8). As usual at the end of each summer, grass (and water) were in short supply and so they were grazing nearer the town than usual. This increased the risk of theft, so they were even more vigilant. The sheep they watched over were prime sheep- some destined for sacrifice in Jerusalem belonging to the High Priest – and these were especially attractive to thieves, and in the darkness, they could get close.

Suddenly without warning a light pierced the pitch black of the night. When they saw the cause was an angel, these bold guardians of sheep became afraid. The angel said "Do not be afraid. I bring you good news which brings joy not fear. In Bethlehem which is the city of David the Saviour, the Christ (the prophesied descendant of King David) has been born. A sign this is true is you will find a baby wrapped in swaddling clothes and lying in a manger". The encounter with the angel brought them into another realm where they saw the angel was not on his own. They now saw the angelic choir and they could hear them singing "Glory to God in the highest and peace on earth to those under the favour of God".

The light and angels disappeared as quickly as they had appeared. The shepherds had all seen the angels and discussed together what they had heard. They decided that there was no harm on trying to find the baby – to see if in one of the stables where there was a manger there just happened to be a baby. After all the angel had said they should go and see for it was a sign for them. They went towards the town not knowing where to start to find the baby. As they got nearer the dark streets of the town, they could see a light shining from a cave nearby. There were a few lights amongst the houses but none normally in what was unoccupied except for animals currently of night. The shepherd s decided to start there, so they moved towards that part of Bethlehem and soon found themselves entering the stable where Jesus had been born.

The light was still burning, and Mary and Joseph were wide awake when the shepherds arrived outside the entrance to the cave. A combination of concern and interest flickered in their eyes as the strangers entered by the wooden gate which was keeping any cold night breezes at bay and made their way into the cave without difficulty. The shepherds looked at the manger and saw the baby as the angels had said, and then in their manner spoke explanatory words to Joseph and Mary who were wondering what the reasons were behind this unexpected intrusion. They had already been through a lot that evening but were amazed at the shepherds' story about the angels' message and song. Mary listened very carefully – she would remember these words throughout her life although she did not fully understand them. For now, she was glad when the shepherds left to return to their work in the fields, so she could sleep until the dawn. It would not be long before Jesus would awake and cry to be fed and she needed to be ready.

Chapter 4

The immediate aftermath of Jesus' birth
(Luke 2: 21-38; Matthew 2:1-12)

Prophecies of Jesus had been written centuries before, but God only knew the plan that was emerging. Satan – the fallen archangel who sought to rule through manipulation amongst the affairs of men – knew nothing of the birth of Jesus until to his horror wise men came into the royal court. Herod was still well enough to carry on his life as usual, so He was in Jerusalem where the wise men would find him. (A future permanent move because of illness from Jerusalem to the cooler fragrant air of Jericho and to death was beyond the horizon currently). The foreigners came with the news of why they had taken two years out of their lives. "Where is he who is born King of the Jews". Far beyond the eastern desert where they lived, they had noticed the message in the stars of a king being born in Israel, and they came to acknowledge him and honour the child as the future king. (Matthew 2:2) Demons linked to King Herod and to those in Herod's court were quick to relay the news they dreaded to Satan their evil master: namely that the Messiah – the saviour of mankind was now on the earth. The immediate result would be the death of innocent children in the vain attempt by King Herod to prevent a rival "King of the Jews".

Before all this occurred, Jesus was circumcised in accord with Jewish custom a week after his birth (Luke 2:21) whilst still in Bethlehem - though by this time they had found somewhere more suitable than a stable to live. They now lived in a house. It would be here that the wise men would come (Matthew 2:11), but at this time the wise men were still many miles away travelling towards Jerusalem to search for the Messiah in the royal court.

A month later Mary & Joseph went up to Jerusalem (Luke 2:22) with their new born child. This was a short visit to the temple in Jerusalem and Joseph and Mary took it in turns to carry Jesus as they walked the five-mile journey from Bethlehem. There was nothing unusual about his. It was the custom to present a firstborn male in the temple. They offered the prescribed sacrificial offering of those who were too poor to buy a lamb for the occasion, so they bought two turtle doves as demanded by the law. (Leviticus 12:4; 8). They had very little money. (The wise men had not yet come with their expensive valuable gifts). Joseph was a builder by trade and income was sporadic and could be low. He was getting a house ready in Bethlehem which required any extra money he might have.

Whilst Herod, his court and the demonic realm in general were not yet aware of the birth of the king of the Jews, there were two people who knew. They listened to God every day and as a result recognised the significance of Jesus' first arrival in the temple. One was Anna, a lady of prayer who tended to be in the temple most of the time. She was old and had had a difficult life losing her husband after only seven years of marriage. The other was a devout man – Simeon by name- who came into the temple at the prompting of God to arrive in time to see Joseph and Mary as they brought Jesus into the temple. Both Anna and Simeon independently acknowledged the special nature and task of Jesus. Jesus was known to God and His servants but unknown yet to his enemies.

Mary and Joseph returned to Bethlehem where they intended to settle.[16] Joseph had already made great strides with the house and his skills as a builder were in demand in the community. There had been

---

[16] When Joseph and Mary return from Egypt they expect to live in Bethlehem (not Nazareth). (see Matthew 2:21,22) It is only because Archelaus being the ruler that persuades them instead to go to Mary's home town, Nazareth in Galilee outside Archelaus' jurisdiction

major building 3 miles south of Bethlehem called Herodium, a fortress and palace completed by Herod under 10 years before. Building was still needed in the area. Life in Bethlehem became for Mary Joseph and Jesus the norm. At this time mother bonded with child and child with mother. It was a time of calm before the storm.

Herod the Great King of Israel (Matthew 2:18ff)

Jesus was born towards the end of the long reign of Herod the Great. He had become king of Judea in 37 BC at the age of 36. He had managed to deftly move from alliance with the defeated Mark Anthony to the victorious Octavian who had kept him as the vassal king of Israel. Herod's appointment as king was an astute move by Octavian – now called Caesar Augustus. Ever since Judea had been subjugated by the Roman general Pompey in 63 AD it had been a mixed blessing for Rome. Augustus recognized that it was better for Rome to exercise power through an alliance rather than make Israel part of the Roman province of Syria, because Rome would be less prone to get immersed in the religious politics of the region and be thus more able to achieve its economic and expansive objectives for the eastern empire. Augustus knew that if the strong religious convictions within the state in its leaders and people could be pacified, the stabilizing of the whole region was possible.

By the time Jesus was born, the early years of Herod's reign was over a generation away. He was now in his sixties, with many wives and children. His first wife Doris he put aside with their young son Antipater to marry in 37 BC an Hasmonean princess Mariamne of royal descent to match his new status as King. Herod loved her with a passion – only matched by the anger Mariamne had towards him after his deliberate assassination of her popular brother to secure his authority. They had amongst other children, Alexander and Aristobulus (who became the father of Herodias). These two sons rather than Antipater were regarded as the successors of Herod[17]. His next wife of note was another Mariamne. She was the daughter of the leading high priestly family of Simon Boethus. Herod hoped by an alliance with the high priest to increase his influence. Herod married her in 29BC and they had a son named Philip. He was also called Herod to show his legitimacy as king. (This is the Philip who first married Herodias). The following year (28BC) after marrying Marianne 11 he took another wife – a Samaritan woman called Malthrace and she bore three children Antipas, Archelaus, and Olympias. Either in the same or a subsequent year he also married Cleopatra of Jerusalem who bore Philip (the future Philip the tetrarch).

When a young man he was athletic and strong. (Josephus wars 1. 23.1.) As Herod grew to be seventy years old (wars v1.23.1) he began to suffer from an undiagnosed chronic kidney disease with an infection which grew worse as he neared his death. When he met the wise men in the early part of 5BC he was comparatively free from the pain which would so assail him later that year that he would be confined to Jericho where he died the following year.

Herod's achievements had been many. He had built the new city which he had diplomatically named Caesarea. Its luxurious palace and state of the art harbour bore testament to the forward thinking and design capability he had. The city with its baths and amphitheatre contained all the elements of a revival in Graeco- Roman culture which he promoted within Israel and beyond. He built for the Jews of Antioch the first paved walkway in the ancient world which had been copied in other cities like Ephesus during his lifetime. He had constructed pagan temples, and amphitheatres in many foreign cities to help the position of Jews within the cities. In his domain he rebuilt the city of Samaria

---

[17] Until they were executed in 7BC following an assassination plot

calling it Sebaste as a fortified city. He also had remodeled and expanded the fortress of Machaerus on the east side of the Dead sea as well as building on the south side of southern tip of the Dead Sea the massive fortress of Masada. He also improved a magnificent palace in Jericho, which he expanded three times during his reign, where he could meet dignitaries from other countries as well as providing a palace where he could retreat from the politics of the city. Whether the palaces were part of a fortress designed to provide security in a time of war or large mansions which could thrive in times of peace, they were all luxurious. Luxury was essential for Herod as the trappings of kingship and so was evident in he had.

All these achievements however were dwarfed in significance when in the fifteenth year of his reign (Josephus Wars 1.21,1) Herod began to renovate and expand the second temple which had been built after the exiles returned to Jerusalem. It was a massive task and would continue long after Herod's death. For the first 10 years 10,000 men were engaged in building the retaining walls for the large temple mount – a pioneering engineering feat unsurpassed in the history of Jerusalem. The main rebuilding of the temple complex was finished 25 years after his death (John 2:31) in 21AD By the end of the decade Jesus the Son of God would come there. (The decoration of the temple, however, would not be completed until 64AD)

Herod's motive in building the temple, was to increase his influence in the religious power base of Israel as he had used buildings to increase his influence in other parts of the Roman empire. He was proud of his political achievements, and he had kept favour with Rome through the civil war and its aftermath as well as helped to end for the time being the war between Rome and Parthian. He had brought prosperity and stability to Israel and for a while it emerged out of the shadow of Syria into an independent kingdom allied to Rome. Herod was not a king in the line of David – but rather in the line of Haman and Agag – enemies of Israel- They were all Edomites descended from Esau. This was a factor which threatened his authority throughout his rule, yet Herod did manage to hold everything together. The nation of Israel, whilst recognizing King Herod was no King David, and not really one of their own, and though many were disgruntled at the high taxes they had to pay to fund his building projects, they respected him as their king. Not since the exile in 586 BC had the nation had its own king. Foreign kings had ruled in Israel for centuries and the people longed for a return to a Davidic monarchy. In the absence of kings, the high priests of the second century had become ethnarchs by bribing their Greek rulers. Now with the rise of Roman authority in the region this had all changed.

Wise men from the East (Matthew 2:1-12)

King Herod the Great was in his late sixties [18]. He was an ill man with less than two years to live. It would not be long after the visit of the wise men that his poor health would prevent him coming to Jerusalem except as a matter of extreme urgency.

The Strangers came to Jerusalem from the East. This was not in itself unusual. Traders from the East often came to Jerusalem who were Gentiles. They arrived outside the city with their camels and donkeys. Their servants did as they had done every day in recent months – fed the animals, put up the tents, set a guard and prepared a meal while their masters went on into Jerusalem. The Magi walked into the city and asked a disturbing question "Where is He who has been born King of the Jews". This caused the city to be troubled.

[18] Josephus Wars 1.33.1

Over a year before [19] (7 BC) the wise men were watching the triple conjunction of Jupiter and Saturn which occurs every 800 years, alongside a star which appeared in the quadrant designated to the Jews. At that time, Herod and the nation had been shaken by the discovery of an assassination plot by his sons Alexander and Aristobulus. After their arrest, the trial dragged on for a few months followed by their execution. A year or more later the effects of this were still being felt in Jerusalem society, because there had been further consequences directly affecting even the highest levels of Jewish society. Despite her protests of innocence, Herod reasoned that the plot must have been known to the high priest's family and therefore to his wife Marianne who had not disclosed anything. The Boethus family which had had the high priesthood in their family for generations was now shamed through their implied involvement in this plot. Simon whose daughter King Herod had married was deprived of the High Priesthood (Ant 19.6.2.) and Joazar one of his family was appointed[20]. A rival family for the high priest' office however started to arise taking advantage of their weakness – the family of Annas. They were able to exercise more influence to rival the Boethus family, and when Archelaus returned from Rome Annas was appointed High Priest. This family would provide the high priests in a near unbroken chain until the fall of Jerusalem. Furthermore, his son Herod Boethus (Philip) who had been a possible heir was forever consigned to never inheriting the kingship. His eldest son by his first wife Doris was declared heir apparent.

---

[19] The first sighting was two years before the magi met Herod (Matthew 2:7,16). We know from Josephus (Antiquities 17.6.4) that on March 13th 4b.c there was a lunar eclipse after which Herod's illness confined him to Jericho until he died later that year. This means the earliest sighting had to be before March 6BC Computer analysis of the skies give a possible explanation for 7 BC The triple conjunction of Saturn and Jupiter was then followed in 6BC with a conjunction of Saturn Jupiter and Mars. (Source Humphreys C.J. Quarterly Journal of the Royal Astronomical society Vol 32 no 4 Dec 1991

[20] For significance of this for the date of the census see the appendix

About the time when the Magi (wise men) were in Jerusalem, Varus the Roman governor of Syria had arrested his next heir Antipater the son of his first wife who had been accused of an attempt to poison his father, so he could become king. Although found guilty, Caesar gave Herod the discretion to execute him or imprison him. He decided to keep him alive in a prison in Syria for the time being, but he planned to execute him publicly when he got better.

Herod soon heard about the question the strangers were asking "Where is he who is born king of the Jews?" No-one could escape the fact that this question was politically charged, and Herod had to intervene quickly. He did not want to raise the thorny issues of succession in a public debate nor fuel any fires of Jewish enthusiasm for a true king of Israel called the Messiah. He therefore arranged a formal enquiry inviting the chief priests who represented the local government and "the scribes of the people " (Matthew 2:4) who since the time Greek rulers of Israel had sought to establish secularizing ways, they had been the spokesmen for the religious ways of life to balance the authorities and so were called in this formal setting.

The Magi stood together dressed in their impressive robes marking them out as distinguished wise men from Persia and Babylon - ancient civilizations of the east where astrology and astronomy were part of daily life. They were in the large palace Herod had built for himself on the west side of Jerusalem. It was a fortress but within it was his palace with state rooms surrounded by impressive gardens laid out with scented flowers, sculptures and man-made streams. They were, so they thought, near to the end of their journey. Two years before they had started to see strange events in the sky and interpreted from them that an important king was being born in Judea. They had taken a year to prepare and arrive there. They had travelled far. The question the men from the east asked was repeated to the king as he sat in his royal court surrounded by his officials. Issues of state were often conducted in the palace in Jerusalem. As the Magi spoke, the court took their arrival seriously especially when they found the basis for their question was their study of the stars, and it began to dawn on them that it might mean that the Messiah prophesied in the bible to come had been born. They found the passage in the book of Micah which stated that he would be born in Bethlehem. They had an answer to their question and so turned to leave. Herod let them go not wanting to whip up any more Messianic hopes and returned quickly to his other duties. Herod, however, turned to one of his officials and privately gave him instructions to send messengers after the Magi as they left to ask them to meet him in another part of his house away from the public eye. They soon overtook the men as they walked away from the palace and led them into Herod's private apartments where they waited for the king to meet them. When he arrived, he apologized for keeping them, but said he wanted to find out more about what they had seen. He offered them hospitality which they accepted and over a meal found out all the information they were basing their conclusions on including how long since they had seen the star. Though he did not show it, Herod was worried. He had valued the title "King of the Jews" for himself and the succession was such a growing concern it was affecting his demeanour, and this was made even worse by the decline in his health. He needed to find out everything they knew so he could make an effective plan to "neutralize" the threat to him and his succession. He was relieved to find it was all within the last two years. Any baby born then would not be an immediate threat. He sent them with his authority to go to Bethlehem as they had been told and if they found anyone to return to him, so he could come and worship him also. Herod had many duties which kept him in Jerusalem which meant he had to delegate this important task to the Magi. They did not see Herod as a threat to the child at all. The Magi went out of the city to complete their journey and journeyed the five miles to Bethlehem. At dusk [21]whilst there was enough light to journey, and stars could be seen in the sky (Matthew 2:9), the foreigners came to Bethlehem and saw the star over one of the houses. Having spotted the house they made their way and discovered that in the house was indeed a child who had been born recently. This combined with the star reappearing that they had seen before they set off on their journey from the East convinced them that this child was possibly indeed the king of the Jews. They made themselves known to Joseph and Mary who had not expected this visit at all. Joseph invited them in, and the house had room for them to stay. They shared a meal and the magi were spiritual people from an ancient world. Though there were no signs of kingship, they did not dismiss any details which Joseph and Mary shared with them and became surer that this child was indeed the "king of the Jews". During the meal they sent one of their servants back to the tents with a message to bring the gifts they had carried over the Arabian desert. When they arrived, they gave gifts of gold, frankincense and myrrh. Their servants returned to their tents whilst their masters settled down for the night at the house of Joseph. Early the following morning, as they were packing up to leave they told Mary and Joseph of a dream they had had in the night that they should not go back to Herod. They had disclosed to Mary and Joseph that they had come from the royal court, and this had held no fears to them. No-one there envisaged the slaughter of the innocent children under two which the king was contemplating. The reason for the change of route was not obvious at the time to the wise men or to Joseph and Mary. The wise men departed eastwards simply obeying the revelation they received   without   question.

---

[21] The wise men could have come early morning, but it is more likely dusk as they stayed with Joseph and Mary in the house and slept (as one of them had a dream Matthew 2:12)

SECTION 2

Jesus' Growing Years From Bethlehem to Nazareth
(Matthew 1:14-23, Luke 2:30)

Chapter 5

Flight to Egypt (Matthew 1:14)

The change the Magi had brought by their visit was not immediately clear to Mary or Joseph. The fact Jesus life was in danger only became manifest through a dream warning them to leave Bethlehem. Joseph had a dream in which an angel of the Lord told him to go to Egypt as they were in danger. He had seen this angel before when he was thinking of divorcing Mary before Jesus' birth, and he knew it was a dream to obey. When Joseph told the dream to Mary, the dream of the wise men to not return to Herod made sense. Now they had to flee. Joseph and Mary got ready and leaving their house behind they took the road directly south to Hebron. From there they went to Beersheba where they left the jurisdiction of Israel behind. They went to the coast from Beersheba to join the Via Maris which took them to Egypt. The journey was more than 200 miles.

There were long established Jewish communities in Egypt. When Babylon had conquered Jerusalem about six hundred years before, thousands of Jews had fled to Egypt and by the time of Jesus there were many synagogues there – in fact the synagogue had developed there which had then been exported back to Israel and to Jews in the rest of the world. Joseph with his wife and family joined other Jewish families who made the journey in search of work. There were various building projects that Augustus Caesar had initiated in Egypt since 30BC when he conquered it. Plentiful work was available. Tradition has it that Joseph found work near Cairo[22]

---

[22] The church of Abu Serga in old Cairo is the oldest church in Egypt (4th century) and reputedly built on the place Joseph and Mary went with Jesus. Augustus expanded and built a massive citadel "The Babylonian fortress" near the pyramids of Giza to guard the southern approaches of the Nile Delta and around it the city of Fustat (later Cairo) grew up. Joseph

So, they met families of many tradesman who were travelling to Egypt and settled into life in the Jewish section of the city. In Egypt they would need to speak Greek – a new language unlike the Aramaic Mary had spoken all her life. She as a woman however could immerse within the Jewish community, so it was Joseph who would need to speak Greek, something Joseph had had to learn as part of his job when working for the Greeks in Autocratoris and other Graeco Roman cities in Galilee. Antipas like his father had engaged in many building schemes and most were buildings within a Graeco -Roman influence and culture, so jobs amongst the Greek speaking was more lucrative and plentiful than those in the traditional sectors of Galilee life

Even this unexpected event of going to Egypt could be traced and reflected in Old Testament prophecy (Matthew 2:15). In Egypt Jesus grew from babyhood into toddler. A year or so later he started to have brothers and sisters, and he also had his first introduction to the Greek language, so that when eventually they all returned to Nazareth, he would have a working knowledge of Greek[23]. Greek was the standard language for the ruling Egyptians as well as Jews, Parthians, Syrians and many others. In Egypt the ordinary Egyptian spoke a demotic, - a sort of popular Egyptian- but Joseph and Mary lived in a Jewish section where all they needed to get by was Greek or Aramaic. Joseph encouraged Jesus in speaking Greek as well as his natural language of Aramaic[24] as it increased his job prospects in the future. Greek was the common language used in all areas of the empire, and young Jews like Mark and Matthew in Jesus' day would be fluent enough to write the gospels in

may have been involved in helping to build the city – the fortress was already built by this time. (see Harold Kramer The Complete Pilgrim: https://thecompletepilgrim.com/author/howardkramer accessed 2017)

[23] Jesus was able to hold a conversation with Pilate at his trial because he could speak Greek as well as Aramaic

[24] Jesus naturally spoke Aramaic Mark 3:17: *Boanerges*; Mark 5:41: *talitha kum*; Mark 7:34: *ephphatha*; Mark 14:36: *abba*; Mark 15:34 *Eloi Eloi lama Sabacthani*

this language, but Jesus had a head start in Greek in a way he would not have done to the same degree in Nazareth. There were times when only speaking Greek would do (not least before Pilate), but for Jesus Aramaic was his first language which he spoke.

Chapter 6

Roman taxation under Caesar Augustus (Luke 2:1,2)

During the years that Jesus grew up as a young boy, "Caesar's tax", as it was called, was not introduced into Israel. Archelaus, Herod the Great's successor in Judea, created a climate which made resolution of this issue impossible. Even before he was officially ruler of Judea, he had offended many. He had executed those caught removing the Roman eagle from the temple gate but when many mourned their death he treated them harshly which raised protests which went as far as Rome. The memory of these two acts soured any future relationship between Archelaus and the religious authorities in Judea. This made difficult any discussion about Judea's relationship with Rome (of which the tax was a major issue) and made it politically impossible to press ahead. In 6AD Archelaus was deposed by Caesar and military rule was imposed. Judea became part of the Roman province of Syria. The immediate result of this was a further revolt and defeat of Judas the Galilean. It was the military governor of Syria Quirinius who would successfully introduce the new tax (Luke 2:1,2) Quirinius was trusted as a man who would get things done. He rose to fame after being appointed in 15BC by Augustus as proconsul over the province of Crete and Cyrenaica. He defeated a warlike tribe in the Sahara south of Cyrene and returned a war hero to Rome where he became consul in 12BC He was trusted and close to Caesar. He had been the guardian of Gaius – the protégé of Augustus for emperor (until Gaius was wounded and died in the wars in Armenia against the Parthians). In 6AD Augustus appointed Quirinius as governor of Syria in charge of a strong large Roman army - the mainstay in the war against the Parthians whose rival empire lay east of the province he ruled. It was this military objective which was his primary concern, yet he also had to turn his attention to introducing Caesar's tax into Israel. The annexing of Judea was for this purpose. Quirinius did this so successfully that by the time Jesus was in his mid-teens, Caesar's tax as it was called was a reality. It was still deeply felt in the population and remained a live issue amongst the populace twenty years later when Jesus as an adult would be asked whether to pay taxes to Caesar or not. Jesus then answered, "Render unto Caesar the things that are Caesar's and unto God the things that are God's" (Matthew 22:21)

Herod's death

Some weeks had passed since the wise men had come to Jerusalem. Herod now lived most if not all the time in his palace in Jericho. His son Archelaus was acting regent in Jerusalem. Some religious fanatics knowing Herod's health was declining, decided to remove a carved eagle (the symbol of Rome) from one of the entrances of the temple, which forced him to make a trip to Jerusalem to judge the perpetrators, but, that was the final time he was there. On March 13th 4BC 29 days before the Passover there was an eclipse of the moon, it happened on the same day Herod had executed those who had vandalized the temple.[25] The connection between the two events were noted at the time as divine comment on the king who was experiencing in the Jewish mind the judgement of God for his sins. Already a sick man he withdrew from Jerusalem to Jericho where he would eventually die. He convened a further meeting (this time at Jericho)[26] a few weeks later to appease some of those upset by the harshness of his judgement. He got his anger off his chest as he told them how much more he had achieved than his predecessors and placated himself by removing Matthias from being High Priest and appointing his wife's brother Joazar instead. As a result, many of those who were under threat of execution were pardoned. Judas the Galilean a young rabbi who had been one of those caught up

---

[25] Antiquities 17.6.4. This was after the census had been taken because Joazar became High priest just before this and he tried to address the adverse reaction to the census when he came into office. See Appendix.

[26] Antiquities 17.6.3

in the vandalism- was not executed as the older influential rabbi Matthias had been [27]. By this time Herod was unable to stand, and he was forced to conduct the convocation from a lying position. Meanwhile his pain was getting worse. It was only eased temporarily through eating. As the days past in Jericho his breathing was affected and in the increasing pain he was suffering he even thought of suicide. On his death bed he heard about his son and heir Antipater (who, as we have mentioned, was in prison for plotting against him) had tried to bribe a guard to let him go now that he had heard his father had attempted suicide and was near death. Antipater was expecting to succeed him on his death. Herod heard about this. He had kept him in prison, so he could execute him publicly when he was well. One of the last decrees the king gave was for his son to be executed. Herod then changed his will defining the succession and five days later Herod died. It was 37 years after the Romans had declared him king and 34 years after he had established himself as king in Judea. [28]

Archelaus (Matthew 2:22)

Born in 23bc, this son of Herod the Great was three years older than his brother Herod Antipas. Archelaus' and Antipas' mother was Malthrace who was from Samaria. Archelaus had only recently become in line for the throne. Just days before his death Herod had made a will granting Judea to Archelaus, and Galilee to Antipas. This was disputed, and so Archelaus and Antipas went to Rome for Caesar to ratify Herod's will.

---

[27] Josephus Wars 1.33.2-4. Antiquities 17.6.2. Judas the Galilean is the same as Judas the son of Sepphoris (the city in Galilee where his revolt was based when Archelaus became king after the death of his father. Varus the Roman general of Syria broke this revolt by destroying Sepphoris. (Wars 2.4.1; 2.5.1) Judas himself escaped and revolted again in 6ADwhen Judea no longer was an independent kingdom allied with Rome, but instead annexed into the Roman province of Syria to get the census completed and tax introduced. Judas took up military force against the Romans Wars 2.8.1. He was a Rabbi teaching a form of Judaism which differed from Pharisees, Sadducees and Essenes Wars 2.8.2, Antiquities 18.1.6 (see also 18.1.1)
[28] Antiquities 17.8.1

Before he went, he had shown what sort of ruler he might be. In the weeks before his death, some religious Jews had sought to remove the golden eagle – because it was an idol – from an entrance into the temple site. It was also the symbol of Rome and Herod inflicted great punishment burning alive those he chose and handing others over for execution. Herod then died, and a lavish funeral was held by Archelaus for his father who was buried in Herodium south of Bethlehem. At the next religious festival in Jerusalem, there was public lamentation for those executed by Herod over the removal of the golden eagle and when Archelaus sought to break up the mob, they turned on the soldiers who ran away fearing for their lives. The mob then returned to their normal duties at the festival worshipping God and sacrificing in the temple. Archelaus sent his whole army to break up the religious festival and send people home causing many to die. The relationships between tetrarch and his subjects continued to decline (Josephus wars 1.7.3) It was this which Joseph heard about which caused him to return to Galilee.

In 6AD after ten years as ruler (Josephus Antiquities 17.13.2. Archelaus was deposed and Coponius was sent as procurator under Quirinius the governor of Syria. It was at this time that Judas the Galilean rebelled against the Roman rule – and the tax (Josephus war 2.8.1)

Just as Augustus had feared, his introduction of a census preparing the way for taxation had bred rebellion. On top of that with Herod's death, social upheaval ravaged the country. Judea had become a dangerous place to travel, Perea had a brigand proclaiming himself king and in Galilee Judas the Galilean had arisen leading a rebellion from the north arming the rebels from the armoury at Sepphoris making the fortified city their base. Archelaus as regent had been unable to stop this and when some soldiers were ambushed, a larger Roman army under Varus responded and defeated the main corps of rebels in 4BC They destroyed their capital (Sepphoris) just outside Nazareth and put its citizens to death or slavery. In this way the immediate fires of rebellion were extinguished. Judas remained at large inciting a further unsuccessful revolt in 6AD when Judea became part of the province of Syria and the census was completed by Quirinius.

Peace had come to Galilee quickly after the defeat in 4BC so that when Herod Antipas was appointed Tetrarch of Galilee a year later, he set about immediately rebuilding Sepphoris to make it his capital city. He built new impressive buildings, surrounded the city with a wall and called it Autocratoris. It would become his capital for about twenty years until he had built by the Sea of Galilee his new capital city which he completed and called Tiberias. Both cities were Graeco- Roman in style and architecture. So, Joseph arrived in Nazareth in 2b.c[29]. just as after Antipas had started to build Autocratoris. It was a great employment opportunity. The building of Autocratoris as "the ornament of Galilee" (Josephus Ant.18.2.7) was just a few miles away from Nazareth.[30] It was a safe place for Joseph and Mary to return.

[29] See appendix re dates

[30] Joseph is called "Builder" in Matthew 13:55. It means someone who makes things. For Joseph this which would include carpentry but would be so much more. Jesus came into the same building profession as his father Mark 6:3.

Chapter 7

Jesus returns to Nazareth

Back in Egypt, Joseph had a dream. The angel of the Lord informed him that Herod the Great was dead and he could now return with his family to Israel. They packed up and went back home towards Bethlehem. Mary, no doubt, anticipated living close to Elizabeth her relative who lived nearby (Luke 1:36,39). As they got back to Israel, they found that the will of Herod had been disputed and for some weeks the royal family had been in Rome waiting for Caesar's decision. Before they arrived in Bethlehem they heard of Caesar's decision to make Archelaus ruler of Judea. Joseph knew he had a reputation for being ruthless like his father, and so chose to go instead to Nazareth to be under the rule of his brother Antipas who had been given the tetrarchy of Galilee. This was a wise decision because anarchy in his domains of Judea and Perea brought out the worst in Archelaus.

So, Joseph and Mary were greeted as they came into Nazareth by Mary's family and friends. Years before they had left with Mary pregnant. Now they returned with Jesus who was just able to walk as a toddler, and Mary was already expecting another child. Mary and Joseph settled down to family life in Mary's home where she had been brought up.

The years went by. Frequently Joseph would walk the two miles or so out of Nazareth to work at Autocratoris. Mary and Joseph had some more children. (Mark 6:3) so by the time Jesus was twelve he was part of a large family firmly established within the community at Nazareth. [31] It was no longer the closed northern village it might have been one

---

[31] After Jesus' birth Mary and Joseph had normal marital relations. They were in Egypt for over a year from early 5b..c. to 3BC , as when wise men come to Herod, he is still in Jerusalem rather than ill at Jericho. It was however a time when succession was an issue.

hundred years before. From Pompey's time, families from the south at his encouragement had moved to Galilee to start a new life. Nazareth however remained an old Jewish village. Jesus was well known in the village and accepted as one of their own. Everyone knew everyone else. It was very different in culture to the modern Graeco - Roman city being built on its doorstep. As Jesus grew up, Nazareth and its surrounding countryside became his world. Galilee was divided into two (Upper and Lower Galilee). They were distinctive areas different in terrain and with their own identities (Josephus War 3. 35-42). Everywhere in Galilee there could be found rich pasture and agricultural land managed by tenant farmers as well as farmers who had owned the land for centuries. Both livestock and agriculture were farmed. Jesus delighted in the countryside around the village set in the hills of Lower Galilee. Jesus experienced the cold in winter[32] with snow on occasions, as well as the heat of summer. Around the village vines and olives grew in abundance, and there were many different trees each with their fruits in season. At an early age, Jesus showed he appreciated goodness (Isaiah 7:15). He loved the bird song at dawn and the stars in the night sky. As he grew up this appreciation of goodness transitioned into an appreciation of good and right and an aversion to evil and wrong. Righteousness marked his thoughts and actions wherever he was.

Lower Galilee was Israel's lushest region known for its sunny temperate climate and its spring watered valleys. The countryside was vibrant with life with every kind of tree and fruit. Small birds were there in great numbers and varieties. Spring was a favourite time of the year when valleys and slopes became oceans of wildflowers and blossoming trees set in a blanket of green which pervaded everywhere. Each year red poppies and the white anemone poppies as well as

The most likely time for this was after the assassination plot of 7BC,(when the next one happens in 5BC he is an ill man)
[32] Josephus Wars 1.6.2

crocuses blossomed bringing added colour to the rolling hills and fertile plains, which were textured with vineyards and fruit orchards. Grapes, figs, olives, pomegranates, oranges and other fruits flourished in its pleasant subtropical climate. Jesus grew up in an area where fig trees and olive trees thrived, but he was also surrounded by walnut trees which only grew in cold air as well as palm trees which only grew in hot climates. (see Josephus Wars 3.10.8.). The walnut trees were often cultivated. They had been imported from Persia two hundred years before and benefited from the times when the temperature dropped below eight degrees Celsius. Walnuts provided not only ready-made additions to deserts and snacks, but with pomegranates were used for dye and ink for writing.

The gradual rise in the land from the Mediterranean compared with Judea meant that the moisture carrying clouds from the west could come further inland than further south in Judea. Lower Galilee averaged 600mm a year which meant rivers flowed with water during the rainy season well into spring encouraging the rich variety of plants and wild life.

Jesus during his childhood as other boys never ventured very far from Nazareth except to go to Jerusalem for the Passover each year (Luke 2:41). Nazareth itself was set in a limestone basin. The white rock was used to build every building in the village including the synagogue. It had been quarried locally from the mountains and brought into the village. Jesus had seen rocks from there brought by cart many times in his young life. Nearby there was a spring where Jesus gathered water for the family. There was always plenty of water from the spring even in the height of summer, and it supplied the whole village.

Climbing up 500 feet onto the hills above the village, Jesus could see thirty miles in three directions. To the north the plateaus of Zebulun and Naphtali, and the mountains of Lebanon with snow covered

Hermon towering above them all. In the foreground across the rolling hills was Autocratoris, the military centre and capital of Herod Antipas. To the west, he could see the rolling hills beyond which lay the coast and the blue waters of the Mediterranean. Sometimes if he happened to be in high enough and the day was clear he could see the high range of mountains called Mount Carmel which lay to the south west. In that direction were Megiddo and the whole plain of Esdaraelon which featured many times in the Old Testament and as his eyes moved around towards the south east, he could see the distinctive dome shape of Mount Tabor and the hills of Gilboa where Saul and Jonathan were killed. The places were in in the Bible stories he had studied in the synagogue and talked about at home. Immediately south of where he stood was Mount Ebal with Samaria beyond. To the east beyond the forested slopes of Tabor were further hills which hid from view the sea of Galilee and the mountains of the desert beyond.

Nazareth was secluded by its natural location, but it was not cut off from the outside world. As Jesus looked down he would see, from his place on the hills, various travellers on the road. To the south was a road that went all the way to Egypt – the way he and his family had travelled when they arrived from Egypt when he was little. A mile and a half away was the caravan route to Jerusalem. At the foot of the hill, there was a Roman road connecting Damascus with the Mediterranean Sea ports and there was always some military or trade convoy to be watched as they journeyed.

Galilee was the northern part of Israel with strong Jewish communities living in much the same way as they had done for centuries but within a culture in which the Roman military were present bringing trade and stability. Since ending of the rebellions in Jesus' childhood, there was no appetite at all for throwing off the Roman mantle that lay so firmly on the land.

By the time Jesus was a teenager Sepphoris had been fully rebuilt, named Autocratoris and walled. It had become one of the biggest and most important cities in Galilee[33]. The city gave Jesus a glimpse into Graeco- Roman city life. Inside its walls It had a theatre and baths and the grand architecture of gates and civic buildings prepared him for some of the towns he would visit in future years.

Jesus was a builder like Joseph. The main material he worked with was wood, making whatever was needed. He learnt some of the skills when a boy. Now in his mid-teens he waited in the market place at Nazareth for work. Sometimes especially when younger he stood with his father, but now it was more often he stood on his own with others as they waited for employment. Many weeks he would have a job which meant he did not have to go the market place. On those weeks his days except the Sabbath would be full working, but there were times when there would be no work for him to do. In 17AD When Jesus was twenty, the opportunity for work locally declined when the rich linked to the royal court left for a new capital city which had been recently built overlooking the sea of Galilee called Tiberias. Jesus remained a carpenter/builder, but it was more of a struggle to get work. He did not travel and leave home to find work elsewhere. There was always just enough to enable him to stay at Nazareth.

---

[33] Autocratoris (also referred to as Sepphoris) served for some of the time as the regions administrative capital, and after the destruction of Jerusalem in 70AD the Sanhedrin met there. The archaeology points to a strong Jewish city. (There were no pagan shrines or references in Memoria).
Mark A. Chancey Dept. of Religious Studies Southern Methodist University February 2003 states "While gentiles were present there (as in all areas of Palestine), nothing suggests that they were especially numerous. They are practically invisible in the archaeological record, and they are not prominent in literary discussions of Galilee, either. Most of our evidence for Gentiles dates not to the first century but to the second century and later, after the arrival of large numbers of Roman troops in 120 CE."

Chapter 8

Jesus aged 12 (Luke 2:40ff)

By the time Jesus was 12 years old Judea was part of the Roman province of Syria under direct rule from Rome with a string of governors - prefects from the military appointed by Rome who ruled the territory from its capital city by the Mediterranean called Caesarea Maritima. It made little impact on Nazareth where Jesus was growing up because Galilee was still ruled as a vassal kingdom of Rome under Herod Antipas. He had negotiated with the Romans so that their military were kept to a minimum within his domain. Most if not all soldiers that Jesus saw guarding premises were those of Antipas not Rome. Roman soldiers in military convoys sometimes were seen moving on the road to and from the coast, but they seldom troubled Jesus or the local population.

Most days while Jesus was growing up, Joseph was out early, and Jesus would be engaged in household chores like other children of his age. When Sabbath came each week, it was different. There were no chores and a lot of family time. There was always the special meal in the Friday evening and attendance at the synagogue in the village on the Saturday morning, after which it was a day of rest until bedtime. Every year the family went to Jerusalem. Joseph as a good Jew travelled every year at the time of Passover to Jerusalem, as did Mary (Luke 2:41). It was a family occasion and they always took the same route via the Jordan valley. Some from Galilee went to Jerusalem in three days through Samaria, but although over twenty miles longer it was safer to go via the Jordan. Although It would take them an extra day to get to Jerusalem than going through Samaria, it was always the preferred route. From an early age Jesus with his younger brothers and sisters had been with them as they went, staying each night occasionally in the open but mostly in a house in one of the towns they passed through.

Some houses were familiar as they stayed there each year as they made their journey to and from Jerusalem.

Jesus at the age of twelve had visited Jerusalem many times. Jerusalem was built where three steep sided ravines join. They are the Kidron, Tyropoeon and Hinnom valleys It was city surrounded by high thick gray walls four miles in circumference which was built along the hills with deep ravines to the south and east and west. At intervals along the walls were massive gateways. As he came down the Mount of Olives towards the water gate across the Kidron valley at its southernmost point, he could see the many flat roofed houses closely compacted together built on the hills and sides of the Tyropoeon valley which cut through the middle of the city separating the temple and the south eastern part of the city – the old city of David -from the western side of the city. It was fully populated, and he could see the group of limestone houses yellow brown in colour from years of sun and wind that sloped downward towards the valley. Jesus knew the area at the bottom of the slope was called the Cheesemakers district. He could also trace the steep and narrow streets as they wound up through the clusters of houses. Jesus knew they that when they were in the city there were many alleyways that he could not see from such a distance away, that separated the houses. There were two bridges over the Tyropoeon valley into the temple. One from the lower city and the other from the Upper city. Jesus had walked up the stairs and crossed the bridge from the lower part of the city, passing the place where the trumpets were sounded to announce the beginning and end of each Sabbath, but he had never crossed the one from the Upper city to the temple. Only the rich and famous used that bridge which was built from the old Hasmonean palace directly into the outer court. As his eyes moved from the lower city to the upper city, the white marble palaces of the rich stood out. At the top of the city, he could see the tower of the Roman fortress attached to the north and west of the temple and as he looked west the palace of Herod next to the west wall. Its northern limit marked by two towers and its southern extent by a third tower. The two towers to the north were built to strengthen and defend the north wall which was the only viable place for military assault on the city. In front of him as he approached Jerusalem was the eastern side of the city and towering above everything else was the temple itself. Its white marble walls surrounding the large temple complex were built on a platform extending beyond the summit of the original hill in an engineering masterpiece. Jesus could see the white masonry stone south facing wall created by Herod: 200 feet from foundation level to just below the roof of the Royal Cloister with special stone blocks some twenty feet in length, with a height of six feet. Looking down from the Royal Cloister the bottom of Kidron valley would be more than three hundred feet below. The temple itself was built to a greater height than anything else in the city so it could be seen from every direction. It was one of the ancient wonders of the ancient world. The temple glinted with gold and the precious stones embedded in its stonework flashed in the sun. It was an impressive sight. Jesus normally approached Jerusalem from the east. The road took them to the east gate of the city[34], the gate of Susa which had access to the temple and to Jerusalem. Sometimes they would go that way. Other times they would join the road from the Dead Sea and approach Jerusalem from the south through Water gate depending on where they were staying in Jerusalem. The city itself was always crowded and it was easier to move outside its walls than within them.

[34] Although destroyed by the Romans in 70AD, it was probably on the same site as the Golden gate now is. It was an ancient gate and remained untouched by Herod. It may have been a double gate one side giving access to a street which went around the temple mount to the sheep gate; the other side giving access by staircase to the temple mount. The total destruction of this gate and the mount means that any conclusions have to be speculative. There is no archaeological evidence.

Jerusalem had a long history but to the Jews it started with King David and since then it had been the religious capital of the Jewish nation. Over the years the city had been destroyed and rebuilt; it had been diminished but now was enlarged. There were unmistakable Roman influences in the city. Herod's luxurious palace just inside the west wall with its gardens baths and architecture modelled the palaces of emperors. The hippodrome (amphitheatre) which although a flimsy but secure structure[35] in open ground was situated to the south of the temple in the area called the plain below the city wall separating the north west from the rest of the city (Josephus (War 2.3.44; Antiquities 15.268). The city of Jerusalem was at the zenith of its greatness emphasized by great technological advances in engineering and architecture. Herod the Great had improved the water supply into the city as well as providing purification pools to the south (Siloam) and north (Bethesda) of the temple site. An aqueduct brought water directly into the city from Hebron.

Jesus and the rest of the family walked in groups with mules carrying the essentials they needed for their travel and stay. His parents were quite used to him being with the wider family (Luke 2:44). Jesus already knew his way around and was safe to leave to his own devices whilst Mary concentrated on her younger children. It had always happened this way on previous visits to Jerusalem. Many times, in Nazareth also Jesus was not at home exploring the countryside around the village spending time with God as he went. Mary knew Jesus could be trusted to be out of sight.

Luke (2:40) describes Jesus during this time as "strong in spirit" knowing his own mind and determined to see a job through and "filled with wisdom" knowing how to speak and how to act in all

---

[35] Whilst there have been no archaeological finds for this, Herod imprisoned people there (Josephus Wars 1. 23.6)

circumstances as well as the way he related with others. So, Jesus grew "in favour with God and man". Even before Jesus moved in power, all could quickly see that "the grace of God was upon Him". Grace stays when we respond to the Lord in life (see same principle in Acts4:32-33). God watches for our responses, and when we welcome him and turn our heart towards Him, His presence comes, and opportunities occur. As we step into those opportunities or respond appropriately to God's presence, the grace of God rests on us and becomes more manifest in our life experience. Jesus now as later was responding appropriately to his heavenly Father building up a history with God so at his baptism the Father would say "This is my beloved Son in whom I am well pleased" Mark 1:11.

On their return journey from Jerusalem Mary and Joseph to their horror discovered Jesus was not with them. Immediately they left their children with their relatives and started back to the city uncertain where to look. They had celebrated Passover as a family and there had been no hint of this. It was now Thursday[36]. They wanted to find him quickly and get back to Nazareth. They went to the place they were staying and there was no sign of him nor did anyone know where he was, it was getting late, so they waited until the morning to start the search. They stayed at the same place they had been during the Passover in case he came back, and Joseph and Mary walked the streets of the city for a whole day fearing the worst. They returned before 6pm when they celebrated the Sabbath together with deep anxiety within. On the Saturday morning they went to the temple. In the southern portico of the outer court (the court of the Gentiles) there was a synagogue, and as a non-resident of Jerusalem, this was the usual

---

[36] Passover was on Tuesday April 9th 8AD (Jesus was probably born in September 5BC) If they stayed just for the Passover or as is more likely remained until the end of the feast of unleavened bread they would be leaving on a Thursday. Staying in Jerusalem just for three days would have involved a Sabbath there

synagogue to attend. They came to the temple well before the meeting started. They started to look in the temple. It was unlikely they told themselves that Jesus would be there – after all he was only twelve. There was no sign of Jesus in the outer court or in the court of the women. Joseph went into the court of Israel and was amazed to see Jesus discussing with the teachers of the law who were there after the morning sacrifice. In under twenty-five years' time, Jesus would be teaching in these temple courts himself (Mark 14:49) using a similar discussion style, responding to questions. On this day those gathered were amazed at the knowledge young Jesus displayed by his questions and answers.

Joseph went up to the group and beckoned Jesus to come. Joseph did not say anything to draw attention. He did not need to. Jesus got up and left the group. Joseph led Jesus down the steps into the court of the women. Mary as soon as she saw him rushed forward and asked the question which had been on her heart all the time they had been looking for him "Why have you treated us like this". Jesus had always been so thoughtful, helpful, reliable and trustworthy in the past. Why the change now? She also wanted Jesus to be aware of the pain he had caused so he would not do it again-, so she continued, "your father and I have been anxiously searching for you". Jesus replied in his straight forward matter of fact way that Mary loved, and which would characterize Jesus throughout his life "Did you not know I had to be about my father's business". Jesus had been there until they found him. He had been doing what His heavenly father had told him. He knew they would come eventually. Joseph quietly led them out of the temple relieved that Jesus had successfully been found. They went back to their guest house to complete the Sabbath. At the end of the Sabbath in the hour or so before the sun went down Mary got food ready and they ate well. None had eaten much the previous day, and they needed their energy for the journey the following day. Early just after 6a.m. before the sun rose above horizon of the earth they set off. They knew they could start earlier and cover the miles at a faster pace than the family ahead of them, and so hoped to make up lost time. They knew the party ahead also would have paused for the Sabbath on their journey and so they walked quickly to catch them up before they reached Nazareth.

They rejoined the family and for Jesus it was a return to family life as usual with younger brothers and sisters as he grew from teenager to adult.

Chapter 9

Politics when Jesus was in his twenties

Just before Jesus reached 20 years old Caesar Augustus died. Augustus during his reign changed the republic into an empire which would last another 400 years. During his reign he exported the culture of Rome out to other countries in the empire building new cities to a Graeco-Roman pattern in which veteran soldiers were settled as the elite. They encouraged Roman influence everywhere. He also took Roman law to the provinces, and his aim was to establish peace through justice backed by military might throughout the empire. To achieve this communication throughout the empire was vital, and so he repaired and improved roads built during the Persian empire 500 years before and built several new ones. All this enabled the more rapid deployment of Roman legions as well as speeded up the transport of trade. It would also aid the rapid advance of the Christian faith in years to come.

Jesus was fulfilling the expectations of those around him for he was still in favour with man as well as God. He was therefore a son who helped his family. He was not married. He worked as a builder (mark 6:3) like his father (Matthew 13:55). Like his father Jesus sometimes worked locally in Nazareth, and other times on nearby building sites. Joseph over the years had built up contacts and now instead of just approaching Joseph for work, they also took Jesus on. Occasionally Jesus worked on the same projects as his father, but this was now less so. He was a young man with developed building skills and would be offered jobs which Joseph might have done as a younger man, but now could not. For the time being Jesus was earning a wage which helped the family finances. There was never much money to go around. By the time Jesus was in his late twenties, his brothers were also bringing money into the home. His sisters were married and left home. Jesus had four brothers. There was James, who after Jesus resurrection would lead the Jerusalem church- and there were also Joses, Simon and Judas (Matthew 13:55; Mark 6:3), neither of whom followed Jesus during his earthly ministry.

Pontius Pilate (Luke 3:1)

Jesus was about thirty years of age when Pontius Pilate was appointed Roman governor of Judea (26AD). He was actually a military prefect, but it was considered more diplomatically sensitive to give him in Judea the political title of governor (John 18:28, Luke 3:1) Judea whilst being part of the Syrian province of Rome seemed more at peace with itself if it could be as far as possible not to be seen as under military rule. The status of Judea as an independent ally of Rome had been lost after the deposition of Archelaus, but by less emphasis on military rule, the sensibilities of the strongly religious Jewish nation were taken into account. Herod Antipas who ruled as a vassal king of Rome the northern part of traditional Israel was valuable to Rome in keeping peace and order in his dominions so trade to Rome flourished and in any diplomatic relationship with the Parthians, whose empire stretched from modern Afghanistan through Iran to the Euphrates river in Iraq. It was the immediate neighbour to the Roman empire and could threaten the Empire's important resources and disrupt trade routes through its lands His father Herod the Great) had been appointed in the year that Parthians had invaded as far as Israel before being driven back the following year by Mark Anthony. Now fifty years on when Pilate arrived in Palestine, an uneasy peace prevailed between the two empires.

So, Pilate with his wife sailed into the harbour at Caesarea. Adjoining the quayside was the palace which would keep remain his official residence for ten years. Whenever his duties required him to go to Jerusalem he occupied the palace in Jerusalem which had also built by Herod the Great. Both palaces contained large state rooms, and wherever he lived, the nearby barracks became the Praetorium (Mark

15:16). Antipas had been given some limited jurisdiction in Jerusalem, but he tried to be away from Jerusalem when Pilate was there. Both Antipas and Pilate lived in the palace when they had to stay in the city.

SECTION 3

The start of Jesus' ministry

John the Baptist began his ministry in the fifteenth year of Tiberius Caesar who had succeeded Augustus Caesar after the latter's death on the 19th August 14AD Tiberius reigned as Roman emperor for fifteen years in September 29AD. Early in Jesus' ministry of power before he had begun his Galilean ministry he was at a Passover (John 2:23). Jesus' baptism by John the Baptist was when John was already established. The Baptism was followed by the forty days in the wilderness, so an Autumn or winter Baptism would be most likely. Jesus therefore was baptized a year after John started. Jesus ministry of power after his temptations in the wilderness began in winter 30AD and the Passover he attended was in the spring of 31AD

Chapter 10

John the Baptist
(Matthew 3:1-12, Mark 1:1-8, Luke 3:1-17, John 1:6,19ff)

Everyone who mattered in the ancient world knew when Tiberius became Caesar. Fifteen years later (Luke 3:1) John started to baptize people in the wilderness. He was there before his ministry began there (Luke 3:2). Perhaps it was the death of his elderly parents and lack of financial support that forced John into the desert to fend for himself, but after he arrived in the desert, John eventually realized the Lord had a purpose for him. He identified with the verse from Isaiah 40 as a "A voice crying in the wilderness" and saw this as his call from God. He knew he had a calling to preach, and the response of those who heard to be baptized quickly followed. So many heard him preach and were baptized by him that history would call him "John the Baptist".

John had been brought up in Judea and it was in the wilderness of Judea (Matthew 3:1) where his ministry was based. He lived near Al Maghtas[37] at the waters of the Jordan just over 20 miles east of Jerusalem. John the Baptist moved from place to place along the Jordan valley never far from water. Jesus found him at a ford used by pilgrims as they came and went from Jerusalem. It was a good place to meet the people who would hear and respond to his message.

At the beginning there were comparative few who came, but news began to spread. When people sought John and heard him speak they were more than impressed. John was a man of no nonsense zeal reminding those who heard of him of the prophet Elijah in the Old Testament. He even dressed like him with a garment of camel's hair tied at the waist with a rope. He had no money and had had to learn survival

---

[37] So tradition has it

skills living near water to drink and eating locusts and wild honey. He had clothed himself with whatever he could find. His outer coat protecting him from the harsh desert winds came from a dead camel he had found. All this provided a context for the message he preached of the kingdom coming and a call to repent in the light of this imminent arrival. This struck a deep chord with the people of Israel and many travelled into the wilderness to hear him.

The Baptism of Jesus Autumn 30AD
(Matthew 3:13-17, Mark 1:9-11, Luke 3:21-22, John 1:28ff)

Autumn rains had ended the dry months of summer [38]. Jesus now in his thirties travelled with many other Jews to Jerusalem for one of the three main religious festivals - the Feast of Tabernacles which in 30AD was September 30th to October 6th. All Jews were encouraged to attend at last one of the big three each year - Passover, Feast of weeks, Tabernacles. This year the first day of the Feast of Tabernacles started on the Sabbath[39], and lasted until the following Friday October 6th. Each year the feast brought a natural lull in the work. It was always near the start of the Jewish new year marked by the Feast of Trumpets (the Rosh Hashanah) which had been held about a fortnight before (September 16th). This was just for one day, so it was less often attended by those outside the immediate area of Jerusalem. In recognition of this trumpets were sounded in other parts of Israel on that day. The Feast of Tabernacles was different. The trumpets publicised the call for everyone to begin to get ready to go to Jerusalem.

---

[38] Jesus set off to meet John the Baptist from Galilee in the late autumn. We deduce this as the schedule: - end of October baptism. 40 days in wilderness after which there was a visit to the temple at Jerusalem (probably for the Hanukkah festivals mid-December), end of January/February Wedding of Cana, baptisms in Jordan, April: Passover (cleansing of temple) May: Jesus' Galilee ministry begins

[39] Jesus' earthly ministry had started before the Passover (John 2:13) so he must have been baptized earlier. The three important religious festivals were Passover, Pentecost and Tabernacles. Of these the latter is the most likely here

Every year Jews observed the feast by going to the temple in Jerusalem. Work ceased during this time, allowing Jesus the opportunity to leave work behind [40]and join others also making their way to Jerusalem. The journey was normally three days but could take four or even five if a Sabbath day had to be observed en route. Most therefore travelled between Sabbaths, making the journey quicker and less expensive. Jesus arrived before the Sabbath which started on the evening before the festival on Saturday September 30th. He discovered some had already been there over a week. They had arrived early to celebrate the day of atonement which had been held on Monday 25th September and coincided with the autumnal equinox. Leaving Nazareth on Sunday, the earliest Jesus had hoped to arrive was late Tuesday, but he knew it would probably be Wednesday before he arrived in the city.

When Jesus arrived in Jerusalem, he stayed in one of the many guest houses. Jewish families living in Jerusalem could increase their income by welcoming fellow Jews into their homes for the festival. As He arrived, walking through the city gates into the narrow streets of the city, he saw the tents which were being put up in readiness for the Feast. They were on the flat roofs of more or less all the houses he could see. It was in one of these tents where Jesus would stay.

Jesus went to the temple each day and it was during his stay that Jesus heard about John the Baptist, even meeting some who had been baptised by him. Jesus determined to find him in the wilderness beyond the Jordan after the festival.

He had time to think about his meeting with John whom he already knew because he was a cousin. John was only six months older than

---

[40] He worked in the building trade (Mark 6:3) like his father (Matthew 13:55) and such work was occasional, being taken on when work was needed. At a major festival with so many absences work demands lessened

Jesus and they knew they were related. The earliest meeting, they could remember was when Jesus had come with his family from Egypt. John had been brought up in Judea whilst Jesus was in Galilee. They had occasionally met during their growing years when the family from Nazareth made their regular trips to Jerusalem and John had grown to respect Jesus. For some years had lost touch. He would soon meet John face to face (Matthew 3:15) by which time he would also knew why the Father wanted him to do this.

Chapter 11

Jesus meets John the Baptist

Jesus remained for the eighth day which was the Sabbath of Sabbaths with its own rituals. Most attendees stayed on for this as the highpoint of the festival. More so this year as the eighth day was also the Sabbath. On the Sunday October 8th Jesus got ready and set out on the road from Jerusalem to Jericho and then continued east to meet John the Baptist. He now knew where to find him at a ford called Bethabara. John (1:28) records that when Jesus came to be baptized he was at a place called Bethany beyond the Jordan to distinguish it from the Bethany near Jerusalem.[41] The village was mainly on the west side of the Jordan, so Jesus stayed there and crossed the ford to hear John preach who was on the other side baptizing those who came.

When Jesus heard about John during the autumn festival[42], he was catching up with what others already knew. In an era without media or printed material, communication only occurred when you met. Jesus like other Galileans only heard about John the Baptist when he came to Jerusalem as most who came to him were from Judea and Jerusalem (Mark 1:15). The fishermen Andrew and John were from Galilee and had heard about John earlier at the Passover in the spring. He was unknown in Galilee even though he had been preaching for about a year. By the time Jesus found John, there were already some disciples of

---

[41] If texts which replace Bethany with Bathabara are correctly giving Bethany (house of figs) an alternative name which means house of the ford or crossing place, then the name Bathabara could be the ancient name before becoming known for its figs, and suggests the place where John baptized was a ford. It was shallower than some other parts of the river as here it was crossable by foot. This could be the Bethabara which is mentioned in Judges 7:24, which was one of the tributaries which fed the Jordan.

[42] It is possible Jesus heard about John the Baptist from Simon the Canaanite and his son Judas Iscariot as they were the only members of the 12 from Judea. They were not disciples of John the Baptist yet Jesus had sufficient relationship with them to make them one of his 12 (see later in the book)

John. Their allegiance to John as their teacher meant that whenever they could they would gather to hear him and follow whatever teaching he gave. In the early days of Jesus ministry disciples of Jesus would act in the same way with Jesus as John's disciples did with John.

At the Jordan Jesus joined the crowds from Jerusalem at Bethabara. This was a shallow crossing: a ford: a place where people for hundreds of years had crossed the river which was at this place about forty feet wide. John had placed himself near this familiar road at the time of tabernacles because people would easily find him. They all came seeking baptism.

Jesus listened to John as he preached and eventually found an opportunity to introduce himself. At this stage, although there were plenty of folk, Jesus was able to get near John the Baptist to ask to be baptised. John knew Jesus and was not convinced he should be baptised. (Matthew 3:14). John wanted a further meeting with Jesus to talk it over once the rush of people had subsided in a day or so. Jesus found somewhere to stay for a few more days where he would return to in later years. Meanwhile John and his disciples were fully occupied with the people coming for baptism. There were questions raised whether John was the Messiah which he denied (John 1:25). He openly declared himself to be a voice crying in the wilderness preparing the way for the Lord, as he called the nation back from past evils to a way of righteousness before God. Jesus waited. John had made clear to Jesus that he needed to talk with Jesus first. Although he did not know Jesus was the Messiah, he knew He was special. October was edging closer to November. Finally, the day came. The crowds had gone (Luke 3:21) and with them his disciples. John the Baptist was alone. Eventually John relented. He could see Jesus was doing this to obey God and he agreed. So, he baptized Jesus in the Jordan where a few days before the crowds had been. No-one else apart from John and Jesus knew the events that happened there. -The voice from heaven, the empowering of the Spirit, and the outward sign of the bird from heaven resting upon Jesus. Others would only know this a few weeks later when John the Baptist told them (John 1:30,31).

People still came, though in less intensity. The crowds would resume in the first or second week of December as people made their way to and from the Dedication Festival (9-16th December this year) which was about forty days away.

For Jesus, he could not stay there. The new power within him drove him to be alone so he could process what was happening inside him within his relationship with the Father.

Chapter 12

The temptations November 30AD
(Matthew 4:1-11 Luke 4:1-13)

Since being filled with the Holy Spirit, Jesus was living at a new level of experience. The blessing of God had overtaken him and overwhelmed his soul. (Deuteronomy 28:2). The Holy Spirit led him into the desert because being away from people and the demands of his old pattern of life allowed Jesus to adjust to all that was now happening within Him. The devil for his part was concerned at the revelation of power which stood against his authority on the earth and sought to "nip it in the bud" before anything could be done. This time of transition in the wilderness for Jesus provided the most opportune moment for Satan. The environment designed to help Jesus adjust also provided the opportunity for temptation.

Immediately after his baptism John lost touch with Jesus. Jesus went into the Judean desert which lies west of the Jordan and descends to the Dead Sea. It was dry scrubland with many ravines – some of them very deep. Nearer Jerusalem this area has a Mediterranean climate, but here in this part near the Jordan where Jesus spent most of the time it had a desert climate. He was in this wilderness forty days. It was never a hospitable place in any season

Jesus left the Jordan behind westwards and climbed into the hills and valleys which make up the Engedi. The semi -desert stretched southwards to the Dead sea. Winter was the rainy season. Although little fell in the year, during the rainy season there could be deluges of rain on odd days which would transform the dry desert for a short time. When it rained, it could be torrential, causing flash floods. Dry valleys would suddenly fill with water. Most days were cloudless, but when clouds came up from the Red Sea it heralded the rain and possible flooding. It was an all-new experience for Jesus to survive in such a climate. Although the rainy season which started every September had not the usual rainfall of other years [43], there were days when Jesus had to cope with the rain and cold.

No-one knew or cared where Jesus was including John the Baptist. John was used to people coming and going and assumed Jesus had returned home. In fact, Jesus went further and further into the desert following one of the streams which flowed into the Jordan climbing up the yellow dry hills as it flowed nearby. It was November, so Jesus had water to drink from the temporary flowing streams in the wadis of the deserts. In the wilderness the commonest tree was the acacia which was only sometimes a strong tree -more often it was only a shrub providing little shade. Jesus walked in the desert seeking shade and survival whilst processing all the blessing God had given him. The yellow tall windswept hills separated by the wadis carved into the rock and deep ravines which cut across Jesus' path. He did find sometimes valleys green with grass pushing through the dry dusty rock in clumps but everywhere was largely unpopulated. If he saw anyone, Jesus avoided them. He spent many hours in thought and prayer as he walked, and whilst resting wherever he could find shade. During this forty-day period he found places to sleep where he was less likely to come to harm from snakes or the wild animals with which he lived amongst during the day Mark 1:13. At times Jesus knew supernatural intervention kept him from harm [44]. Shade out of the sun by rocks or in caves could be dangerous, but when everything was pitch black at night, there were great many more dangers. He drank water from the brooks but by the end of this time, he was lacking food and it hurt. During these days he had been tempted but towards the end of the 40-

---

[43] John the Baptist would have to move northwards in the spring because of the lack of water in the winter months which was the rainy season.
[44] Mark 1:13

day period he had three significant temptations from Satan himself directly questioning his position and trying to evoke sinful responses – a tactic he had successfully managed since the garden of Eden.

Jesus moved around the deserts as King David had done when fleeing from Saul a thousand years before. Towards the end of the forty days he was still in the deserts making his way towards Jerusalem for the Dedication festival. Satan caught him when he was at lowest. After fasting for weeks in the desert he was hungry- his natural desires providing the opening for the temptation. "Make the stones bread if you are the son of God". Jesus refused. Satan tried another tactic for the next temptation. It was from an interaction with his human spirit. Jesus had a vision. Like Ezekiel who had travelled to a mountain at the command of heaven to see the new city of God in a vision, so Jesus found Himself on a mountain surveying the world's glory. This time the vision was from Satan who showed him what he regarded as his property - the glory of the nations, with the offer to hand all this over to him if Jesus would worship him. This was a genuine offer. It was the same deal He had given to the Beast who was the power behind the nations (Revelation 13:2). Jesus refused this. He was not going to bow the knee to Satan at all. Around the same time [45] Jesus went to Jerusalem for the feast of Dedication which that year was from December 9th to 16th it was nearly at the end of his forty days. (Luke 4:9). Jesus joined the road which went from the Dead Sea to Jerusalem. He went through the old gate of Jerusalem called the Dung gate and went up the wide main paved street past the pool of Siloam which used to be the only major source of water in the city fed by the Gihon Spring until the aqueducts had been built by the Hasmoneans and now the Romans. The street was full of carts and there were shops and stalls on the side of the road

---

[45] Temptation 2 and 3 are in different orders in the gospels because they were at the same time.

where people were gathered buying. It was always busy even in winter time. The paved street passed by the western wall of the temple mount before exiting the city at the north west of Jerusalem. Jesus entered the temple site using one of the many entrances to the site. whilst Jesus was in the temple. Jesus found himself up in a high place of the temple looking over the parapet into the Kidron valley three hundred feet below. He was near where his brother James thirty years later would be martyred when thrown over that same wall [46]. It was a vantage point from which Jesus could see the Mount of Olives as well as many parts of Jerusalem. Jesus knew it was not far from where he stood that he had seen trumpeters announce religious festivals. It was at this time that Satan spoke into his thoughts. It was only afterwards he recognized because of the temptation that Satan had caused him to be there. Whilst he looked down, Satan put a thought in his mind suggesting he should throw himself off the temple as a sign. Jesus stood firm and so each temptation failed. Thirty-six years before at the time of the religious festival, not many miles away, the Holy Spirit had come on his mother and he had been conceived. Now he was to move into his full adult ministry. The last day of the feast had been on the Sabbath. The season of his temptation were over. He had been in the wilderness for forty days and the time of trial had ended. On December 17th he packed up and left Jerusalem in peace returning to the Jordan.

---

[46] There was no need for Jesus to access the restricted access of the upper levels of the temple towers or upper story. Both would have required planning whereas Jesus only had the thought from Satan when he saw he was in a high place. Suicide was possible from the Royal Cloister (which was open to everyone)into the Kidron valley. It happened with James and could have happened to Jesus. Source for martyrdom of James is Hegesippus Christian convert in mid second century in his last book quoted by Eusebius

Chapter 13

John the Baptist v The Royal Family
(Luke 3:19, Mark 6:17,18, John 3:23,24)

Whilst Jesus was in the desert there was a watershed moment for John's ministry. John heard the news of the marriage of Antipas to Herodias and promptly condemned it as adultery. Many agreed, and John became a household name and celebrity overnight. Crowds started to come from Jerusalem and the surrounding towns to hear him and to be baptized whether there was a religious festival in Jerusalem or not.

In the winter of 30AD Herod had quickly divorced his wife and married Herodias who was recently divorced from her first husband. There was no time to make even a dignified space of time between the two events and it caused an outcry. This was the political platform on which John the Baptist rose to prominence becoming a household name in Jerusalem and Judea. In the eyes of John, the Baptist and those who agreed with him, the divorce of Herod Antipas from his first wife – a Nabataean princess, Phaesalis, daughter of Aretas iv - was not the issue. Divorce happened to some and whilst not the perfect way, was acceptable. The real problem was marrying Herodias who was his brother's wife whilst his brother still lived. It was only acceptable to marry your brother's wife if your brother had died. This act of Antipas in the eyes of many religious Jews was equivalent to adultery.

Crowds came out to be baptized by him and his message and popular support was more than an irritation to both Antipas and his new wife. His popularity and respect amongst the religious Jews meant Antipas had to careful how he acted, and anyway John was most of the time in Judea which was outside Herod Antipas' jurisdiction. Rome ruled Judea, and Antipas had spent most of his political life trying to gain favour first with Augustus who did not hold him in high regard and then Tiberias with whom he had more success, though at the cost of strained relations between him and the Roman provincial governor of Syria under whose military authority Judea and Galilee existed. So, all the political signs were for Antipas to tread carefully, and he heeded them, so John the Baptist was able for the moment to preach unhindered. His denunciation of Herod's marriage to Herodias was not the only thing he preached about. His message was one of personal righteousness to become ready for the revelation of the Messiah. As his fame continued to grow, he became a thorn in the side of Antipas and Herodias which they could not silence.

The history behind the marriage of Herodias to Antipas[47] is as follows. Herodias on the execution of her father Aristobulus in 7BC, by her grandfather Herod the Great, found out it had been arranged for her to be betrothed to Herod Antipas' half-brother Herod Philip 1, who was now named heir to Herod the Great after Antipater. [48] When her father was killed she was only eight years old (born in 15BC) , and she was betrothed to Herod Philip (in his late teens), who was a son of Herod the Great by his wife Mariamne II, the daughter of the High Priest. Herod Philip like the other sons of Herod the Great lived in Rome as well as Judea. It was beneficial to be known in the Roman court circle. She was betrothed to Herod Philip to provide family stability which was essential especially after her father Aristobulus' execution. Herodias when she was old enough, would become Herod Philip's wife. She too was in Rome with her younger brother Herod Agrippa.

Four years later Herod the Great died. Herodias was just 11, when she first met Antipas. He was sixteen and in Rome to contest the will of his

---

[47] the actual dates when Herodias divorced Herod Philip or when Antipas and Herodias were married is unknown. The date of the fifteenth year of Tiberius in the gospel narrative referring to the time when John started his ministry does give us a date for this.
[48] Her father had lived in Rome and on his execution her brother Agrippa was brought up in Rome under the protection of Tiberius' favourite son Drusus.

father Herod the Great. Herodias and Antipas fell in love. Antipas stayed with his mother as he was still under 18, but whilst there his mother died, and he was looked after by guardians whilst the emperor made up his mind about the contested will. The decision by Caesar took some weeks and during this time their romance blossomed. The decision of the Roman emperor was to bypass Herod Philip who was linked to the high priest's family which had been implicated in the earlier plot of Herodias' father to assassinate the king[49]. Instead He affirmed the last will of King Herod and appointed Antipas as tetrarch (a vassal king) of Galilee and his older brother Archelaus tetrarch of Judea. Antipas had made a pact to marry Herodias [50], but Emperor Augustus "advised" Antipas to marry the daughter of the Nabatean King. This was the will of Caesar and to ignore it brought the peril of death. Caesar Augustus valued such alliances marriages could make across the borders of the empire as it could help foster peace.

---

[49] Towards the end the of the reign of Herod the great a conspiracy to assassinate him was discovered. His spurned wife Mariamne III was the daughter of the high priest. The sons Alexander and Aristobulus (the father of Herodias) by the Hasmonean princess Mariamne 1 (who had been executed some years before) were executed. The High Priest family Boethius were also implicated as Herod decided that such a plot could not have been hatched without the knowledge of this family. This brought about the end of the influence of the Boethius family and the rise of the rival priestly family of Annas who remained in authority throughout the new testament period.

In 12 BC Alexander and Aristobulus were executed for attempting to plot against Herod the Great. Herod Philip the son of Herod and Mariamne II was unconnected with the plot. He married Herodias. In 5BC Herod the Great's first son- the named heir-Antipater who had been in exile for some years – only returning a few years before- hatched a plot to poison his father. He knew he had been declared Herod's successor and was trying to speed up his succession. On his execution for treason, Herod Philip who had been named no 2 in the line of succession became a potential heir, but the connection between him and the disgraced Boethus high priestly family continued to disqualify him. After Herod the Great's death his will bequeathing Judea to Archelaus and Galilee to Antipas and Decapolis to Philip the tetrarch, was upheld by Caesar.

[50] Josephus Antiquities Book 17 chapter 10

Herodias, however, had fallen in love with Antipas and could not forget him. She was already betrothed to Herod Philip, a man seven years older than Antipas. Herodias remained in Rome and at the right time became the wife of Herod Philip, but her heart was always for Antipas. At the age of 28 In 13AD she became pregnant and had a daughter in 14ADby Herod Philip who they called Salome after her grandmother on her mother's side, the strong-minded sister of Herod the Great, but she was unsatisfied. She wanted to be Antipas' queen. Divorce and remarriage was a much easier thing to do in Rome than it was in Jerusalem. Herodias had a useful precedent for a wife taking the initiative to divorce her husband Herod Philip when the time arose. Her grandmother Salome had divorced her first husband in contradiction to strict Jewish laws (Josephus Ant 15.7.10). The problem was not at her end of the agreement. It was Antipas who delayed the marriage. He was politically astute and knew the possible adverse consequences both within the people of Israel and from the powerful Nabatean kingdom his wife's father ruled. But his main concern was that to divorce Phaesalis would directly disobey Augustus Caesar who had told him to marry her and could easily bring about his exile or execution. This fear was reinforced when his brother was exiled in AD6 and Judea was turned into a Roman governorship. He therefore did not take any steps to fulfil his promise to Herodias. Antipas started to rule in northern Israel without her. When Augustus died in 14AD, marriage to Herodias became one step closer, but that same year Salome had just been born and it was impossible to fulfil his promise. Antipas and Herodias still waited until events forced his hand. In 27BC Tiberius retired out of Rome to Capri and for two years Sejanus the leader of the elite praetorian guard ruled Rome. Sejanus attacked the Jews in Rome persecuting them to a greater degree than any previous denunciations of the Jews [51]. This had become dangerous for Agrippa and Herodias.

---

[51] Diaspora; Jews amidst Greeks and Romans by Erich S. Groan page 35

Although Tiberius was unaware of the truth, six or seven years earlier Agrippa's close friend Drusus who was being prepared to succeed Tiberius had been poisoned by his wife who was having an affair with Sejanus [52]. It was quite possible that Sejanus in his persecution of the Jews in Rome would target Herodias (and her brother Agrippa) because their links with Drusus made them known targets. To make matters worse, her brother that year (in 30AD) had had to leave Rome running away from his creditors which increased the likelihood of being "noticed" by the secret police. Any security Agrippa might have brought her with the powerful in Rome was now ended. Herodias wanted her and her daughter out of Rome and she wanted Antipas to fulfil his promise of marriage to her. This time Antipas responded. Fifteen years after the accession of Tiberius, Antipas now in his late forties finally took the plunge and married Herodias. So, Herodias escaped from the threat of Sejanus[53]. Their marriage however was still a big political gamble.[54]

---

[52] Tacitus Annals IV.7,8

[53] The persecution of the Jews in Rome until Sejanus' death in 31AD)

[54] The biblical dating Luke 3:1 is the only known source for the date of the marriage. In 36AD there is specific reference made to this after the defeat of Antipas by Aretas following the death of Philip the tetrarch in 34a,d, which shows the popular negative comment about the marriage that John the Baptist spoke is accurate. There is no reason to doubt the biblical dates as the events happened only six years before the battle. As the defeat shows there were no Roman soldiers in Israel. They were in Syria just beyond Philip's territory. Antipas needed Philip on his side which he did so by giving him Bethsaida in 30AD -in the 34th year of his reign (30AD) Philip issued a coin calling himself founder. The only city he founded was Julias which was the expanded and renamed city of Bethsaida. This gives a possible date of the wedding of Antipas to Herodias

Chapter 14

The first of Jesus' disciples (John 1:35-51)

When Jesus arrived back from the wilderness, he noticed straight away how many more people there were than when he had left. He knew he could not stay there very long. He needed to return for a family wedding. He planned to leave in a couple of days [55] so he could arrive at Galilee in time for the Sabbath. These two days (Monday and Tuesday December 18th,19th) were to prove highly significant. John the Baptist recognised him almost immediately he arrived. Jesus was on his way to the place he had stayed before he had been in the wilderness. When John saw it was Jesus (John 1:29), just as his mother when he was in the womb had prophesied at the coming of Mary, so now John prophesied at the sight of Jesus: "Behold the lamb of God who takes away the sin of the world!" This was a phrase first said under inspiration that day which he would repeat the following day to two of his disciples who were Galilean fisherman John, the brother of James and another Galilean Andrew the brother of Simon. When they heard John the Baptist, they followed Jesus to find out more. John the Baptist's public statement started a process whereby some of John's disciples began to transfer to become disciples of Jesus. The forerunner John was not anxious about this. He saw himself as pointing the bridegroom out, and was content with the results (John 3:29)

John and Andrew were Galileans like Jesus was, and they immediately became friends. Simon who Jesus would call Peter was being introduced by his brother to John the Baptist for the first time. Peter was travelling back to Galilee from Jerusalem – having been at the same Dedication festival which Jesus had attended. Jesus also met two other

---

[55] It was probably the Sabbath which meant Jesus stayed the two days until Sunday

Galileans whose names reflected the Greek culture that had invaded Israel. One was Philip from Bethsaida – the same town where Peter and Andrew had grown up (John 1:44), and the other was Nathanael son of Ptolemy who was from Cana[56]. Jesus explained that he was also going to Cana for a family wedding. It was not long before Jesus invited them all to come with him to the wedding and Nathanael had invited them all to stay at his home. Jesus was now part of this group of Galileans and friendships were formed quickly. They all decided to travel together. They set off early. The temperature was cool (especially at night) During the day it seldom got above 15 degrees C. They walked steadily but with minimal delay. Cana was about 70 miles away and would be a good stopping place for those going onto Capernaum. They would spend the Sabbath at Cana. The wedding would be on the days following. They covered the distance well, only stopping overnight on the Wednesday and Thursday nights. They started each day at 6:00. m. as the sun was rising and would finish each day before sunset at 4:30pm At this time in winter they only had nine or ten hours of daylight. They walked following the well beaten worn dry mud paths which characterised many of the roads of the day. They covered about twenty miles a day.

As they travelled the Capernaum fishermen ribbed the "Greeks" and it was not long before Nathanael was known more by his Greek sounding surname Bartholomew (son of Ptolemy). On Friday morning the disciples walked up out of the Jordan valley into Galilee[57]. They were now on home territory. When they reached Nain at the foothills of Mount Tabor instead of striking west along the valley of Jezreel to go to Nazareth situated in the hills to its north a journey of only three miles or so across the hills, they kept on the main road which navigated the

[56] See John 21:2
[57] The disciples were those mentioned in John's gospel - Andrew, Philip, Nathanael and John. There may have been others.

best level way through the hills. Though about fifteen miles, it was the preferred route to take to Cana which was only just over 8 miles north east from Nazareth[58]. They soon saw their destination in the distance. Cana was situated with a commanding view over the Bet Netofa valley 300 feet or more below. It was afternoon as they picked up their way up the southern slope from the valley to the town. They passed a complex of caves where people in ancient times lived and the shelter it gave was still used. They continued to walk and they all looked onwards to the rest that beckoned as they saw the houses ahead. They came onto the main street in Cana where main roads converged. Cana was the gateway to Upper Galilee and the north south road intersected with a road which to the west went first southwards through Nazareth before striking about 30 miles west towards the Mediterranean. Eastwards the road went six miles to an important town called Magdala situated on the coastline of the sea of Galilee and then turned north-easterly following the coast round to Capernaum (a further 6 miles) The road was always busy. Much of the fish that was exported from the Sea of Galilee to Rome came through Magdala where there was a major salting works. It was then taken sometimes along this road to the port of Ptolemais on the Mediterranean or by choosing a southern fork in the road some miles west of Cana, it was possible to reach Caesarea Maritima. Cana itself, though not large, was bigger than Nazareth though the houses looked similar being built of limestone in a similar style. Nathanael introduced Jesus and the others to his family who welcomed them into their home. As the sun began to go down, they got ready   to   celebrate   the   Sabbath.

---

[58] The site of Cana is disputed. Khirbet Kana (meaning the ruins of Cana) was held as the site of Cana by Theodosius in the 6th century onwards. This is the view adopted here. See "Searching for Cana where Jesus turned water into wine by Tom McCollough Biblical Archaeological review Nov/Dec 2015 vol 41 p 31-38

SECTION 4

Jesus' Pre-Galilee Ministry

Jesus would be known throughout Israel because of his ministry which started in Galilee, but he was baptised outside Galilee and his ministry of power actually began outside Galilee

Chapter 15

Cana December 30AD - first week of January 31AD
(John 2:1-11)

The wedding was an important family occasion. It was when the bridegroom came to the bride's house to take her as his wife back to his house. It was a time when the bride's family wanted to create a great send off for their daughter. It was important for the daughter but even more important for the standing of the family in the village that it went well. Jesus' brother[59] had been some years ago been betrothed to a girl from Cana. Now was the arranged time for the wedding. As Jesus went to the place where the wedding was, there was no difficulty in discovering where it was. The house was decorated for the occasion. Everyone in the town knew where it was and most came. Jesus and his disciples were greeted as bridegroom's family. It made everyone happy. The bridegroom's family were outnumbered by the large number from Cana. It was good to balance this up a little by some additional family coming on the bridegroom's side. Sometimes bridegrooms would arrive at the bride's house with few family. It was always a greater honour for the bride's family when the bridegroom's party was large. It reflected a strong family into whom their daughter was being married, and their attendance meant acceptance and support. John and James were relatives of Jesus' family so there were blood relatives amongst them. As soon as Jesus arrived at the wedding, he greeted his immediate family. He introduced them to his disciples and vice-versa. John and James as relatives were distant relatives and Mary was pleased to meet her nephews and find out how her older sister Salome was getting on. A year or so before she was married, Salome had married Zebedee a man

---

[59] Or a close male relative, because Jesus' mother was involved in a wedding outside her home village and she was able to order the servants to do things and they would obey her. She was not just an ordinary guest there.

from Capernaum. Over the years he had become quite wealthy through his flourishing fishing business. The other disciples were also made welcome. No-one realized at the time, but this would be the last family wedding Jesus would attend. It was also the first occasion where the new power of the Holy Spirit would be demonstrated.

The celebrations continued. Mary as the bridegroom's family was only helping when asked. The organization was after all the bride's family's responsibility There were more people than the bride's family had anticipated and after some hours they were already starting the last stock of wine kept for this occasion. Mary heard the whispering behind closed doors about this. Jesus bringing so many with him may not have helped the situation. The family of the bride provided the wine but when Mary heard that the wine was running out, she sought Jesus to remedy the situation thus avoiding any possible negatives on what had been so far, a normal family celebration. The anxiety of the bride's family at the possible shame had caused the news to leak out to Mary. Mary quietly approached Jesus. "Woman my hour has not yet come" was Jesus' necessary reply to his mother. He could not make Kingdom activity subject to family whims and he knew the Galilean ministry lay in the future. However, Jesus also knew that the Father was in this request because he knew what to do. His mother had already detailed some helpers to obey whatever Jesus said. He told them to fill the limestone jars – so typical of the Jews of that time (–rather than the clay pots used by the Romans) with water. The helpers were good. The jars were large- too heavy to move, yet they brought water and filled them to the brim. When no more water could be added, they told Jesus what they had done. Jesus did nothing until new wine was called for as the wine that was there had run out. Jesus told them to draw some out and take to the wedding's wine taster. He was the master of ceremonies providing focus and fun at such big occasions. One of his jobs was to announce the new wine had arrived and to taste it first for him to make comment upon it before it was served to everyone else. They ladled some of the water (now made wine) into a jug and brought it for him to taste. They poured it into his cup as he stood up for all to see. He drank it in front of them all and announced it was the best wine yet. No-one except the servants knew. So, the wedding passed without difficulty. The next day following the wedding, Jesus with his disciples and his mother plus some of his siblings went to Capernaum. James and John had invited Mary and Jesus to their home. They knew Salome the mother of James and John would be welcoming. They had had no contact for years. John had not known Jesus was a relative until they had arrived at the wedding. During the journey his disciples had found out about the water becoming wine. They were amazed.

Family visit to Capernaum (John 2:12)

Mary now a widow continued to follow with interest the development of her son Jesus. She wanted to spend time with both her sister and Jesus.[60] At Capernaum Jesus and the rest of his family stayed at his aunt Salome's house with his mother. [61] Any disciples of Jesus who were not from Capernaum would have been put up either at the same place or in another house. The family of Zebedee was part of Jesus wider family., and they had come from a family wedding in Cana, and there was every expectation that they would stay a month or so, but they were not there very long at all (John 2:12) much to the surprise of the family. It was

---

[60] There is no mention of Joseph at this time or later. Mary (without Joseph) is with her sons at Capernaum trying to meet Jesus, and also later at the cross with other women. Mary (without Joseph) is at the tomb with other disciples of Jesus and is probably also present with the disciples at Pentecost following the instructions of Jesus when he ascended. Joseph by contrast is not mentioned at all. Joseph his father was dead. At his crucifixion Jesus assigns his mother into the care of one of his disciples – something he could not have done if his father was alive, and his father did not die during Jesus' years of ministry (there is no funeral during his ministry). Although deceased , but the family still drew their identity from Joseph (John 6:42),

[61] As at the marriage of Cana, whilst the disciples of Jesus exist, Jesus is treated by his mother as one of the family. The relationship between Jesus and family was changing but had not yet evolved to the point when he is active in ministry

late January or even early February when his mother returned to Nazareth with her other children. (Luke 4:14). They had completed their stay. One of the reasons for the early departure is that Jesus went preaching in other synagogues rather than spend time with them. They saw that Jesus would not be taking charge or providing for Mary. The relationships between Jesus and the family had changed because Jesus had changed. His focus was now on his ministry which Jesus was actively developing, even speaking at some synagogues in the area. This was not welcomed by everyone in the family. but Mary was very capable in managing every difficulty and helping the rest of the family stay together in peace whilst watching Jesus emerge into his calling which would become a national ministry. She returned home to meet her new daughter in law. She had given the newlyweds some space from the family, but now they would resume their life with a new addition to the family in Nazareth. Jesus' absence from home was being filled by one of her sons with his new wife living there. They would manage and manage well.

Jesus was now in his thirties and his brothers and sisters now in their twenties and early thirties were established and fully independent. Although his brothers might have wished him to stay (Song of Songs 1:6b) and look after everything at home, there was now no longer any obligation so to do. Jesus knew the will of God lay in the ministry of the Kingdom of God. Jesus also did not stay in Capernaum but nor did he return with his family to Nazareth. Instead for the next few weeks he taught in the synagogues (Luke 4:15) in Galilee living in no one place during this time.

Chapter 16

The Passover Wednesday April 25th 31AD Feast of Unleavened bread 26th April – May 2nd 31AD (John 2:13)

It was now April, and sometime well before Passover, Jesus set off for Jerusalem. (John2:13). The ministry so far in Galilee whilst the right thing to do, had not led to much. It would be some months before the crowds would seek him wherever he went. For now, Jesus was little known, and he walked alone [62]. Passover was always at a time of year when the evidence of spring was all around them in the countryside green replaced yellow, and all kinds of fruits were coming into season. The pink blossom of the almond trees added colour. Pears and blood oranges were in plentiful supply.

Setting off early for Jerusalem was not unusual. Jews from other parts of the Mediterranean often were very early, if not the first to arrive. They came to Jerusalem taking advantage of the ships now sailing again after the winter when adverse winds enforced all shipping to cease. Jesus took the road southwards from Capernaum area following the shoreline of the Sea of Galilee and travelled on the main Roman road past Tiberias southwards to Bethshean (an ancient Jewish city now rebuilt as a Graeco- Roman city) on the border of Galilee. Jesus joined other pilgrims travelling southwards down through the Jordan valley towards Jerusalem. This route was not only 23 miles longer than the direct route through Samaria which some Galileans took (Josephus Antiquities 20.6.1.), but also considerably hotter. There was also at the end of the journey a steep ascent to Jerusalem. The bulk of the 3,400-foot change

---

[62] Only John records this. There may have been few disciples with Jesus at this time. There is no mention of disciples until after the feast (3:22). The disciples are only recorded during this time as remembering the significance of a recorded saying Jesus made during this time in Jerusalem.

in elevation (Jericho lies 812 feet below sea level and Jerusalem 2,600 feet above sea level) occurs within 15 miles. The steep road from Jericho winds through a desolate wasteland of barren rock with twisted canyons and cliffs. There were also perils from wild beasts especially in the Jordan valley, but it was the preferred route because the Jordan was a constant source of drinking water, and there was the large number of villages and towns in the Jordan valley where hospitality was available. This could not be said of Samaria.

Jesus stayed overnight in one of the villages as he made his way towards Jericho. When Jesus reached Jericho, he turned west making the steep ascent up to the dry Judean plain to gradually ascend to the mount of Olives before descending the other side to Jerusalem. Since his youth had come this way to Jerusalem for the main Jewish festivals. This Passover[63], however was the first since he had been baptized in the Spirit. Jesus was in Jerusalem over a week before the arrival of most visitors. Thousands came from all over Israel and beyond, so even before Passover, the ancient city of Jerusalem was heaving with visitors. At such times worshippers in their hundreds converged on the temple. There were, however, many entrances and so there was no delay in Jesus' coming into the large paved area on which the temple was built. [64] Though later referred to as the court of the Gentiles, Jesus knew it as the mountain of the house. (The only named courts of the temple were in the temple itself). The open pavement stretched over a tenth of a mile in each direction and was paved with the finest variegated marble. Colonnaded porticos or cloisters bordered the large open space.

---

[63] Jesus would experience only two more seasons of Passover (John 6:4 when he fed the 5000; and John 11:55 when he was crucified).
[64] Jesus cleansed the temple here and just before his betrayal. The temple mentioned here is the building containing the sanctuary, inner court and outer court set in an enclosed paved area called the court of the gentiles. Jesus threw them out of the outer court (known as the court on the women) to find a place in the paved area of the temple site which was the usual place where people bought and sold.

Particularly grand was the colonnaded royal porch to the south with its carved Cedar roof and four rows of white marble monolithic columns with Corinthian capitals (162 in all) which provided three aisles of which the middle one was wider than the other two. Within this portico was the administrative centre of the outer court so from its shade would emerge priests who were always there to help. They would advise pilgrims on the right sacrifice and help the temple activities. Money changers, animals for sacrifice as well as other gifts were for sale were there. Ever since the second temple had been rebuilt there had been various stall selling helpful produce for pilgrims. Herod just formalized it a little by creating space for a large market amidst the columns. The synagogue in the temple was also situated nearby there. Jesus moved northwards across the marble pavement towards the temple. The crowds seemed to get even larger as he walked. Priests and the rich pilgrims who lived in the western part of the city walled off from the rest of Jerusalem came via the bridge they had paid for over the valley which separated them from the temple and the Roman tower of Antonio. Other Jews had had to climb the steps from the valley bottom to the gate on the south west corner. The rich came into the paved area through the gate of Coponius. Other pilgrims – both rich and poor came in through the sheep gate in the north or from the gate in the east (The gate of Susa), but these were less than the flow of people from the other entrances. Most gates to the temple site were on the south side and most of those in the city used these. The numbers in the outer court were visibly swelled by those who entered the temple site that way. All the entrances to the outer paved court they came through you only discovered once there. There were tunnel entrances linked to stairs which led from each southern gate under the royal porch directly into the court of the Gentiles When Herod had extended the mount with retainer walls he had also created the two tunnels one on the left and on the right from the south facing wall. One of the "Mole" (Huldah) gates[65] was double arched and the other, on the right triple arched to distinguish them. Stairs led up to each gate. Entrance to the temple was through the triple arched whilst exit through the other allowed for rapid movement of the crowd. Another tunnel entrance near the Gate Beautiful was not used by pilgrims. This was used by Roman soldiers from the adjoining barracks (the Antonia fortress) so they could be quickly deployed onto the temple site if there was a disturbance[66]. At every major festival there were always battle-ready Roman soldiers battle able to be deployed (Josephus wars 5.5.8) quickly via the tunnel and via the upper colonnades that linked the fort with the temple. This did not offend the Jewish religious sensitivities. Pagan soldiers in the outer court was acceptable as it was open to non-Jews, though few as such were ever there. Large impressive marble slabs four and a half feet high engraved in Greek and Latin warned of the death penalty to any non-Jew who dared to enter the actual temple which was surrounded by a raised terrace in the middle of the paved area. Jesus went up the fourteen steps, which only Jews could walk, onto the terrace lined with a balustrade which bounded the temple. He was now on the same level as the doors into the temple. There were four gates on the south and north three of which were used by the priests and men to get directly into their court (the fourth gate went into the court of the women). Jesus along with most of the crowd made their way up the steps on the east side of the temple and followed those in front through the principal door called "Gate Beautiful". It had large brass impressive doors (50 cubits high and 40 wide) of the temple which were wide open to receive

---

[65] One tunnel still exists in Jerusalem and is used to reach the mosque which now stands there.
[66] in Acts 21:27-32 when Paul was taken out of the temple building - through the Gate Beautiful- into the outer court and the doors of the temple were shut. The crowd sought to kill Paul there and then as the marble notices stated but the soldiers accessed the paved area through the tunnel to arrest Paul

the crowd. As he went through the gate Jesus went past two treasure chests for the half shekel tax, into which some near him threw a coin. This was one of the ways money was raised for the upkeep of the temple. Jesus had entered the court which was as far as Jewish women could go. This was the largest of the courts of the temple. It had four sixty-foot square courts on the outside corners of the area and the space in the middle between these was a large open space 200 feet square (Mishnah Middoth 2,5). The smaller courts at the corners of the court were marked out by columns and in front of these were eleven treasure chests for the voluntary offerings of money. and it was open to all Jews male and female. To one side of the court Some men were shaving the heads of some male pilgrims in accord with Nazarite vows. In other parts there was dancing, music and song. Children with mothers in attendance moved with the elderly and infirm. The next courtyard was for male Jews only. A magnificent circular staircase of fifteen steps led to the Nicanor gate which was decorated in silver and gold beyond which was the narrow hall filled with beautiful cloistered columns called the court of the Israelites. In this court of the Israelites was an incense altar and it surrounded an inner courtyard where only priests could go. Here the sacrifices occurred and beyond that was the temple sanctuary hidden from view by a heavy priceless curtain decorated with a map of the known world where only the priests could go. Jesus never went here. This area contained the incense altar seven branched lampstand and the table for the shewbread. Beyond that, hidden by another heavy curtain was the holy of holies. While it may not have had the full splendour of Solomon's temple, but it was much larger and very impressive. Josephus describes it as follows "Viewed *from without, the Sanctuary (the temple building) had everything that could amaze either mind or eyes. Overlaid all round with stout plates of gold, the first rays of the sun it reflected so fierce a blaze of fire that those who endeavored to look at it were forced to turn away as if they had looked straight at the sun. To strangers as they approached it seemed in the distance like a mountain covered with snow; for any part not covered with gold was dazzling white..."* (The Jewish War, p. 304) The gold and white marble pillars supported the weight of vaulted roofs. The architecture of the whole building was stunning. Rich tapestries adorned the walls which Josephus describes as depicting "the whole vista of the heavens" in the purple, blue, and scarlet colours of the Old Testament tabernacle. It was impressive and a source of pride to many Jews of Jesus' day.

Before him was the curved steps up into the court of Israel, but Jesus stopped. He saw some had set up stalls within the temple making the most of the increased business major festivals gave them to sell and exchange money. This was after all the treasury, but this was a place to give to God as part of their worship. Not a place for selling or exchanging money. They were even in the open courts at the corners of the court of the women as well as in the main area. He sat down and quietly made a whipcord. He then stood up and attacked the stall holders forcing them back down the steps. He also drove out of the temple those who were selling sheep and oxen for sacrifice as well as those changing money from the "pagan" currency into temple coins. He forced them back down the steps to find a less lucrative or advantageous position in the court of the Gentiles where buying and selling had taken place for hundreds of years. No-one who was there as Jesus did this, objected to the principle of this, for everyone knew that this was right. No-one should be selling in the temple itself. Even the temple "police" did not arrest him.

Many approved of this action by this zealous man. Jesus was not the only one to have done this. The Galileans especially were pleased to make a statement against the rule of the Jerusalem authorities. They had no love of the "southern" orthodoxy which despised them for being Galilean and at the same time continued to adapt to Hellenic and Roman customs.

As Passover approached Jesus met disciples including the friends he had left in Galilee (So John 3:22) who now joined him in Jerusalem. Jesus shared in the Passover with the family he was staying with. They were just one of the Jewish families who opened their home every Passover to visiting Jews. It was a source of extra income for them. Jesus did not form any in depth relationships with any he stayed with in Jerusalem. He was just one guest among many to the hosts. He stayed during his life at various places but the one he stayed this year was owned by one of those who had close links to the Sanhedrin or at least the party of the Pharisees. One night after Jesus returned from the temple during the feast of unleavened bread -the feast which immediately followed the Passover- there was a knock on the door where Jesus was staying with some of the disciples. It was dark. Outside was an older man who had come to talk with Jesus at an unexpected time of night. The owner of the house welcomed him in and Jesus met him. He found out this man was well known and one of the Pharisees on the Sanhedrin – an important man in Jerusalem. He visited him by night, so he could not be easily recognized. Nicodemus Ben Gurion was wealthy and a celebrity. He had risen to fame through a miraculous answer to prayer. Although his family knew him as Bunai son of Gurion, everyone else called him Nicodemus. Jesus had also done one major miracle – turning water into wine, but although Jesus was not moving in the miracles he would later, the kingdom manifested wherever he went. Nicodemus who had only seen what Jesus did in Jerusalem from his cleansing of the temple onwards had witnessed enough of them to make him curious and eager to meet Jesus. The synagogue or family contacts were the normal way news travelled. So, when Jesus started to be talked about, Nicodemus wanted to meet him. It only took a few enquiries before he knew where he was staying. Nicodemus was well known, and he had no wish of drawing attention to himself or to Jesus at this time. He came with the intention of finding out who Jesus was.

Jesus was unknown. He had not been brought up in the circles of the Pharisees. He was not from a powerful family of influence.

When he had sat down with Jesus he began "No-one can do the works that you do unless God were with him". (John 3:1) Nicodemus recognized God was with Jesus in a remarkable way. The words he heard he did not fully understand, but when he left the house, Nicodemus was never the same again. He knew Jesus was special. (see John 19:39)

Nicodemus was not the only one who had been affected by what Jesus did during the Passover. He had created quite a stir in Jerusalem which was reported and remembered with affection for some months in his home region of Galilee (John 4:45). Even whilst still in Jerusalem Influential people offered welcome and friendship. Such offers held the promise of provision and opportunities to take up, but Jesus refused to agree to their proposals (John 2:24). They were similar offers to the one Satan had given him on the mountain, and Jesus would not take any apparent short cuts to bringing the Kingdom. It had to be the Father's way alone. Jesus returned to the Jordan

Chapter 17

At the Jordan May 3rd (John 3:22-35)

Jesus and his disciples left Jerusalem and made their way back to the familiar place where John the Baptist had been baptising. They found John had already moved northwards to Aenon near Salim but some of Jesus disciples already had places to stay in the area where John used to be so Jesus stayed with them [67]They shared the Sabbath together on the evening of the following day. Jesus already knew he could no longer stay any period at Nazareth – a sentiment he would share with those he travelled with when returning a few months later (John 4:44) but now was not the time to go to Galilee. There was no place to stay there at the moment, whereas where he was, he was welcome. Jesus was content to stay in a place which he knew was not his final calling. Because there was no other viable option, Jesus knew this must be God's will for the present.

It was May with the usual hot dry summer to come. The normal rainfall during the winter had not been as abundant as the previous year. Spring at the end of the rainy season should have been a time when there was plenty of water in the rivers but already the water level was too low for John to baptize the crowds where he had been for some months. John decided, after the difficulty of baptizing the crowds coming to Jerusalem for the Passover, to move immediately northwards (see John 3:23) to Aenon [68]where the natural springs ensured there was plenty of water. Rain that had fallen months before in the western hills had seeped through the limestone to form springs. This was the main source of water for John. The crowds now came more frequently so that

---

[67] Note John 3:22 Jesus "remained with them" - not they remained with him
[68] Aenon means "Springs". John the Apostle identified this place as near Salim (Some suggest the Shalom of Genesis 33:8 en route from Peniel to Succoth on R Jabbok about thirty miles east of the Jordan some miles north of Bethabara)

many hundreds had been baptized. They had come in larger numbers since John's accusation of Antipas had made him a household name. Baptising many people was no longer just around main festivals as pilgrims made their way to and from Jerusalem. It was now all the time. Crowds came from the Passover festival to be baptized at the ford crossing, to find that John had moved to Aenon. When they found that Jesus and his friends were there (John 3:23), rather than travel further, they asked to be baptized and the disciples (who had been disciples of John) baptized them. People continued to come for baptism even when most pilgrims attending the Passover had returned home. His disciples baptised those who wanted but Jesus himself met people quietly on a one to one basis. He did not teach publicly nor did he in any way upstage John. Since being baptized, Jesus had started to move in spiritual gifts and the days he was there enabled him to grow in maturity in the practice of them. Such maturity only comes by doing, and Jesus became proficient in words of knowledge and experienced in healing and deliverance by the time he returned to Galilee through his time here.

Although Jesus did not baptize (John 4:2) the distinction between him and the forerunner call of John the Baptist was lost to the crowds (John 1:26). Because Jesus' disciples were actively baptising, it took only a short time before Jesus was likened and compared to John the Baptist (John 3:26). The numbers coming to the place John the Baptist used to be were far greater than those who found him at Aenon near Salim. It was obvious that the disciples of Jesus were baptizing far more than John (John 3:26, John 4:1,2). When Jesus heard this, he decided to move from the Jordan (John 4:1) Jesus had no wish to adopt the call of John. John had a specific calling and Jesus respected this position. He had no intention of staying any longer.

He knew John was a forerunner, so He saw in this a sign that his hour had come for he was now more successful than John and was rivalling his reputation. Jesus knew this had to stop. In addition, from a human point of view he needed to distance himself from the Baptist's ministry to develop his own ministry. As Jesus was pondering such thoughts, news came to him that John the Baptist had been arrested (Mark 1:14). John by moving northwards had put himself into the reach of Antipas who ruled Galilee and Perea. John was in a border region between Decapolis[69] and Perea. Antipas had acted quickly when he found out where he was. He had made some agreements with Philip the tetrarch who ruled the Decapolis region to allow him to bring his military onto his territory. He had no wish for the Roman legions stationed just beyond Decapolis to get the wrong idea of what Antipas was doing when doing military maneuvers outside his domain. Antipas then arrested John, imprisoning him in the fortress Machaerus[70] a mountain fortress on a high precipice on the eastern shore of the Sea of Galilee. John was taken down into its dungeons away from public view.

For Jesus John's arrest was confirmation that the time had now come to move back to Galilee. He acted immediately leaving the Jordan with his disciples to go to Galilee (John 4:1-3).

---

[69] It is probably at this stage that Antipas handed Philip Bethsaida who would transform it into his capital city. from his 34th year (31AD). Philip issued a coin in that year celebrating the fact he was a founder. The only city he founded was Julias which used to be Bethsaida. See Arie Kindler's article "The coins of Philip of Bethsaida" Arie Kindler Coins of Tetrarch Philip and Bethsaida, https://bethsaidaarcheologyorg.files.wordpress.com/2017/01/1999-kindler-coinstetrarch
[70] Josephus Antiquities 18.119

Chapter 18

The move to Galilee May 31AD
(Matthew 4:12, Mark 1:14, Luke 4:14, John 4:1-3)

The arrest of John the Baptist put Jesus and his disciples in potential danger of arrest also. They had been linked together in the public eye. So rather than following his normal route - up the Jordan valley northwards back towards Galilee, he chose the alternative route through Samaria. (John 4:34).[71] This was a longer route from the Jordan, but by avoiding the area where John the Baptist had been captured Jesus ensured he was not arrested. So, Jesus and the disciples went back to Jerusalem and then northwards to reach Anuathu Borcaeus – the last Judean city before Samaria where they stayed the night. They then set off the next day to walk across the rolling hills and valleys of Samaria

The woman of Samaria May 31AD (John 4:4-42)

It was four months before the feast of Tabernacles (Harvest. John 4:35)Although as we have seen external circumstances forced him to take this route (John 4:4a), the Father was unfolding His plan. The journey through Samaria was uneventful until they reached the site of ancient Shiloh. This was where in ancient times Jacob had lived for a while. There was a deep well there which originally had been dug by Jacob. 500 yards to the north was the tomb containing the bones of Joseph brought out of Egypt with Moses (Joshua 24:32). The tomb of Joseph was on land bequeathed by Jacob. They were surrounded by history. To the west looking nearer than it was lay Mount Gerizim and on the bottom of its northern slopes was Shechem the ancient city of refuge for the central mountains of Israel, nestling between mount

---

[71] Hence John 4:4 "he needed" to go through Samaria

Gerizim to its south and mount Ebal to its north. They were east of the valley where the road they would take would go up the valley between the two mountains. He could see Ebal directly before him and as his eyes turned south west he saw Shechem at the foothills of Gerizim (the holy mountain to the Samaritans) which rose majestically just beyond the city. The view of the mountains had not changed since Jacob had lived and looked at the same view. Samuel too had walked these parts on his frequent journeys from Shiloh and Shechem to Bethel and to his home at Ramah in the south near Jerusalem and Bethlehem. They would soon walk the ancient road through the valley past Mount Ebal and then strike northwards towards Galilee, but for now they must pause in their journey. The well seemed the perfect place to stop. It was well built and promised water. Their initial delight, however, soon turned to disappointment when they realised that the well was so deep they could not get any water out of it. They knew water was there, but they had no bucket to put down and get some. It was a typical summer day. The temperature was above 30 degrees C and the few small clouds in the blue sky did nothing to hide the burning glare of the sun. Jesus was dehydrated and weary. He stayed there near the well whilst the others went into town to get provisions. They had already covered many miles that day. They had made good time to reach Sychar and from here they would walk northwards to Samaria at the other end of the pass. They had now just under 50 miles to walk to reach Galilee. But for the moment Jesus could walk no further.

The disciples went over the sandy rocks towards the nearby town[72] to buy some food. Jesus knew they would be gone for a while. Jesus sat

---

[72] This is not Shechem. John 4:5 says this is a city of Samaria called Sychar an expression used of an obscure city rather than the well-known Shechem , the capital city of Samaria, which was nearby. The city is unknown though today there is a village called Askar with a spring on the lower edges of Ebal about half a mile from where Jesus was. The view taken here is that this is the town where the woman comes from.

down on what once had been a field owned by Jacob and bequeathed to Joseph – a field the latter had never seen. Now Jesus would claim that inheritance (John 4:5 [73]). As he stood on the ancient land, Jesus could open an ancient spiritual well.

As often happens at such times, events reflected ancient events. Leaving Jesus by the well the disciples went, unaware of a woman who was already on her way to get water for her and her family. This woman would become the catalyst for the gospel, being the first to bring it to her home region. Elements of this meeting with Jesus would reflect the first meeting of Jacob with Rachel and indeed the mother of Jacob Rebekah's first meeting with the servant of Abraham when he first chose a wife for Isaac (Genesis). Both were at wells and watering thirsty animals. It was this well that Jacob proudly built in later life after winning the ground by his own hand (Genesis 48:22)

Jesus thirst grew as he waited in the sun. The woman ignored him as she came to the well, got her bucket attached to the rope to put down the well. Jesus asked her for a drink. She did not know he was the source of all life (John 1:2), the Messiah- who asked for a drink. Without a word she put a cup down into her bucket of water and gave Jesus some. The woman for her part was surprised that anyone should talk to her – especially a Jew. She had noticed him as she got close and could see he was a typical Jew. Galileans especially were often seen making their journey to and from Jerusalem. The woman walked the half mile trip from Sychar every day, but she had never had a Jew ask her for a drink before. She came to the well as she could get the water she needed in peace. There was a spring in the city itself[74] but it was always in demand and it was a struggle to get what she needed there especially

---

[73] It is significant that the text references the history of the land in establishing the location first and only then mentions the well around which the narrative unfolds.

[74] Modern village Askar contains a spring

when there were others who would bad mouth her or threaten her. Her personal life had much to be desired, and there were women in the village who had personal issues with her. The well was deserted at this time of day and therefore never a problem. None of this she told Jesus. The inner question of her heart was why Jesus had asked her a Samaritan to give him a Jew some water, so she asked him. She had come prepared with rope and a bucket, but unprepared for the conversation which followed her question and would change her life. Jesus reply was that if she knew who was asking her, she would be asking him for the water of life. Life on the inside was what she wanted. Without her disclosing anything about herself, Jesus knew everything and spoke to her such words that had such an effect on her that she left her water pot which she had been filling so she could go quickly to the city. She went where the men were gathered (John 4:28) to share important news and so needed to speak it directly to them. (There was no guarantee that the women would listen to her or act on it). The men she spoke to, were the important people in the town: what they said counted. They listened, came out to Jesus (4:40) and formally welcomed him into their town. The hospitality and respite in the journey was very welcome. This was the first time in Jesus experience of kingdom ministry in a different culture. During these days he taught all who wanted to hear, and many believed through what he said (John 4:42ff).

After two days John 4:43) they left Sychar behind. They did not wish to be in Samaria during the Sabbath so after saying their "goodbyes" they walked on towards Galilee. The first stage was 7 miles north west through the valley of Shechem until they came to a wide stretch of land resembling a basin bordered by hills which stretched out below them. In the middle of this "basin" was a large steep hill on which was the ancient city of Samaria, rebuilt and then expanded by Herod the Great and with the town spreading out below it. It was now called Sebaste. The road northwards went to Galilee and so they reached Cana without difficulty. Cana was well placed to visit other places in Lower Galilee. It was on a main route from the coast to the Sea of Galilee where roads from the south joined them before going northwards in to Upper Galilee. Cana had frequent travellers passing through in many directions, so the group of men walking into town was not even noticed. Nathanael took them to his home where they stayed for the Sabbath. On the following day, those from Capernaum and Bethsaida departed eastwards whilst Jesus remained. Jesus' ministry was very small, by its later standards. Jesus was welcomed not because of his connection to John the Baptist. Most people in Galilee could not care less. On his arrival in Galilee by those who had witnessed what Jesus did when He was in Jerusalem during the Passover festival a month before. (John 4:45; see John 2:23-25). Jesus had plenty of places to stay.

SECTION 5

The start of Jesus' ministry in Galilee

Chapter 19

It was 6 months since John the Baptist had baptized him. Jesus was now anointed in power and some in Galilee had witnessed this in Jerusalem and talked about him to their families and friends. For the moment Jesus was an interesting person -an item of news - rather than anyone to be sought after or followed. No-one had yet discovered the greatness of his person or the uniqueness of his teaching. That would come later. Jesus started his ministry to Galilee from Cana. He was welcomed into homes wherever he went so there was somewhere to stay for the Sabbath and he could teach in the synagogues. The welcome he received seemed in contrast to the revelation which he had shared with his disciples on the journey. Jesus had told them to expect local Galileans to despise what he said. "a prophet is not honoured in his own country" was the proverb Jesus spoke. John 4:44-45) To the disciples it might have seemed at that moment the revelation was not true. Welcome was important to Jesus, for it dictated where He went in Galilee. Jesus came to Cana and stayed again with Nathanael's family until each Sabbath he would go and stay in another village speaking at their synagogue.

The nobleman's son June 31AD (John 4:43-54)

As we have seen Jesus during the week was in Cana living at the house of Nathanael. A nobleman from Capernaum heard he was there and sought him out because his son was sick. He travelled with the state of his son's illness heavy on his heart and with the specific intention of asking Jesus to heal his son[75]. He had heard about Jesus and his power to heal, and even his servants back in Capernaum knew of his plan to find Him. He like many other wealthy men travelled this trade route

---

[75] It is likely that he also had business to do in the area and came laden with items to sell.

many times. Cana lay on the road from Capernaum to Port Ptolemais which, because of its extended harbour was the main port for Galilee. He found Jesus around midday (John 4:52) and asked if He would travel with him in his cart to heal his son (John 4:47). Instead of getting up and going with him, Jesus just stated that the young son was healed and remained where he was. Within the hour after meeting with Jesus the nobleman was on his way back towards Capernaum (John 4:50) hoping to cover the 12 miles to Magdala and the 6 miles to Capernaum before sunset. Unknown to him his son began to get well at the very time Jesus spoke. When the nobleman's household (his family and servants) were sure the nobleman's son was now out of danger and well recovered, servants were dispatched to tell his father. They were concerned the nobleman was now bringing Jesus on an unnecessary journey. More than one servant were sent (John 4:52) (It was safer to travel in groups even in Galilee). They set off riding as fast as they could to find him. Meanwhile the nobleman was on the road back from Cana past the watershed ridge and descending through the brown fields and olive groves towards the sea of Galilee. They were not sure who saw who first, but they met each other about half way between Cana and Capernaum in what is called the valley of the doves below Mount Arbel just outside Magdala sometime between 3pm and 4pm. It was with great joy the nobleman heard his servants' news. As they had shared their stories, the nobleman quickly realized his son got better at the same time as Jesus had said "Go your way. Your son is well". In his heart he now knew that Jesus' word was true, and his son had been healed. Jesus was indeed the healer! Together they went through Magdala (Migdal) over the plain of Gennasaret (Tabgha). When they got back home to Capernaum they quickly told all they knew. News about Jesus spread to both family and servants. Faith blossomed in his house for it was his whole household (family & servants) who believed (John 4:53). From there this incident spread to others especially those who attended the Capernaum synagogue. John heard about this and wrote it down later in his gospel. Jesus heard from his disciples in Capernaum about the son being healed. It may have helped to provide an encouragement for Jesus as he thought about the next stage to possibly live in Capernaum. The news of this event shared amongst the Jewish community in Capernaum is likely to have been in the background when they, sometime later, discussed asking Jesus to do the same for a Gentile – the centurion who built the synagogue in the centre of the town when his servant became ill. (Luke 7:1-10) and may have also helped the ruler of the synagogue at Capernaum seek Jesus out when his daughter became dangerously ill. More fruit would follow from the healing on the nobleman's son.

Nazareth June 31AD (Luke 4:16-30)

Jesus set off on the road from Cana to go to his home town of Nazareth. He went through Autocratoris and then southward on the road Joseph and he had walked many times as he came into Nazareth from the north. Here Jesus was in familiar surroundings. He greeted his mother and intended to stay for the Sabbath when no Jew travelled and so in the evening Jesus celebrated with his family the traditional meal at the start of Sabbath. There was a mixture of emotions. Jesus taking part like he always had in the home again had a nostalgic feel about it, for everyone also knew life had moved on and it could not be the same. Joseph was dead, and life at home was moving on. His brothers and sisters were getting on with their lives and his mother was transitioning from being an active mother with children at home and a husband into a place of widowhood[76]. In her inner heart Mary knew Jesus was starting the ministry prophesied about him by Gabriel at his birth. She recognized the differences Jesus was now in after being filled with the Spirit, but she and Jesus had developed an understanding.

[76] There is no direct reference to Joseph after the birth narratives and he is certainly dead by the time Jesus on the cross designates her to be looked after by John, and there is no reference to Jesus attending a funeral of Joseph during his earthly ministry.

Their relationship worked. Her care was from a distance. She was not demanding of him and she had learnt to respect the words that would come like lightening from his mouth and the choices in life he made. For her part she would support in whatever way he chose to live. She determined to not put any demands on him even if family or neighbours said she should. Only once did she go back on this decision.[77] Jesus now had disciples with him most of the time and she was not always able to provide for them. Her lifestyle was poor but for a few days she would manage and manage well.

Jesus had obeyed the Jewish rules [78]since a boy, so he would not travel far on a Sabbath remaining in the town. If he had to leave a town on the Sabbath he would certainly not walk more than a mile on that day[79]. He like everyone else attended the synagogue. He had known this practice if he could remember. He came into the room with rows of benches around three of the walls. Nothing had changed. He sat down where the men sat in the front benches. Jesus knew most of the adults as he took his seat. The local people wanted to hear him for they had heard about him especially what happened when in Jerusalem where Jesus had done wonders which had amazed even members of the Sanhedrin (John 3;1). He was the local boy who was starting to become a celebrity in the area. So, Jesus was invited to read from the scriptures at the synagogue service. Jesus made his way to the place where he had seen so many people before him stand to read and speak. It was right in the middle and he could be easily seen (and heard) by everyone. Jesus took the scroll that was handed to him by one of the officials there. He found Isaiah 61 and read from it. He then closed the scroll and gave it back to

[77] Mary came with his brothers to try to interrupt Jesus ministering when he lived in Capernaum Matthew 12:46,47

[78] There was never any controversy about Jesus' strict observance of the law until his healing ministry began on the Sabbath

[79] Acts 1:12 describes the distance from Jerusalem to Mount of Olives as "a Sabbath day's journey". The mount of olives is 400 yards from the south edge of Jerusalem

the synagogue authorities who kept the precious scrolls safe. The preliminaries were over, now all the synagogue's attention was on Jesus and what he would say[80]. Jesus started "today this scripture is fulfilled in your Hearing". What Jesus said, everyone agreed afterwards was amazing. They could not believe one of their own, uneducated could at least match those who were learned... Some thought they had never heard anything like it. It was the authority and confidence with which he spoke that surprised them as well as his deep knowledge of the scriptures. They were astounded that a builder's son could speak like this. He was as good if not better than anyone they had heard before. Those who heard Jesus that morning, later told their families and their relatives who lived in other villages what a good speaker he was (Luke 4:22). The atmosphere suddenly changed when Jesus seemed to drift into heresy. He attacked the special status they enjoyed as Jews. Some in the synagogue rose up in anger and grabbed him and took him out of the synagogue and there was nothing anyone else could do. All his mother could do was watch as they took him out of the village southwards to what is now called Mount Precipice in the cliffs of Kedurmim just outside the village high above the valley of Jezreel. They went with the intention of throwing him over to his death. When they got to the place their resolve seemed to weaken. There was a great crowd and debate about the best way to punish him. In the confusion Jesus slipped away hiding from them in an ancient cave which still exists today that he had explored as a boy. Jesus waited until nightfall before going back into the village. Jesus knew the synagogue members, and they knew where his family lived, and although the anger might have already settled down so that some were relieved that Jesus had not been killed, nevertheless his escape from their hands meant he could not return to his home (Luke 4:28,29). He did not want to make things difficult for his family. Until the visit to Nazareth, all had been

[80] Luke 4:20

going well. In Cana Jesus had been welcomed and praised (Luke 4:14). And this was also true of Nazareth at the start. But now Jesus had to leave. The incident at Nazareth had decided that! (see Luke 4:31). [81] He went to Capernaum.

---

[81] At this time Jesus' ministry was more about preaching than about healing. Crowds following him seeking healing was for the future. It was the content of his teaching which had caused the adverse reaction against Him. (For the moment there was no controversy over his actions on the Sabbath). Jesus was behaving as a normal Jew on the Sabbath. There was as yet little expectation on Jesus to heal and Jesus did not regard this as unbelief. (Later it would be different. (Mark6:6)) At this stage miracles were sporadic so there was no expectation or unbelief. God's purpose grows and the manifestations of His purpose change from season to season. In the future there would be great seasons of healings and demonstration of the kingdom of God in Jesus' life. Jesus' task was to obey the Father in whatever way he was told (John 5:19), and for now it was proclaiming the kingdom through preaching and teaching. Jesus in every synagogue he visited announced the kingdom. There were several small cities and villages in the hills around Cana including Nazareth and Jesus visited some of them. Wherever he went It was the authority as he spoke that people noticed and what people talked about afterwards

Chapter 20

The move to Capernaum June 31AD
(Matthew 4:13, Luke 4:31)

Jesus set off immediately for Capernaum. The welcome he had from those in Capernaum contrasted strongly with his experience in Nazareth. Jesus set off early as soon as it was light enough to walk safely, and before too many people were awake. The birdsong at dawn was the only sound as he left the place of his upbringing. He had a walk of forty miles and he would walk most that day, staying in the large city of Magdala where there would be many places to stay if he could manage this before nightfall. The following day he would follow the shoreline of the freshwater lake called the Sea of Galilee northwards as he walked on the ancient road- the "Via Maris"- to cover the six or so miles to Capernaum. As Jesus started the cool night temperature was quickly being replaced by the warmth of the June sun. Jesus knew it would probably climb into the mid-eighties degrees Fahrenheit by the afternoon especially as he descended towards the Sea of Galilee. In June there was thirteen hours of sun so the extended daylight at this time of year meant he could cover more ground each day. The most direct route was to go to Cana and then from there on the ancient road through the Arbel valley, a mountain pass which cut a passage to the Sea of Galilee. The road was steep and often slippery when damp, but there had as usual been no significant rainfall since May so everywhere was bone dry. Jesus still needed to be careful as he walked. There was also a possibility of robbers on any journey you took but this was increased when you walked alone. Some robbers escaping from justice were rumoured to live in some of the ancient dwellings high in the precipitous cliffs which towered above the path he walked. Wild beasts could also be a problem. Jesus arrived at the Arbel valley without incident and followed the Arbel creek as it flowed towards Magdala. He passed the caves of Arbel high in the cliffs inhabited in prehistoric times, but he saw no-one. There were few people in this mountainous region. The Lower Galilee region as a whole, however, was more densely populated than most other areas of Israel. Jesus followed the road into the town of Magdala which was an important fishing town[82]. Josephus calls it Taricheae "the places where the fish are prepared", because it was here that fish were salted in large quantities for export to the rest of the Empire. (Josephus War 18.9;) Jesus walked through the streets into the market place. It was a rich city and in days to come he would visit the new synagogue which boasted some old mementos preserved from the second temple. Not far away to the south was Tiberias the new capital of Antipas which had been built just over ten years before around 17 natural springs on a mountain slope overlooking the lake of Galilee. Tiberias already eclipsed Magdala, though some of its residents still refused to have anything to do with the new city just four miles south of them. Jesus joined the road from Tiberias as it weaved its way along the coast of the Sea of Galilee to Capernaum. Unlike the narrow goat trails or wider hard beaten paths that Jesus often walked, this was a well-made limestone rock road which was even paved in places. The Via Maris, as it had been called for years, was used for trade and in places had recently been upgraded as a military road. It linked Egypt with Syria and continued to Mesopotamia. This road was wider and easier to walk on and brought him to a stone's throw of Capernaum. Jesus entered the town, walking through its narrow streets. The houses were simple as they were in Nazareth. He noticed a heavy basalt millstone which the rich had in Nazareth to mill their grain and knew that it was here in Capernaum that they were made. In Capernaum there were many more houses. The town stretched northwards about half a mile where the main cemetery

---

[82] Magdala was large enough to be fortified and became a major base against the Romans at the rebellion in 70AD (Josephus Wars 3:10.1)

marked the towns boundary. The main part of the town had narrow alleys between the houses. Each quarter of the town was marked by a main street which went both east west and north south. The town looked very different and was much larger than Nazareth. Southwards the houses eventually thinned out to houses near grain fields and olive groves where there were also many oil and grain mills which marked the end of the town.[83] It had expanded during Jesus growing years and was a busy place. Jesus was reminded that fishing was its major industry as he walked past houses with fishing nets drying on their roof terraces above, identifying the houses belonging to fishermen. There were many. Some houses had stood there for well over a century. The houses themselves were typical. Some small one room shelters but most in this prosperous town had more than one room. It was not unusual for houses to grow bigger to accommodate the next generation as they married and themselves had children. Family was a central base of society there. Capernaum was a distinctly Jewish town as Nazareth was a Jewish village[84]. But business forced more interaction between them and non-Jews – people who now lived in the area from other parts of the Roman Empire. Some were retired soldiers and others rich well connected in Roman society. These were good customers and so many of the top Jewish business men spoke Greek as well as Aramaic when necessary. This was not unusual though more common in bigger cities like Jerusalem where there was a larger military presence and in the cities of the Decapolis. Jesus, as we have seen, knew Greek from an early age, so when he needed to be bilingual[85] it presented little difficulty to him.

---

[83] https://en.wikipedia.org/wiki/Capernaum

[84] There have been no archaeological finds to suggest anything other than Jewish culture in Capernaum (or Nazareth)

[85] John a fisherman from Capernaum wrote in Greek. Zebedee his father knew Greek as did the leaders in Jerusalem who talked with Pilate and the Roman authorities. In this way it

In Capernaum most people usually spoke Aramaic, but he would however be introduced to many more cultures and backgrounds than in Nazareth. Visitors stopped at the town to resupply themselves on their journeys with dried fish and other essentials.[86] Trade caravans to and from Damascus would pass through the town as they journeyed nearby along the Via Maris. There were also local traders who travelled from Capernaum to Caesarea Maritima or other ports on the Mediterranean coast and engaged with many different culture and nationalities. This helped to create a more cosmopolitan culture in Capernaum than Nazareth.

Jesus drew little interest as he walked through its streets. He saw the brand-new synagogue that had been built in the centre of the town (Luke 7:15). He continued past the limestone and basalt which made up many of the outside walls of the houses. The stone had weathered to produce brown or in some cases red patches on it so each street he passed through looked different. Jesus did not stop. He wanted to introduce himself to Zebedee's family. Jesus went along a few more streets towards the water. No-one in Capernaum lived far away from the water. The town stretched north south along a pebble beach shoreline further than the distance from the outskirts of the town to the lake. The landscape was so different from the environment of Nazareth far away from the sea. Jesus turned towards the house where he knew James and John lived. His aunt Salome welcomed him into the house. He would stay there before finding his own place the next day to live in the town.

---

was similar to Egypt where the main political and economic drivers would speak Greek though some of the populace would only know the local language. A further incentive for the spread of Greek in the time of Jesus was the fact that Jews had been dispersed all over the Greek world and still came to Jerusalem each year.

[86] At the lake shore, where Peter and other fishermen worked, archaeologists have discovered a fish sales area

SECTION 6

Jesus' Galilee Ministry from Capernaum

Introduction

There were three phases to the ministry of Jesus whilst based in Capernaum. Each phase lasted only a few weeks.

1st Phase: Matthew 4:18-22 He taught occasionally in the synagogue at Capernaum and visited the surrounding towns. Although in a different context, some things for Jesus continued the same. From the first week he had arrived in Galilee he had taught in local synagogues. In Capernaum that same pattern of ministry continued. At this stage it was localized having two characteristics. (1) link to his disciples (2) not too far to walk. Resources to pay for hospitality were extremely limited and he could not be too far away from Capernaum. During this phase he called Simon Peter & Andrew, James and John to be his disciples. It includes the first teaching about the Kingdom which is called the Sermon on the Mount (Matthew 5-7) where he first drew those he had met in Capernaum and the surrounding region to meet. The place Jesus chose was in response to the numbers (Matthew 5:1) and may therefore have been unexpected. From this time on crowds followed Jesus wherever he was.

2nd Phase: This was followed by a further dimension of power and a wider scope for mission. This all started one Sabbath in Capernaum with an exorcism at the synagogue whilst Jesus was teaching. This led to a decision to extend His ministry throughout all Galilee in the same style as his earlier more localized ministry settings (Matthew 4:23). The events of that Sabbath changed everything. Jesus went throughout Galilee and invited people back for further teaching at Capernaum. As` a result large numbers of people came seeking him at Capernaum. After a leper had been miraculously healed, Jesus needed to develop further strategies to be on his own. Jesus and his disciples had to discover new ways to live. In Capernaum He had to enter secretly to stop being swamped. (Matthew 8:1-3). In addition, He frequently went into the desert to pray (Luke 5:16) living in the desert for days on end. The spiritual retreat was a practice which he would later involve "the twelve" in as they would go where he went.

3rd **Phase:** overlaps phase 2.

Phase 2 had prepared the way for new structures to emerge which would enable the ministry to grow. Phase 3 covers the time from the formation of "the 12". The announcement of who are members of the 12 was done at one of the gatherings of disciples – in this case the sermon on the plain. (Luke 6:17-49). Around the time of his choosing the 12 Jesus had to leave his home in Capernaum Mark 3:7- Mark 4:1 Matthew 13:11 to live in a house in Gennesaret. His healing of a man with a withered hand on the Sabbath in the synagogue in full view of the Jewish community caused active plots to kill Jesus. It was too risky to stay in the town. He moved a few miles down the coast and lived by the sea.

After the 12 are sent out on their return the demands of the crowds` can no longer be managed and from this time on Jesus is fully itinerant no longer based at Capernaum.

Chapter 21

Calling of the first disciples June 31AD (Matthew 4:18-22)

Jesus soon found Salome's house and her family helped Jesus to find a house to live in[87]. They had many contacts in the town and as in every place the local Jewish community was very close. Once settled with the help of some of his friends Jesus began to adjust to this new environment.

One of his closest friends was Simon who he would nickname Peter. He was married and lived in Capernaum. Simon Peter's mother in law was now a widow[88]. She had always ruled the home, but Simon ran the family fishing business. He had one or two boats which when he was not using them, he would hire them out to others. There was a regular income coming into the home. It did not need Simon there all the time. Fishing was a prosperous trade with any fish caught in high demand. When he got married and moved to Capernaum, he had become a fisherman which was the common trade both in Bethsaida where he was born and in Capernaum. He had recently started a new business partnership with James and John (Luke 5:10) who were backed by their father Zebedee who had his own lucrative and long-established fishing business. Simon brought with him useful contacts from Bethsaida, and so had helped to expand the business to both cities.

The disciples he had known from the days of the Jordan, were now back in familiar surroundings with family and friends closer to hand. There was no-one seeking them for baptisms. Whilst at the Jordan, they had been busy. Now all seemed to change. Jesus did not let them remain

---

[87] Mark 2:1 references his house in Capernaum.
[88] It may be that Jonas was alive in Bethsaida and Peter's mother had returned to her home town of Capernaum because of some trouble, but it is more likely that Jonas died either in Bethsaida or in Capernaum, because there is no direct mention of him.

inactive. He invited those he knew to accompany him as he visited the towns and villages in the Capernaum area that had a synagogue. Included in the list of places visited were Bethsaida (about six miles from Capernaum) where Philip and Simon (and Andrew) came from and Chorazin (two and a half miles northwards on the hills overlooking the sea of Galilee). Out of all the places Jesus visited at that time Chorazin, Bethsaida[89], and of course Capernaum is where Jesus went most.

During these days Jesus often went down to the seashore. The Sea of Galilee was a lake that stretched 13 miles from north to south and was eight miles wide. Its waters were called the sea of Gennesaret in the north and the sea of Tiberius in the south[90]. It was always beautiful. There was at the edge of the sea a small pebbly beach with a sprinkling of small shells which were so numerous that they caused a white glister in the sunlight. He looked out over the sea framed by the undulating mountains around its shore. The shapes of the mountains would become very familiar to him. No crowds accompanied him as he walked. The ministry of Jesus was just around the Sabbath and the synagogues. Some days Jesus did little except pray. It was early on a Friday morning in July that Jesus walked by the seashore with a purpose to start to call disciples to follow him. Jesus was still new to the town. On the following Sabbath Jesus was going to another synagogue. This time he wanted to invite friends to accompany him every time he went – not just in the forthcoming trip but every trip. Those he had in

---

[89] Bethsaida would quickly change during Jesus' third year of ministry. The coins issued by Philip the tetrarch mark him down as a founder in his thirty fourth year of his reign which gives the date (31 AD) when Bethsaida changed into Philip's hands and he started to build it into the city Julia named in honour of the mother of Tiberias who had recently died.
[90] Both terms are used in the gospels, but rather than suggest they were just alternative names for the whole sea of Galilee , I suggest they were terms to describe which part of the Sea one was in: Gennesaret to the north and Tiberias to the south.)

mind were Simon Peter, his brother Andrew[91], with James and John the sons of fisherman Zebedee, who had already started a fishing business with Simon. Jesus was already planning to the next stage including signposting interested people back to a teaching gathering back in Capernaum. He needed help with this and these would help the ministry to grow.

He made the short usual journey to the water's edge and discovered many fishermen after a night's fishing mending their nets. He saw Andrew and Peter first. They were some distance from the boats themselves making up nets for their boats. They would not be going out fishing that night as it was the Sabbath, so they were getting everything ready for the following week. It was at this moment that Jesus asked them both to follow him which they did, leaving their nets still unfinished (Matthew 4:20). They had already seen enough of Jesus to recognize it was an invitation which they could not refuse. The commitment they were making at this stage was ambiguous. They were committing to follow Jesus during the next visit he would make. The commitment they were making would emerge into much greater significance when Jesus chose them to be one of the twelve, but that was not yet. The three of them walked along the seashore where they recognized Zebedee's boats – He was wealthy - certainly compared to Jesus' own family.He owned many boats with a good workforce to fish from them. Peter's own business had not got the capital behind it to employ people as Zebedee did, so he hired his boats out to others when he was not using them. As they approached they saw James and John in one of the boats sorting out the faulty nets, laying them out in the sun, so the linen would dry correctly. Jesus asked them to follow him and

---

[91] Andrew was called in the same way as the others but did not make it into the "three" who were with Jesus even when the rest of the twelve and other disciples were not included. This was probably because of his youth or he may not have been able to come on every trip so the relationship with Jesus did not develop to the same degree.

they too immediately stepped out of the boat leaving their father to complete the task with his servants and joined Peter and Andrew who were standing with Jesus. They knew the task was to be with Jesus and to become "fishers of men", and they gladly accepted. They set off together for the nearby town where Jesus would proclaim the kingdom. From this first calling would emerge the three fishermen Peter, James and John who would become the first disciples to be with him all the time. The synagogue-based ministry that had first started in Cana could now grow further.

Galilean Ministry June 31AD (Matthew 4:23)

He went with his disciples northwards over the rolling hills to a large city set inland about two miles from the shore amidst dark rocks formed many millennia before. This was Chorazin which was built on the volcanic layer which lay above the limestone of the region. It was summer. Looking down from the hills on the Sea of Galilee the water was a beautiful blue. With the green, yellow and brown vegetation showing forth at this season around the coast. The harvesting of the wheat in the Gennesaret region southwards was already over as harvest is about a month earlier there that elsewhere in Israel. From a distance the lake gleamed like a sapphire. Beyond were the Eastern Mountains which could be seen clearly beyond the lake of Galilee. As expected it was a clear summer's day. He turned his head back to the path they were walking. Inland were other mountains to see which came into view as he walked higher. The heights of Naphtali piled up in the north and above them all the summit of Mount Hermon could be seen. Jesus walked over open moorland where sheep grazed as he approached Chorazin. It was the dry season and the day was hot well into the mid-30s Celsius. They entered the city and were grateful for the shade the buildings provided. The town was in such a different setting from Capernaum. Most of its buildings were built of the same dark basalt rock they had passed as they approached the city. The stone was black, grey and brown as the metals oxidized. Jesus and the disciples were welcomed. Jesus would visit Chorazin many times. The following day they went to the synagogue and Jesus taught there. Next day as Jesus left the city, he could still see the familiar turquoise blue of the lake as he walked back down the hill towards Capernaum. The visit had been very successful.

The disciples Jesus had called, had opened the way for Jesus to do more. He was now able to begin to establish a threefold base for the ministry, using Capernaum, Bethsaida (the home town of Simon Peter and Andrew) and Chorazin. (see Matthew 11:20-24; Luke 10:13-15). His first introduction to Bethsaida was when Peter and James and John took Jesus there by boat. It was the best way to get there and Philip and Andrew accompanied them. They had stayed in the family home of Philip. Peter and Andrew had not lived in Bethsaida for some time, but there were members of their family there.

For some months Jesus and his disciples stayed in one of these three towns every Sabbath. Sometimes when Jesus visited Chorazin, they went onto Bethsaida instead of Capernaum by walking six miles around the north west corner of the lake to where the Jordan river flows into the lake. There on a hill about a mile upstream was Bethsaida.

Each Sabbath, wherever Jesus was, he proclaimed the kingdom of God by word and deed. If he went more than a mile from Capernaum, because of the Jewish rules of Sabbath day travel, for Jesus to visit the synagogue he (and his early disciples) would need to be able to stay for at least two nights (Friday and Saturday nights) as travel was limited to when it was daylight (John 12:35). In the beginning the time they spent was from arrival on a Friday afternoon to departure on the Sunday

Many miracles happened during this time (Matthew 11:20). Sometimes they stayed an extra day or two because of the miracles that occurred, but it was primarily a Sabbath based ministry at this stage. Jesus would spend other days away on his own as he prayed in unpopulated parts in the hills of Galilee or in the deserts beyond Bethsaida.

Whenever Jesus went to any town or village he now always went with the three disciples Peter, James and John. Sometimes there were other disciples who joined them like Andrew and Philip and, when in the Cana area, Nathanael were there, Other disciples were not always with Jesus like Peter James and John were, but accompanied him many times. Jesus knew them well. Out of these disciples, the twelve would eventually be chosen.

Wherever Jesus went, he healed whoever he found that was sick in the village (Matthew 4:23). It would only be later when they brought the sick to him. (Matthew 4:24). This only started after the first gathering Jesus held and then continued to be a growing aspect of his ministry.

Chapter 22

The first Teaching Gathering in Capernaum June 31AD (Matthew 5:1-7:29)

News spread fast in Galilee and beyond. Testimonies of the wonderful deeds of Jesus caused the fame of Jesus to spread beyond the borders of Galilee so that even Syrians could be seen in the crowd who came to Capernaum for the first Gathering. "Great multitudes" of disciples came. (Matthew 4:24,25). At this stage Jesus was known as a prophet (John 3:1) who healed.

Hundreds gathered to be taught. Some had heard about Jesus when they were at Jerusalem, others from their relatives as they heard the stories of the healings that had occurred during Jesus visits to the towns in Galilee. The testimonies of healing were many. Epileptics and those who had suffered strokes as well as the paralyzed were included amongst those who were healed. In addition those oppressed by demons had also been set free. (Matthew 4:24). Jesus had by now experience of some whose conditions were openly demonic. They were disturbed, having distressing behaviour in word or actions. Jesus had so far only met such privately or in small village contexts. Nothing had happened in synagogues on this scale (yet!). In such cases the characteristic of the demon was evident to all, but Jesus had also had experience of others who had illnesses which seemed purely physical but were only healed after a demon was cast out.

Jesus had been preaching the kingdom through signs and wonders as he travelled to the towns of Galilee proclaiming and bringing the Kingdom of God, now the gathering was where his teaching ministry would be exercised. Everyone who came was already a disciple (Matthew 4:25). Jesus did not know how many would come. On the Friday some of the disciples started to arrive to spend the Sabbath at Capernaum, so Jesus already could tell there were going to be a lot of people. He knew many more would come for the Gathering on the Sunday after the Sabbath. They had accepted his invitation which Jesus had given those he met as he travelled around in Galilee and some even came he had met in Jerusalem. Those that had been invited brought others with them. When he saw how many had already made the journey and from where they had come (Matthew 5:1a), he decided to hold the gathering towards the top of a hill on open land just south of Capernaum 500 feet above the shore. It was less humid than in Capernaum and away from the hubbub of the town. It provided the space for Jesus to teach the crowd of disciples who would come. He explained the locatiuon to his disciples who then told those as they arrived in Capernaum. It meant climbing up a hill, but at the top was a cave above which was a perfect place to speak whilst the crowd could sit on a wide-open space about six feet below. He went there and sat down and waited for them all to come. They came as families. These were all age gatherings [92] (see John 6:9). Jesus throughout his ministry welcomed all. It was a sizeable crowd of a hundred or more – both male and female.

The Sermon on the Mount June 31AD (Matthew 5-7)

Jesus looked at the crowd as they gathered. He recognised most there- in fact Jesus knew most of them there on first name terms. Peter, James and John and Matthew (who recorded what was said for us to read Matthew 5-7) as well as all the future twelve (Acts 1:21-22) were there. Local disciples from Capernaum and the surrounding district mingled with those who had travelled much longer distances. They were all disciples. From the start Jesus' ministry attracted people wherever he went. (Matthew 4:25) Some had known Jesus when he was at the Jordan, others at Jerusalem but most had seen him in Galilee. Some

---

[92] There is no reason to assume the feeding of the 5000 crowd was different in socio-composition to other ones

Jesus did not recognise. These came from places Jesus had not yet visited – Syria and the Decapolis areas which bordered Galilee. They came with family or friends though one or two had come just because of what they had heard about him. They were all Jews and open to follow Jesus. Jesus had not yet become known enough to attract the sceptical religious authorities who would later confront and question him.

When they arrived, he taught them (Matthew 5:1c). Jesus chose this occasion to teach the values of the kingdom of God. It was a foundational declaration about being a disciple in the Kingdom of God. Those who came were eager to listen and to learn (Matthew 5:1). On this important day there were no requests for healing nor teaching after questions from the crowd. Jesus had planned what he was going to say. Jesus taught from a seated position – something which he did throughout his ministry when he could. [93][94]

Capernaum synagogue June 31AD (Mark 1:21)

The Kingdom of God manifests in various ways (Hebrews 1:1) and Jesus had to learn to respond to all His Heavenly Father purposed. Sometimes there was an extra overflow of power or a greater significance in events for Jesus personally. Such was the first Sabbath after Jesus returned to Capernaum after the first gathering.

The events of that day would prove to be significant for Jesus Himself and His ministry. As we have seen Jesus had been preaching in

[93] This was the first of similar gatherings that Jesus held in the earlier and middle stages of his ministry until his popularity and sheer volume of numbers meant this tactic became no longer viable. At this stage disciples were still a general body of people -both men and women. (It would not be until the calling of Matthew- sometime after Matthew heard the sermon on the mount which he records in his gospel- that the 12 were formally formed).
[94] This was the "sermon on the mount" (Matthew 5-7). The traditional location for the Mount of Beatitudes is on the north-western shore of the Sea of Galilee, between Capernaum and Gennesaret (ancient name Ginnesar first mentioned in 1 Maccabees 11:67 just south of Capernaum). Its highest point is 58 metres (190 ft) below sea level, which is approximately 155 metres (509 ft) above the surface of the lake.[1]

synagogues in the area. The crowds coming to Capernaum from all over Galilee for the gathering impressed many in the synagogue and Jesus had been invited to preach at the synagogue in Capernaum. Although Jesus had preached in many of the synagogues in the area, this synagogue was probably the largest one in which he had so far preached, and it was certainly the newest one, having been built in recent months. It was in the centre of the town not far from where Simon Peter lived. It was not the first time Jesus had been invited to speak at the synagogue (Luke 4:31,32). Some in Capernaum had been with Jesus whilst he ministered in neighbouring towns and villages. Others had heard about what he had done in Jerusalem and at Cana. It was not long before Jesus was invited to speak on the Sabbath at their synagogue. They knew he was from Nazareth – and possibly heard of the adverse reaction he had received at Nazareth- but what happened in that small village was of no relevance in Capernaum. They were very different from the rural communities up in the hills of Galilee and regarded themselves as superior even to other towns in Galilee (Matthew 11:23). Whenever Jesus had spoken in their synagogue, he had been well respected. Those who heard him had been impressed by the authority with which he spoke. What they heard did not ruffle any theological feathers or teach revelatory truths which astonished them. What was new was the certainty which accompanied what he said. It would be much later in Jesus ministry that people would say "no man ever spoke like this man" (John 7:46)

The Sabbath started as a normal Saturday but with God's power no day is ever "normal". Since Jesus' baptism, and his arrival in Galilee Jesus had demonstrated that he was "full of the power of the Holy Spirit" (Luke 4:14). Supernatural power operates at a level the mind cannot anticipate or understand, and so it was when Jesus taught in the synagogue on this Sabbath, a demon manifested as he taught (Mark 1: 21, Luke 4:33ff). Jesus as a good Jew had attended this synagogue

130

during every Sabbath when in Capernaum. Already he had taught in the synagogue prior to this event, but it was that day that the demon manifested. Finally, the evil entity had to rise from its dwelling place in the life of its victim. The demon spoke through the man and reflected the view of the culture. "What right have you got to speak in Capernaum when you are from Nazareth". This was quickly followed by an impossible threat "did you come to destroy us" - because you know you cannot until the second coming- and thirdly an unsettling comment "I know who you are the holy one of God". All this was designed to throw Jesus onto the back foot so the authoritative faith he moved in would be undermined allowing the demon to stay undisturbed. Jesus would have none of this. He spoke specifically to the demon to Come out and it had to obey - coming out with a scream but leaving the man unhurt (Luke 4:35) much to the relief of friends and family there with the man at the time. None had seen such a thing before and the news of this event would be told so much that there would be no place in the local area that did not hear about it. (Luke 4:37 It was at the synagogue and not on the streets where the kingdom had been seen and experienced. And it could not be dismissed. The declaration of the kingdom made earlier in the week at the sermon on the mount had released a new level of authority which the demonic realms felt first.

The Kingdom manifested in power when Jesus was invited to teach. Although the Holy Spirit lived in fullness in Jesus, for the Kingdom to manifest there had to be avenues for preaching, teaching or healing so the spiritual gifts could be activated. Jesus had not been a long time in Capernaum before the Kingdom manifestation grew to a point of action; news of which spread all over Galilee (Mark 1:28). This in turn prepared the opportunity for new places to visit (Mark 1:39). Jesus recognized a new level of action in the anointing and he started to think what was needed to stay at the new level. For the sake of the captives, the Father intended him to remain at this new level of power. The answers to his questions would only come after prayer and there was little time for that during the day.

Healing of Simon Peter's mother -in-law June 31AD
(Matthew 8:14, Mark 1:29-31 Luke 4:38ff)

After the service Peter had arranged for Jesus to share a meal at his home. Peter's mother in law who was now a widow, ran the home. She had always been pleased that her daughter had married Peter. She valued a man in the house and it had suited Peter. He ran the family fishing business whilst she and his young wife ran the home. He was from Bethsaida – a fisherman by trade - who was now able to build a better business in Capernaum than he could have done in the town where he had been born. His mother in law was also keen to have the support of her daughter in the home and so the arrangement had worked well for some time. She had agreed to host Jesus and the rest of Jesus' friends that Sabbath. The house was not far from the synagogue, but as they entered the house, Peter was surprised to find his mother in law was ill. In the synagogue the men sat at the front and the women were at the back, so Peter was not even aware that she was not there. Peter soon found she was in bed with a fever (Luke 4:38-40). This was unexpected, for otherwise Peter would never have brought everyone for lunch. Jesus when he found out, went to the bedside of Peter's mother in law and rebuked the fever and she was immediately able to get out of bed and serve them. This day was already proving to be very special indeed and it was not over. As the sun started to set marking the end of the Sabbath men and women – some with other members of their family started to come to the house. They had heard of the events of the day and so brought those who were ill to be healed. (Luke 4:40) They came with different needs – some were diseased (Mark 1:34), some with mental illness, but they all came because they thought the cause of their conditions was demonic (Matthew 8:16) and they had heard or seen what Jesus did in the synagogue that morning. Not all were demonized but Jesus healed all who were sick as well as casting out demons (Matthew 8:16) All were healed. It was not possible to invite them into the house. Peter and the family did not want these people to come inside. So, Jesus went outside to meet them. He soon found there were too many people to do anything other than minister to them in the street (Mark 1:33). Jesus healed all who came, and then afterwards after saying "Goodbye" to Peter went back down the now familiar streets to his own home.

Jesus' ministry was from this day on no longer limited to the synagogue. That day had heralded a further stage in his ministry. Whilst he would still base his ministry in the synagogues of Galilee, from now on there would be an increase of opportunities during the week for people to be healed or taught and the gospel of the kingdom proclaimed.

The narrative about Jesus also changed as a result of the events in the synagogue that morning (Mark 1:28). His authority over the demonic was now equal in the eyes of the public with his proclamation of the kingdom. Theories and disputes about the source of Jesus' authority over the demonic realm would dog his steps wherever he went (e.g. Mark 3:22, John 8:48)

After this Sabbath it would be a few hours before everyone in town knew about Jesus' healing ministry. Jesus awoke before the town did (Mark 1:35) and before any crowds could gather. He found a place away from any houses and prayed. It was during this time of prayer Jesus heard the Father unfolding to him the next stage in His plan – which was to take the kingdom in the whole of Galilee using the same model he had already done in Capernaum. As we have seen Jesus had already spent time in the neighbouring towns and villages around Capernaum. Now he was to go much farther afield. It would involve him being a longer time away from the town and visiting communities where he did not yet know anyone who lived there. Both these provided new

133

challenges of faith. Jesus needed welcome to have a platform for ministry and hospitality. Jesus knew that the Father wanted him to preach (Mark 1:39) the kingdom all over Galilee and that He would provide.

Peter had been woken early by people knocking on his door. They had come for healing. Peter ran to Jesus' house to find he was not there. He asked other disciples who also did not know where he was. Someone suggested they should look for Jesus in the place he would go to pray outside the town. They went and indeed found him. They told Jesus that already there were people looking for him (Luke 4:37) with the expectations that he should be there to meet their needs (Luke 4:42). So soon the expectations of others had already formed around what Jesus should do. From the beginning Jesus refused to respond to the expectations of others at the expense of obeying the Father. He immediately told Peter and the others of his decision to go on mission.

Disciples in Capernaum when they heard what had been decided tried to prevent him from leaving. They wanted more of what they had seen the previous day. It was not easy, but Jesus knew he had to leave to preach in the other synagogues of Galilee (Luke 4:44). Jesus went with the disciples not knowing what would happen. All he knew was he would speak at the synagogues wherever he went. What they found was that what had happened in Capernaum was repeated elsewhere – healing and exorcisms continued to follow the preaching of Jesus. All those who heard Jesus recognized he spoke with an authority, and now the demons felt it too and reacted. When they manifested Jesus cast them out. So, Mark records, "he travelled throughout Galilee preaching in their synagogues and driving out demons" Mark 1:39. The narrative around Jesus began to change even more from a "preacher with authority" to "a healer who casts out demons". Controversy and debate would change to these new areas, and would remain with Jesus whilst he was in Capernaum and Gennesaret

Chapter 23

Wider Galilean Ministry June/July 31AD
(Mark 1:39, Luke 4:44)

Over the next weeks Jesus visited all the places within reach of Capernaum, Bethsaida and Chorazin. Each town was now a base from which he went to proclaim the kingdom. Jesus would leave Capernaum to visit towns before ending his journey at either Chorazin or Bethsaida. In this way Jesus was away from Capernaum for some days at a time. Twenty miles from each was the maximum distance he would cover as this was a day's journey. Many wonders had been done in Bethsaida the home of Philip and where Simon Peter and Andrew were born and Chorazin (Matthew 11:21) as well as Capernaum at this time.[95] There were more wonders done in Capernaum and Chorazin and Bethsaida than anywhere else (Matthew 11:21) because Jesus spent more time there. Jesus proclaimed the kingdom of God in many other towns from these three bases. Although people had come from Jerusalem, Judea and Decapolis[96] to the first gathering (Matthew 4:24), but Galilee was Jesus' focus for the proclamation of the Kingdom (Matthew 4:23). Galilee was divided into two distinct areas Lower and Upper. To the north and west of Capernaum lay the higher mountains, and deeper valleys of Upper Galilee. Jesus had never been to Upper Galilee in his life. Now he would walk through new terrain and go towards Mount Meron, the largest mountain of Upper Galilee. He would travel from Bethsaida towards

---

[95] The implication from Jesus' statement in Matthew 11:21 is that Bethsaida and Chorazin shared a similar time and quality of signs and wonders as Capernaum so it is highly likely that Jesus spent as much time here as he did in Capernaum.

[96] Bethshean, the ancient Jewish city 33miles south of Capernaum south west of the Sea of Galilee seven miles south of Tiberias was called in Jesus' day Scythopolis and was the only city of Decapolis in Israel. Jesus would have gone through or near this town to Jerusalem and it is probable that those from Decapolis came from this city

The greater rainfall in Upper Galilee made much of the landscape green longer in the year in contrast with the often-dry yellow brown summer scenery Jesus was used to. One of the main cities in Upper Galilee was the fortified city of Safed (mentioned in Judges as part of the tribe of Naphtali Judges 1:17) only fifteen miles or so from Capernaum (nearer from Chorazin) over mountainous terrain. This ancient Levite city in the ancient territory of Naphtali was sited over 900 metres above sea level, and was the highest city in Israel at that time. It was very hot in summer but also very cold in winter. Upper Galilee's hilly terrain meant more distance separated towns and villages, so Jesus visited many but not all at this time. As Jesus made his way into Upper Galilee he saw different flowers from his home area as they blossomed on the hillsides. Grass and trees were also more plentiful. Pleasant streams ran through mountains and wooded valleys. Waterfalls, some of them very spectacular, were also a more common feature than in lower Galilee as the water made its downward journey through the steep hills.

Lower Galilee was more densely populated than Upper Galilee. Jesus went southwards from Capernaum six miles to Magdala, a significant Galilean fishing town just north of Tiberias and then west a further six miles to Cana. He would mainly travel the sun- beaten well-worn paths of Galilee, but occasionally he would travel by boat to some of the small towns and villages around the Sea of Galilee. In this way even Kinneret seven miles south of Tiberias near the South west shore of the lake was reachable. But Jesus could not visit all of Galilee.

During his travels some disciples started to travel with Jesus, and this increased when disciples who lived locally joined them. Because Jesus at this stage had a synagogue-based ministry he came to the town and stayed for the Sabbath before returning to either Capernaum, Bethsaida or Chorazin. During these weeks a core group emerged around Jesus who tended to be there most times. There was no "twelve" at this stage – just a group of male and female disciples who sought to follow Jesus and help where they could with some of the practical issues that arose. Jesus alone was involved in teaching or healing. When Jesus returned to a town often on the day following the Sabbath, the disciples dispersed to their homes again to return to work and spend time back with their families.

It was during this time that Jesus met and healed Joanna who was the wife of Chuza the steward of Herod. Chuza and Joanna had come from Rome with Antipas. They lived not far from Magdala in the new capital Tiberius completed by Antipas ten years before. They had first looked after Antipas in his teenage years after the sudden death of his mother in Rome [97] and they alongside their son Manaen (Acts 13:1) had accompanied Herod Antipas back to Israel when he had become tetrarch. Chuza now a man in his late sixties had proved himself trustworthy as a worthy guardian tutor and administrator and so Herod had employed him as his steward when he became king. They had shared the journey with him for thirty years. Joanna who was probably in her mid-fifties – a similar age to Jesus' mother Mary- had become ill and had sought Jesus out and was healed. As a result, she supported Jesus from her wealth and connections in his ongoing ministry. It was also at this time he met Mary from Magdala who he delivered of an unusual number of demons (Luke 8:2, 24:10; Mark 15:40,47, Matthew 28:1, John 19:25; 20:1-18). Jesus usually found that when the chief one went if there were any others they all went at the same time. In Mary's case the demons were separated, dwelling in different parts of her life requiring the deliverance of each one. Mary was thoroughly healed and would become one of the main contributors of finance and logistics as Jesus' ministry progressed. Magdala was an important port town on the lake (sea of Tiberius), and still retained its importance despite the rising influence of the smaller town Capernaum

---

[97] Josephus Antiquities Book 17 Chapter 10:1

or being in the shadow of the new capital city built by Antipas just a couple of miles away which he called Tiberius. Mary delivered of the demons living in the wounds of her life, was rich enough to support Jesus and the disciples in their travels. She and other women provided money, took time to organize food, did the cooking when needed and joined with the many other disciples who went with Jesus This became even more significant after Jesus chose the "twelve". Their help with the logistics and other practical arrangements allowed Jesus the ministry of the Kingdom of God to grow.

By the autumn he had proclaimed the kingdom from Magdala to the border towns of Galilee in the south to towns up to fifteen miles north of Chorazin like Safed a fortified town which at an elevation of 2,950 feet is the highest town in Israel. Jesus also visited in that area a group of ancient towns gathered nearby such as Pina Rosa and Hazor[98] in the marshland of the southern Hulka valley overlooking lake Meron. Jesus ministry throughout this time was based around the synagogue, but as the weeks passed, the ministry began to become an everyday ministry.

---

[98] It was not any longer the major city of the Old Testament as it never fully recovered from its Assyrian destruction in the 7th or 8th century BC

Chapter 24

The Second Teaching Gathering July 31AD (Luke 5:1-12)

Wherever Jesus went, people saw the kingdom manifested and became his disciples. There was such a rapid growth of disciples who needed to be taught, Jesus organized another teaching gatherings.

Although this was only the second teaching gathering, there were already more expected than the first gathering. Jesus knew the space where he had met before for the Sermon on the Mount would be too small, so he chose a place on the shore south of Capernaum. Hundreds of people (note Luke 5:1 "multitude") came spreading out along the shore in the Gennesaret region. This would become the normal place where Jesus would teach when in Capernaum. It worked for small and large numbers. Jesus started to teach as soon as he arrived, and as he taught the crowds grew. The shore was ideal, and so for some hours Jesus taught on the shore of the lake. There were however a lot more people at these teaching gatherings than the groups Jesus normally taught when he had travelled in towns and the numbers attending outgrew any previous time. People had come from all over Galilee and all at the same time. Jesus soon realized that teaching hundreds required a different method than teaching twenty or thirty. He had to think fast as to the best way to teach them. They could hear him, but they could not see him and so many were easily distracted. Also, Jesus valued eye to eye contact with his listeners as he was used to in the synagogues. Jesus noticed some fishermen mending their nets adjacent to some boats. The nets used were the trammel nets which were nets which only work at night because as soon as it is light the fish recognize the net and avoid it. The fishermen had not caught anything that night but were making sure the nets were secure and laying them out to dry in the sun to prevent the linen, which made up the nets, rotting.

Jesus did not recognize them from where he was on the beach but realized how useful a boat would be. The shoreline is extensive. Jesus realized that if he were in a boat, the crowd could spread along the shoreline. More would see and hear him that way. The place was on the shore of the sea of Gennesaret just under three miles south of Capernaum. Jesus could be heard and seen by everyone. He suggested the plan and found that one of the boats was owned by Simon Peter who could take him out without any difficulty. Other people used his boats (for a price) to fish, so when Jesus found this, he asked Peter to get the boat ready, so he would speak to them sat in the boat. Everyone in the crowd waited and watched as Peter took some of his work colleagues and hauled the boat down the beach into the water. It had not been long since they had pulled it out of the water after an unsuccessful nights fishing with James and John who owned the other boat (Luke 5:10,11) beside his on the beach. And he walked in the waves pulling the boat behind him to bring it around to where Jesus was. Jesus got into the boat and sat down whilst Peter rowed it into position and anchored it. Jesus taught until it was time for people to go back to their homes to eat.

It was not yet the extended teaching session that would be common later in Jesus' ministry, but the ingredients for the future were all there as Jesus taught about the kingdom. At this stage healing was less noticeable than the teaching. In a few weeks there would be new challenges as the crowds would further swell with those coming for healing. For now, Jesus simply had to teach.

When He had finished, Jesus turned to Peter in whose boat he was in and asked him to launch out into the deep. Jesus wanted to repay the debt he had incurred by using the boat and wanted him to be able to get some income through catching fish. Peter and those in the boat who often fished with him looked at each other. Peter explained they had been fishing all night and caught nothing. Jesus said cast your nets out over the side. Fish filled the nets almost immediately and Peter and his friends (Luke 5:9) were amazed. They called out to James and John on the beach who quickly got in to their boat. They were his business partners and they often worked together. They grabbed the net from their boat, so the weight of fish did not break the net, and together they rowed back to shore. They had to be careful because the weight of fish in the net was pulling the side of each boat nearer the surface of the water. If it got much further the boats would sink. When Peter saw this, he was absolutely amazed. He said, "Go away from me Lord for I am sinful man". Inside Peter's heart he saw the lack of commitment he had given to Jesus. He had chosen to fish all night even though he knew Jesus was teaching in the morning. He had been with Jesus during his travels but in going fishing had returned back to his old life when he got back home. He realized now that this was wrong. Jesus' response was to affirm the calling he had given him. "Do not be afraid" and then repeating the words of his call "From now you will catch men". This event made such an impact on Peter and James and John that they left the fishing for good and followed Jesus. They hired their boats out to others, so income was still being coming into the business. From now on Jesus could rely on these three always being with him wherever he went whether on a ministry trip or back at Capernaum. The "three" as a permanent structure was now sealed. It would prepare the way for "the twelve" who would share the same commitment. But even when the twelve were formed, the "three" would still be retained. They would be there when Jesus prayed privately, (Luke 9:28) and would be witness to remarkable events not seen by other members of the "twelve" (e.g. the raising of the daughter of Jairus from the dead (Luke 8:51); and the transfiguration of Jesus Mark 9:2,9).

Chapter 25

The healing of the leper
(Mark 1:39-40; Luke 5:12ff, Matthew 8:1,4 July 31AD)

Jesus was now accompanied by Peter, James and John wherever he went. Other disciples also joined them as Jesus went from town to town in the local region staying at Bethsaida or Chorazin as well as Capernaum. It was at the end of one such trip as he was on his way back and not far from Capernaum[99] when a leper approached him to ask if he would heal him. Leprosy was a disease which could infect others and so lepers lived lives of an outcast outside normal society. It was bold of this man to come so close to Jesus and Jesus recognised that faith lay behind the interruption. The man had made a statement of his faith "If you are willing you can make me clean", and Jesus as usual replied without hesitation within the same parameters of the man's faith. "I will, be clean" and then he touched him[100]. This contravened every rule of how to relate with lepers.[101] Jesus touched him because he was no longer a leper. He was backing up his word of command for the disease to go with the action to seal in the healing. The leper was healed instantly. Jesus then told him to keep quiet about the healing, and to go and ask for a medical checkup from the religious leaders to make sure he was healed so he could be reinstated back into Jewish society. (Mark 1:44). Jesus knew the man did not have to say how he was healed. (It was possible for skin conditions to clear up on their own so the people

---

[99] the leper is outside Capernaum either on a usual route which Jesus took from either Chorazin or Bethsaida which would mean he was returning from Upper Galilee or on the Magdala road if from Lower Galilee

[100] See Luke 5:12 This could have been Chorazin – see Mark 1:39-40. Chorazin was probably situated in the hills about two miles inland from the sea of Galilee (about 3 miles from Capernaum).

[101] The real leprosy caused by mycobacterium leprae bacillus was present in Jesus Israel. See Gibson Final days of Jesus page 34,35

he went to see did not need to know it was Jesus who had healed him). Jesus did not want this healing known at that moment. News would disrupt the ministry of the Kingdom. Jesus knew that although this happened outside Capernaum, it was near enough for news of the healing to travel into Capernaum making things more difficult. No longer would only those who the Father was sending come: his new-found celebrity would draw them. No longer did those who came, come out of need for healing or seeking truth: Curiosity would draw them. In this context argument, skepticism and controversy would breed. The leper however told everyone. It was a story which he could grab the attention of those he met, making up for the long time he had been an outcast. For Jesus, the time of relative peace, free from controversy, was now over. The news from the leper indeed hampered the ministry of Jesus. It complicated things. This would be the last week of "normal life" that Jesus would have in Capernaum. Once the news of the leper's healing was known Jesus rapidly became a celebrity in the town with its attendant demands. People came from every direction (Mark 1:45). To cope with this, Jesus departed from Capernaum for days at a time either on mission or into the deserts to pray (Luke 5:16), and when He entered Capernaum, he did so secretly. (Mark 1:45).

Back in Capernaum
(Mark 1:39-40; Luke 5:12ff, Matthew 8:1,4)

As Jesus left the leper behind to go back to Capernaum he did not yet have to concern himself about the future consequences. It would take some days before the news of the leper's healing trickled back into Capernaum. For the moment nothing changed as he walked past the familiar dwellings that marked the edge of the town of Capernaum. He and the others with him could return to a "normal" life for a few days. The next major event in their schedule was the third teaching gathering where his disciples would meet on November 8th. Jesus got on with life outside a ministry context until the following Sabbath (Mark 1:21) where he taught in the synagogue.

Chapter 26

Centurion's servant July 31AD (Matthew 8:5-13, Luke 7:2-10)

Jesus had not been in Capernaum long, before some of the Jewish authorities from the synagogue approached him with a request from the centurion who had helped to build the brand-new synagogue in the centre of Capernaum which mattered so much to the people of the town. One of his slaves was very ill. He was paralyzed, and in some mental distress. The dignitaries from the synagogue knew about Jesus and where he lived. They passed on the centurions request and added that because he had helped so much to build the synagogue that they were keen for Jesus to respond to his request. Jesus should treat him as one of their own and so respond. The earlier healing of the nobleman's son may have been in the back of the minds of some who talked with Jesus. It might even have reached the centurion's ears birthing faith in his heart that Jesus could do the same for his son. Anyway, Jesus immediately went with them in the direction of the centurion's house who lived just outside the town near the Via Maris[102]. One of the leaders sent someone to run ahead to tell the centurion that they were on their way with Jesus. It was a little distance to travel to his house in another part of town. Whilst still some distance away from their destination, a slave came from the centurion's house met them. He approached the Jewish authorities who were accompanying Jesus. Slaves were a part of ordinary life. In Nazareth and many Jewish towns there were none but were always present whenever there were Romans. In the new cities in Israel where Greeks lived, slaves were the backbone of society; a normal part of the life. The centurion was in a part of Capernaum separate from the rest of the Jewish town. He was an upright man,

---

[102] The major trade route that passed by Capernaum was the reason for the Centurion's deployment. He was strategically placed should Roman intervention be needed.

respected in the local community – in fact any Roman living in Israel could not get away with some of the excesses that were in Roman society elsewhere. Such scandal would incur great punishment from the Roman authorities who would not wish for any disturbance or excuse for rebellion from its rule. They stopped as the slave met them who told them the message the centurion had given him. He wanted Jesus to be told to just to say the word (like he had done with the nobleman). He said you do not need to come. I just say the word and it is done and I know you can do the same. So, Jesus never met this centurion. What the slave said brought everyone to a standstill. Jesus said he had not seen such faith even in Israel and did exactly as the centurion had requested and they heard later that the centurion's son had indeed been healed.

Galilee of Jesus' time was a mixture between communities largely unchanged for years and new secular cities with a strong Greek-Roman influence. These were few. There was in addition small fortresses which acted as watchtowers staffed by soldiers under Herod Antipas' authority to help prevent trouble. Most were high up on top of hills where a fire would be lit to call for urgent military intervention. Galilee was strongly Jewish and before 70AD the Roman empire made minimal impact on their Jewish culture. Capernaum did have a centurion stationed there who had the authority to get things done and to respond when needed. Capernaum was a thriving town through fishing the wide variety of fish present at the Sea of Gennesaret part of the sea of Galilee[103]. Much of the fish that was landed either at Capernaum or Magdala was salted and exported to other parts of the empire including Rome itself.

---

[103] It has been assumed by many that the Sea of Galilee, sea of Tiberias and Sea of Gennesaret are interchangeable names for the same thing. But just as the same valley is called the valley of Jezreel in the central and east part and the valley of Megiddo in the south and west part , so the Sea of Gennesaret in the north becomes the Sea of Tiberias in the south.

Chapter 27

Healing of the paralytic
(Mark 2:1-13; Matthew 9:1- Luke 5:18ff)

The disciples were coming for the third gathering (Luke 5:17) and this time it attracted people who were not disciples of Jesus. Religious leaders from the region - Pharisees and teachers of the law – who came with disciples from their synagogue. They came from all over:- Galilee, Judea and Jerusalem (Luke 5:17). It was the day after the Sabbath, but many came to Jesus' house early. Amongst those who came were some who were ill. Amongst those who arrived early were some religious authorities. They had observed the Sabbath at Capernaum and were now checking Jesus out. They were curious about Jesus and troubled by his influence as Jesus was not well educated or from a strong religious background – a total unknown to the authorities. None of their fears would be allayed by their visit. They had made their decision to come after they heard about the controversy following Jesus' healing of the sick man near the Bethesda pool. (John 5:15-16) Jesus' unorthodox approach of healing on the Sabbath day, and seeming flouting of the regulations was a major concern and they were also worried about whether the source of his actions was really from God. Jesus and the twelve knew that many others would be coming, and a meeting had already been arranged at the usual place just south of Capernaum for later in the day to allow those who had spent the Sabbath in their own towns to reach Capernaum

They had expected a large number for the teaching but had not anticipated the large numbers that had come already to Capernaum after the festival. They crammed into Jesus' house. The needy who were there, Jesus healed one by one. As each healing occurred, it became clear to those who looked on that "the power of the Lord was present to heal" (Luke 5:17) even more than usual. This spurred some local disciples from Capernaum to think of a friend who lived nearby who was paralyzed. They got up and left to bring him. They picked him up as he lay on his bed and brought him to the house. By the time they got there the places they had sat were filled. In fact, so many had come that many were standing outside unable to get in at all. They tried at first to get in but found it as impossible as those who had tried earlier. They needed to create a corridor through which they could bring their friend, so even if one of them had managed to get into the room there was no hope they could bring their friend there. They adopted an alternative plan, making their way up the outside stairs at the side of the house onto the flat roof that characterized nearly all the houses. At the part of the roof directly above where they estimated Jesus to be, they removed the protective tiles and then started to dig up the hardened clay beneath.

Below them the meeting was friendly even though it was crowded to the doors. Jesus had moved from healing (Luke 5:17) to teaching as he demonstrated the kingdom of God. There was no offence in what he said, though not everyone would become one of his disciples. As He taught, parts of the roof started to be disturbed. Jesus stopped speaking and looked up as a hole was made and then enlarged in the roof to allow a man to be let down on a bed by ropes. As they let down their paralyzed friend Jesus recognized the faith of his friends. Jesus saw this as a sign the Father intended to heal him, so Jesus asked his heavenly Father in his heart how he should proceed. Into his mind was revealed the cause of his paralysis. It was not from the body but from the soul. Guilt had paralyzed his soul which had spilled into his physical body. So, Jesus said to him "Your sins are forgiven". This worried the authorities from Jerusalem. They questioned in their minds "How could Jesus say, "Your sins are forgiven you" for only God can forgive sins". He then faced the crowd, addressing the questions they had in their hearts, and said "is it easier to say your sins are forgiven or to say rise take up your bed and walk. But so, you know that the Son of Man has power on earth to forgive sins "– he turned to address the sick man "rise and walk". The man got up and walked. Everyone was amazed. They made space for him. Accompanied by one of the disciples, the man learned to move again using muscles which had laid dormant for so long. He pushed his way through the crowd to join his friends who had rushed down from the roof to meet him. This did nothing to allay the fears of those who had come to check him out. In fact, they saw Jesus say to the paralytic the same words which had caused the trouble in Jerusalem "Take up your bed and walk". A concern was growing in the hearts of some there. Jesus resumed his teaching.

By the time his family came to see him, there was no way they could get in. They would try again later when the crowd gathered on the seashore at Gennesaret for the main teaching session

Call of Matthew (Matthew 9: 9-13 Mark 2:14, Luke 5:27ff)

The healing of the paralytic brought the meeting in the home to an abrupt end. There was a roof to repair – probably by one or two of those disciples of Jesus or friends of the healed paralytic. Meanwhile Jesus and the others moved quickly out of his house with the crowd following walking the mile or so out of Capernaum to the shore of Gennesaret which was to become the usual place Jesus would teach. The route took him by the booth at the town end of the harbour. In the booth was sitting as usual Matthew taking the fish due as each catch was landed. Jesus leant in and said Follow me" and Matthew immediately "shut up shop". There were others who could receive the tax due. Jesus knew the family and had spoken to Matthew previously on many occasions. Jesus knew Matthew's half-brother James[104].They

---

[104] Matthew's half-brother James was also one of Jesus 'disciples. In any of the gospels they are never described as brothers like James and John. They shared the same father (Alphaeus). It is likely that James was older than Matthew (Levi) (as James had a son Judas

had been both invited by Jesus when he had taught the sermon on the mount (Matthew recorded this teaching in his gospel in later years). He and his family already were well acquainted with Jesus, and Jesus had often seen Matthew down by the harbour collecting the dues in kind for his boss before the fish reached the market. and followed with the others to Gennesaret. Jesus called him to leave his job and become full-time disciple. He readily accepted and joined the other disciples who followed Jesus as they went towards Gennesaret,

Matthew was from a wealthy background and was well connected and he invited Jesus and the other disciples to come for a meal in the evening at his house after the teaching was over. Matthew also invited some of his business friends – who were tax collectors- to the meal. This was the right context for Matthew to announce and communicate the new position he was in and to stop any false news about his leaving his work. Giving news in a context of a social meal was always the best way. Jesus and his disciples looked forward to the celebration meal at the end of the day. Jesus who had only a house with a damaged roof would also stay at Matthew's house for a few days during the teaching gathering. This caused quite a local scandal when they saw Jesus going to and from Matthews house. Religious Jews avoided the houses of tax collectors (see Luke 5:30, 19:7).

(known also as Thaddeus (Mark 3:18) or Lebbaeus (Matthew 10:3) -to distinguish him from Judas Iscariot) Luke 6:16, Acts 1:13 – one of the disciples). They were sons by different mothers.

Chapter 28

The Third Teaching Gathering July 31AD
(Luke 6:17-19, Mark 2:13)

So that same day late morning they met on the shoreline a mile or so outside Capernaum for the start of the teaching gathering. Jesus taught until the sun started to go down and the crowd dispersed back to Capernaum until the following morning when they would gather again on the beach. The gathering would last this time two days. The enthusiasm amongst the disciples was tangible as they waited for Jesus to teach. This was the Gennesaret region and its coastline stretched three miles from Capernaum southwards towards Magdala. Josephus called it the well of Capernaum because of the abundance of water from springs which flowed into the lake there. Jesus had led them to a place on the shore near where the sermon on the mount had been preached on the cliffs above. He chose an inlet now called "Sower's Cove[105]". It was a natural amphitheatre, and the crowds could hear Jesus clearly even if they were on the cliff top or spread out down the shoreline. They came to hear him (Luke 6:17) and Jesus taught from the boat as he had a few weeks before. This time they also had come for healing (Luke 6:17) and so Jesus returned to shore to lay hands on the sick. The healing ministry of Jesus was manifest in this gathering healing those with diseases (anything from eye diseases and gangrene to leprosy) and setting free those who were tormented by evil spirits (Luke 6:17,18). Since they had heard about the leper being cleansed less than a month before, their expectation to be healed by Jesus of their diseases rose. News of the leper's healing had travelled everywhere and had been recently talked about amongst the Jews at Jerusalem during the Feast of Tabernacles. As a result, in this gathering there was an equal emphasis

---

[105] Tradition states this was the place where Jesus taught.

amongst the disciples for Jesus to heal diseases as there had been for Jesus to bring deliverance from the demonic. Jesus' healing ministry was still growing and in days to come there would be creative miracles when those born blind would see (John 9), and limbs would be restored (see for example Matthew 15:30), but for now those who had suffered through disease were all healed. Then Jesus dismissed the crowds so that some could return home. Many had squeezed in the gathering on their way back from the Feast of Tabernacles. The next Gathering would be held at the same venue at the turn of the calendar year. Not everyone went back to their homes for the Gathering had an additional meeting with Jesus the following morning at the place where the sermon on the mount had been preached some months before. He chose this place to introduce the twelve, because the crowd were less and could be accommodated there below a small hill where he could not only be seen but where the crowd could be close enough to see the faces of the twelve so there would be no doubt who were the chosen members who made up the twelve, so there could be no future deception of others leading the disciples astray

The Sermon on the plain July 31AD
(Luke 6:20-49 Mark 3:13 Matthew 10:1)

Jesus left "Sowers Cove" behind as he climbed up the mountain alone in the fading light. At this time of year Galilee was more humid than Jerusalem which was dryer and cooler. The cool of the evening was welcome as he made his way upwards. In the silence he could hear the gentle flowing of a waterfall nearby, but by now the light was too little to see much beyond where to put his next step. Near the top of the mountain was a cave which looked over the sea. It was here Jesus prayed. He prayed alone all night to the Father about the immediate plans and heard from him revelation about the way the new structure would work to enhance mission and strengthen the development and nurture of all the disciples. Although he had already heard from the

Father who of the disciples should join him as one of the twelve, he remained in prayer for them in their new calling. He listened in prayer to receive any more instructions of what he should say to them. Jesus also committed his ministry to prayer, which was rapidly gaining strength with new challenges. It was after all only six months since the first teaching gathering and already they were in a very different place with crowds everywhere they went even more numerous than before (Luke 6:17ff Mark 3:8). The responsibilities were growing. On the mount it was cool. He wrapped his clothes tight around him as he prayed and watched the night sky as it moved from dusk to dawn.

The sun rose just after 5am and Jesus knew in under three hours the twelve would arrive. They arrived uncertain what Jesus intended, but were already used to just doing what he said and discovering the reason later. When they all were there, Jesus explained his idea. It was not the first time they had heard many of the elements Jesus said, but never with such clarity. Jesus explained the commitment required on their part - the new part of which was that they would start to do the things Jesus had been doing. This matched the hopes they had had when they had first become disciples. Indeed, the hope of every disciple was to become like their master (Matthew 10:24; John 15:20). He explained about the harvest of souls he wanted to reap in Galilee and the rest of Israel. He outlined that the first step would be to go to each of their home towns where they would organize hospitality and after that had been completed they would be sent out to different areas in twos without him to do as they had seen Jesus doing. The full details of their sending out would be explained fully when the time arrived. For now, it was sufficient to paint the broad strokes of what was required. They listened and readily accepted. Jesus told them he would announce this immediately to all the others who were assembling below them in front of the cave

The crowds of excited disciples came to a place just below the top of the Mount Eremos[106] which was just over 500 feet above the lake. Jesus taught affirming again the basics of the Kingdom. The teaching Jesus gave here contained many elements of the original sermon on the mount because Jesus wanted all his disciples to be fully founded in the same soil of the Kingdom and it provided the right context in which to announce the twelve.

Jesus introduced the twelve who stood with him, so all could see them bringing them forward one by one so everyone would recognize them. Jesus ensured through this public appointing of "the 12" that they had recognition, respect and authority which would facilitate both Jesus' and their future ministry. From now on wherever Jesus went, the 12 would be also. The meeting finished, and everyone returned to their homes.

The twelve chosen July 31AD
(Mark 3:16-19, Luke 6:12-16, Matthew 10:2)
The calling of Levi (Matthew) was the immediate precursor to the formation of the 12 so in that sense Matthew is the last of those formally called to follow Jesus before the 12 came into existence. Events from the choosing to the sending out would be many and so varied that Matthew focuses on the events at Capernaum and then the teaching Jesus gave, whilst Mark and Luke seek to bring both events and teaching together. Luke included events that happened in some of the towns they visited with the twelve. The twelve are listed in Matthew, Mark and Luke.

---

[106] This is the traditional site for the sermon on the mount. As it was placed between Capernaum and Gennesaret, it is the most likely location for both sermon on the mount and sermon on the plain

The twelve had relationships already existing which were respected within the 12 because they are reflected in the named order. The list starts with Simon Peter, James and John the sons of Zebedee, (these three together were already an inner circle around Jesus) Andrew (the brother of Peter), Philip, Bartholomew (Nathanael friend of Philip), Matthew, Thomas, James son of Alphaeus (the older half-brother of Matthew who is also a son of Alphaeus. He is a different generation to Matthew (and a different mother as Matthew and James are not described as brothers like the sons of Zebedee). James has a grown-up son Thaddeus (Judas) who is also one of the 12) Thaddaeus (Judas son of James Luke 6:16), Simon the Zealot and Judas Iscariot (another father and son combination [John 6:71, John 12:4 (KJV)].

From the start Jesus had intended to go through all of Galilee (Matthew 4:23). Now with the twelve he could extend the reach of the ministry. He had done what he could from Capernaum, Bethsaida and Chorazin. Now he had additional places to move out from - the home towns of the twelve (Matthew 11:1). The first stage of their mission was that Jesus would visit with the twelve every home town. When he had done this, he would then send them in twos back to their home area to do what he had done from Capernaum, Chorazin and Bethsaida. Going from each home town as a base into the neighbouring communities until every place hears the kingdom.

This next stage was a massive step up organisationally from what had been happening[107]and could not happen without further support from the wider circle of disciples (Luke 8:2ff) both in manpower and money (Luke 8:1), as they would be away for extended periods of time requiring money for both food and hospitality. Jesus knew the support was in place, so the ministry could proceed. Over the summer Jesus and

---

[107] Matthew 9:35 repeats the phrase in Matthew 4:23 because what Jesus started before the 12 were formed can now be fulfilled now he has this new structure in place

the twelve continued to go to the towns they had been before but now the twelve began to help with the ministry of Jesus as well as exercise some leadership when required over other disciples which joined them. Jesus also went to towns unaccompanied by anyone else when they went to more remote places where they had not been before. Jesus now he had the twelve with him was able to expand into new parts of Galilee

To the west of Capernaum ran the road through Cana to the sea port of Ptolemais. The coast was 27 miles from Nazareth and Jesus had never had any reason to go far much beyond Nazareth westwards into the hills or coastal plain of Galilee. The population was denser in Lower Galilee than most other parts of Israel. Outside the main cities there were many small villages, which together formed a population of many thousands. Beyond Nazareth there were small communities in the Jezreel Valley along the Kishon river and near the many springs. On the coast there were small fishing villages one of which one would become Haifa centuries later. These were all communities separated by the geography and history of the region, yet they were all Galileans who as Jews shared a common heritage. Most shared a pragmatic approach towards Rome tolerating the secular Graeco Roman cities built in their midst (e.g. Sepphoris (Autocratoris) and Tiberias) whilst actively seeking to preserve their Jewish way of life. Jesus also intended to go northwards from Cana where Nathanael lived, to the border towns on the boundary between Upper and Lower Galilee. Included in this were fortified towns like Bersabe located on a steep hill (472M) above the ancient west-east road which connected Acre on the north coastal plain (near modern Haifa) to the Sea of Galilee.

Chapter 29

Controversy with the Scribes and Pharisees July 31AD
(Mark 2:15, Matthew 9:1ff)

Before the ministry of Jesus and the twelve had even got underway - In fact whilst some who had come for the gathering were still in Capernaum, there was controversy. Not everyone was well pleased with what they had seen or heard from Jesus. They had had their fears confirmed by Jesus' nearly blasphemous claims (2:6-7) as he had healed the paralytic and were soon reaching a conclusion that Jesus was dangerous. The grumbles amongst the religious were increased by the company he was keeping especially now Matthew the tax collector was so publicly welcoming him into his home. Jesus had stayed with Matthew as he had no house in which to live for the next day or so. The roof of his house was soon repaired, but a full repair required first the clay to be hardened with the sun before the tiles could be put on. For the moment Jesus and the disciples were staying at Matthew's house. The Pharisees asked the disciples about Jesus eating with people like Matthew (Matthew 9:11). Eventually one of the disciples told Jesus who when he heard it, spoke openly to those who had secretly been asking questions behind his back. He stated an everyday truth to challenge their judgement of him because he was staying with a tax collector and eating with sinners. Jesus said, "Those who are well have no need of a doctor but those who are sick". Jesus then said what he was doing was in line with scripture by quoting from the Old Testament (Hosea 6:6). "But go and learn what it means "I desire mercy and not sacrifice". He then finished his reply by talking about his own personal call from God "For I did not come to call the righteous but sinners to repentance".

The fast of Tammuz July 26th 31AD (Mark 2:18-22)

The friends of Jesus asked questions about his disciples. He had just chosen them as his twelve and so Jesus was asked about their behaviour. The specific issue him. It was the fast of Tammuz. This was a three-week mourning period when Jews remembered the destruction of Jerusalem by the Babylonians. Pharisees and the disciples of John joined other Jews in a fast, but they saw Jesus' disciples were not observing this at all. Most of the disciples of John were visitors to Capernaum, old friends of some of the twelve, who had known Jesus from the start of his ministry, and most knew of the connection between him and their leader. They approached Jesus and asked him about this.

More Controversy with the Scribes and Pharisees July 31AD (Mark 2: 23, Matthew 9:1ff)

It was the Sabbath[108] Jesus was with the twelve preparing for the next mission trip. On that Saturday they were talking together as they walked through the countryside just outside the town. It was a pleasant route which allowed for conversation which was not always possible in the town. Since the leper's news Jesus had had to be careful where he went in the town. The path they took went through some fields of wheat (Mark 2:23-27, Matthew 12:1ff, Luke 6:1) which were still to be harvested even though it was past Pentecost. This was not unusual as some years the harvest could stretch into July[109]. They had taken this route before the previous Sabbath on their way to the synagogue. On that occasion the disciples had plucked the grain and they had not been criticized by those who saw them, but since Jesus had continued to stay

---

[108] Most versions of Luke 6:1 omit the one Greek word translated as " second Sabbath after the first" KJV (also Latin Vulgate). The word is only used here so the meaning is unclear. I translate it as this is not the first Sabbath that they did this

[109] Readers digest book entitled Jesus and his Times page 100-101 quoted at http://www.joybysurprise.com/harvest_times_in_israel_.html accessed 2018

at Matthew's house , criticism was growing. The previous week no-one had made any complaint, but this week it was different, Strict Pharisees referred to their activity as winnowing which was forbidden on the Sabbath. The Pharisees felt they were fully justified to raise the issue with Jesus. Jesus confounded them by his answer, the elders of the synagogues and Pharisees in Capernaum were becoming ever more concerned about Jesus.

SECTION 7

Jesus' Galilee ministry from Gennesaret

Already Jesus and the twelve were away travelling to different towns and villages in Galilee, but when they returned they no longer returned to Capernaum but to Gennesaret, a well-watered plain just south of Capernaum where Jesus had taught the crowds before. Now he lived in a dwelling amongst others built amongst the fields.

Chapter 30

The healing of a man with a withered hand August 31AD (Mark 3:1-6 , Luke 6:6-11)

Jesus and the twelve were going throughout Galilee and were away from Capernaum for many days. The controversy between Jesus and the religious authorities, however, continued to fester. Although Jesus was no longer living at Matthew's house, the controversy did not abate. It came to a head on a Sabbath a few weeks later (Mark 3:1). Jesus with the twelve and some other of his disciples sat on the benches in the synagogue as he had done many times before. Jesus noticed a man who had a withered hand there. Jesus asked the man to stand and stretch out his arm which was healed before their eyes. This public act of breaking the Sabbath in the synagogue itself was the final straw for the authorities who finally agreed that the only course of action was for Jesus to die. This was not a new idea, but those who were the first to suggest such a resolution to the problem were regarded as "hot heads". Many had tried instead to seek a less radical solution. They had tried by pressure, arguments and subtle persuasion to try to stop Jesus breaking the law as they saw it; but all to no avail (John 5:16a). They now threw their lot in with the few who had from the beginning spoken of murder. Jesus was not unaware of what was being discussed about him. The synagogue retained few secrets. He knew that living in Capernaum was now no longer an option as murder was easy in its dark narrow streets. Instead he went to live a few miles to the south of Capernaum by the sea in Gennasaret (Mark 6:53.).

Jesus withdrew to the sea from Capernaum August 31AD (Matthew 13:1 Mark 3:7)

As soon as Jesus knew what reaction there as to the healing, his decision to move from Capernaum to the sea was immediate (Matthew

12:15). Jesus was off as soon as he heard that his life was in danger (Matthew 12:15). He moved to the place near Capernaum where he had taught the crowds. Jesus and the twelve knew it well. Gennesaret was an open fertile plain fed by streams which flowed from springs. It was a mile in width at its greatest extent and stretched about 3 miles along the coastline south of Capernaum. It provided open space away from Capernaum making assassination less likely. There was a harbour at Gennesaret [110] but it was much less busy than Capernaum itself. Jesus rented a house to live in (see Mark 3:19) nearby and the twelve joined Jesus there.[111]

[110] See https://www.ritmeyer.com/2014/12/04/harbours-of-the-sea-of-galilee/
[111] Mark chooses to detail who belonged to the twelve at this point before Jesus went on mission with them

Chapter 31

As we have seen during the summer Jesus had set off with the twelve to visit the towns and cities from where they came. Jesus knew that as they went to their home town each of the twelve would have to step forward into some responsibility. He was growing them in ministry. Each "home town "where Jesus went was surrounded by other towns and villages. At each place they stayed for a few weeks while they ministered in the places nearby in a similar way to how Jesus had already operated from Capernaum and then Chorazin and Bethsaida.

There were now just the final few to visit before they would go to Jesus' home town which was to be the last one. Jesus would remain in the Nazareth area whilst the six teams returned each one to one of the regions where they all had visited during this time to build on what Jesus had started. One of the places still to visit was not in Galilee. It was in Judea. They had kept this visit until they went to Jerusalem for the feast of Tabernacles. The feast of trumpets on October 6th 31AD marked the start of the Jewish New Year and was celebrated in Capernaum and other towns in Israel. This also marked the time for Jesus and the twelve to get ready and so they started out for Bethany.

Bethany was a mile and a half east of Jerusalem and was the village where Simon the Canaanite and his son Judas Iscariot came from (Matthew 26:6, John 12:4 KJV). Jesus had not yet done any ministry in the village though during his life he had been through it many times on his way to Jerusalem. Jesus had been many times to Capernaum (home of Peter, James and John), and Bethsaida (home of Philip John 1:44 and where Andrew and Simon Peter came from) and had also ministered at Cana (home of Nathanael John 21:2).

Nain October 31AD (Luke 7:11-14)

Jesus and the twelve were from the beginning of their formation transitioning to becoming fully itinerant. The days were over when He was going out and coming back to Capernaum. There were disciples now in most places they went, so there was support everywhere they went, but they could not burden anyone. So, ministry was expensive. Provision was now available in a greater degree than before through a network of supporters. Chief amongst these disciples were three wealthy women – Joanna, Suzanne and Mary Magdalene (Luke 8:2ff) who gave of their wealth and sometimes joined the twelve and the other disciples as Jesus moved around the towns. In the past any ministry visits would be all about proclaiming the kingdom, whilst teaching disciples and those considering becoming disciples was done back in Capernaum.

They went to Nain (Luke 7:11) in Galilee on his way southwards to Bethany in Judea which was just outside Jerusalem. Nain was about 8 miles south of Nazareth, so it was a village with which Jesus was familiar. The journey to Nain was 25 miles from Capernaum. and being a day's journey was the first place to stop on their journey. Its location lived up to its name – Nain means beauty. Mount Tabor lay six miles to the north and formed a back drop to the village. This village was one of the last villages before the southbound traveler left the Galilean plain.

Jesus and his disciples skirted the west side of mount Tabor watched by the soldiers on the watchtower far above them. They followed the path which brought him by the sepulchre tombs cut into the steep rocks about a quarter of a mile west of Nain. As Jesus approached the village itself, he and the twelve saw a group of people coming in their direction out of the village. The group were walking following a cart pulled by oxen. It was only when they got near they realized that on the cart was a body. This was a funeral cortege going towards the cemetery which

Jesus had just passed. Jesus noticed the grieving mother. There was no man near her, so she was a widow facing a future of poverty without support from husband or son. The despair etched in her soul showed in her face and demeanour. He could not allow them to pass by. He stopped them and spoke directly to the dead boy as he lay in full view on the cart to get up. The boy responded and before anyone could say anything, Jesus picked him up and gave him to his mother. They stopped; speechless whilst Jesus turned and went on his way.

John the Baptist sends disciples to find Jesus October 31AD (Luke 7:17 Matthew 11)

They stayed at Nain, and whilst there were approached by some of John the Baptist's disciples. During the summer they had come for the gathering held during the fast of in July. They had asked why Jesus and his disciples did not fast whilst the Pharisees and they did. Jesu had replied in language which John the Baptist had also used about him being the bridegroom and John as being a friend of the bridegroom (Luke 5:34; see John3:29). One or two of them had gone to John in prison and shared what Jesus had said. They had been given a task to ask him a question when they next saw him. John asked, "Is Jesus really the Christ". John had been in prison for nearly a year. Jesus replied by sharing some of the recent miracles that had happened including the raising of the widow's son just a day or so before. (Matthew11:4). No-one anticipated that in only a few weeks after he heard Jesus' words, John's life would end in execution [112].

---

[112] Herod was definitely born before 20b.c, but the precise month or year is unknown. According to my chronology John was executed in 32BC a year before Jesus was executed. Herod's party was held before Passover (Jesus feeds the 5000 at Passover time just after he has heard of John's execution) in the weeks post the feast of Purim at the end of March as Herod quotes from the story of Esther which was always read during that feast – The words he speaks to Salome are the same as King Xerxes said to Esther at a party she was holding in his honour. The occasion therefore was at the start of April when the Jewish royal year

At Nain they were not far from the wooded ravines which marked the transition from Galilee to Jordan rift valley and they would follow the streams as they flowed into the Jordan. From Nain Jesus travelled twenty miles towards the Jordan Valley descending by the path which took him into the fertile valley of Beth Shean. In the head of this valley in a strategic location at the junction of the Jezreel and Jordan valley was Scythopolis the capital of Decapolis (the only city of the Decapolis group which was situated in Israel). Jesus had many links with people from the Decapolis cities for many came to see him in Capernaum. The majority of those came from this town as it was relatively easy to travel to Capernaum from there. It was just 17 miles from the Sea of Galilee. Scythopolis is not mentioned by name in any of the gospels and was a city built after the Graeco Roman style of other cities in the empire. Its buildings had transformed the ancient city of Beth Shean into a Roman cultural centre in Decapolis. Still Jewish in nature, it also had a distinct culture influenced by the Roman Empire. From there Jesus followed the Jordan river as it flowed southwards. He walked down the Jordan rift valley towards Jericho from where he took the usual road to Jerusalem to arrive in Bethany – not at the home of Mary and Martha - but rather at the home of Simon and his son Judas (Iscariot). (Matthew 26:6; John 12:4KJV)

Bethany October 31AD (Luke 7:36-50)

Jesus and the twelve arrived in Bethany to stay at the house which was still called "the house of Simon the leper" [113]as it had been labelled to warn people when he was ill, and the name still stuck to the house. Simon was now no longer a leper so there was nothing restricting him

began when appointments to office began. It was for a celebration of Herod as King that the dignitaries gathered. Salome was born in AD14 and so was 17 or just turned 18 years old when she danced at the party.

[113] He may not have gone through the various rituals associated with cleansing a house from leprosy

being part of the 12 and he already took a full part in the community so many came for the meal where they would meet Jesus. He was now called "Simon the Pharisee" locally and known as Simon the Zealot amongst the disciples (Acts 1:6). Zealots came from Judas the Galilean who had revolted between the census and the tax being introduced to Israel. It was an offshoot from the Pharisees.[114] and its philosophy was growing in popularity amongst them. They believed they should have no ruler except God [115]. This would grow greater and be a major belief behind the rebellion against Rome thirty years after Jesus death. The titles Simon had been both a compliment of his devout religious heart but could also be used disparagingly of the religious political allegiance. How Jesus first met him we do not know, but it could be he was a leper who had been healed by Jesus. He and Judas were from Judea whereas the other members of the twelve were from Galilee. Simon as a zealot was more open to the religious leaders from Galilee (after all his zealot founder was from there).

Jesus visit to Bethany was not without incident. As they ate together, a local woman came in. She had been there to help, but she wanted to anoint Jesus. She was grateful He was there and that she had been allowed to be part of such an occasion. Her past had been difficult. She had made mistakes, wrong choices, and bore regrets. She was also despised by those who knew her (Luke 7:39). But now because of Jesus she knew in her heart a newness – a forgiveness- which required some show of gratitude (Luke 7:47). She brought an alabaster flask full of fragrant oil. She intended anointing the head of Jesus, but much to her surprise she could get no further than his feet. She approached Jesus,

---

[114] One of the values of the philosophy of Judas the Galilean was that they do not value dying any kind of death nor heed the deaths of relations or friends (Josephus Antiquities 18.1.4) so if Judas Iscariot was influenced by his father, Jesus talk of his future death would be irrelevant
[115] Josephus Antiquities 18.1.6

but more was happening than her mind perceived. As she got near Jesus tears welled up and flowed down her cheeks. She stopped, blinded by her tears which rolled down her cheeks and through the mist to her horror she could see was making the feet of Jesus wet. Without a second thought she let her long hair drop out of its tidy tight binding to fall to her shoulders, so she could kneel and wipe the tears off with her hair. Jesus let her do this remaining reclining with feet outstretched as he ate with Simon the Pharisee and his friends. There was no rebuke from Jesus. Something about his acceptance moved her. She kissed his feet as he ate at the table and anointed his feet with the oil. The fragrance of the perfume filled the air. Her actions were unnoticed by the others who were talking with each other and eating what was a very good meal. Simon however noticed what was happening. He knew this woman and could do nothing. It was up to Jesus to tell her to stop it. After all Jesus was the master, and he a disciple. Also, Jesus was no Essene and so might be enjoying this strange act by this woman and as his guest he should not interfere. The mixture of thoughts and emotions within Simon turned to a negative thought about Jesus. "If he really were a prophet, wouldn't he know what I know that she is a sinner, and would he not act like I would have done". As soon as he thought like this, Jesus interrupted his thoughts. "Simon, I have something to say to you". This got his attention. Simon replied "Rabboni" (My teacher)– the normal way his disciples addressed him (Luke 7:40, John 20:16). Jesus then told a parable about two debtors who both owed money: one a lot and the other a little. He followed up the parable with a question If both were let off the debt who would love the master more. Simon answered the one who was forgiven most. Jesus then contrasted the actions of the woman at his feet with the non-action of Simon in basic hospitality. Washing the feet was a normal necessity when walking in sandals on dusty roads. Everyone did it but not Simon. He had forgotten to do what the woman was doing. This woman, Mary by name, was unknown to Jesus at the time, but a year or so later she would try again to anoint

Jesus properly as she had intended to do but with even more expensive perfume trying to make better, in her view, this failed attempt.

Jesus and the twelve stayed in Bethany visiting nearby villages before going into Jerusalem.

Chapter 32

Jesus in Jerusalem for the Festival of Tabernacles October 20th to 26th and the Eighth day 28th 31AD[116] (John 5:1-45)

The Feast of Tabernacles lasted a week. Jesus joined others in the journey to Jerusalem. He set off in good time to arrive before the start of the feast which this year began on October 20th which happened that year to be a Sabbath. Of all the Jewish religious festivals , Passover, Pentecost and Tabernacles were the main ones that most Jews attempted to attend at least one of them a year. Jesus had been to Passover since he was a child. This year had been no exception going to Jerusalem before his Galilean ministry had started. This Feast of Tabernacles was the first occasion he had made the journey to Jerusalem since his full time Galilean ministry had begun.

It was autumn. The warmth of spring was a long way off (see John 6) and Jesus stayed an unknown guest in one of the many houses in the city. October was pleasant temperatures for travelling as it was free from the summer heat, but felt cold after the sun went down. Any rain that fell would tend to fall in Galilee, so once Jesus had descended into the Jordan rift valley he knew rain was unlikely. Jesus had experienced rain in Galilee and knew how sudden and fierce it could be. It would continue to hinder his progress once the rain had passed. Paths would become mud and rocks slippery. The temperature averaged about 66F, though even now there would be times when the temperature could reach 75F. Nights were always cooler (57F) and Jesus was grateful for the coat he wore over his woven tunic.

---

[116] John does not specify which Jewish feast it is. Some commentators therefore say it is the feast of weeks, but the events described in Galilee from Passover would take longer than the 50 days from Passover to Pentecost (feast of weeks). Tabernacles is most likely.

Jesus arrived in Jerusalem and attended the temple each day alongside thousands of other pilgrims who were also there for the feast of tabernacles. This year the eighth day which was regarded as a Sabbath of Sabbaths separate from and yet concluding the festival was delayed by the actual Sabbath which was October 27th 31AD On that Sabbath day Jesus was walking near the sheep gate at the north of the temple. At this place just outside the temple site walls, not far from the Roman fortress adjoining the temple site there was a pool. The pool was called Bethesda (John 5:2). It was a twin basin with one portico on each of the four sides and one separating the two basins [117]. The five porches provided shade from the sun so the sick gathered there. Jesus came down to the terraced levels which were steps the length of the pool and which continued into the water. He noticed a man lying there (John 5:6). It may have been his posture which first caused Jesus to notice him because most there were going about the rituals of purification or sitting on the steps. Whatever the initial reason that caused Jesus to notice him, Jesus at the same time knew that the Father was in this, and that he was being called to heal the man. Jesus approached the man and asked him if he wanted to be healed. Jesus knew God would not override free will and so the man would have to give his assent. If he chose to remain ill, there would be no healing. The man told Jesus he studied the movement of the water for evidence of the angel's presence, and if he saw the water move, he had tried as quickly as possible to enter the water in the hope of healing, but someone else had always managed this before him. As it was water used by many for ritual cleansing before entering the temple site, he hoped that this "holy" water could facilitate healing by a visiting angel. He had been trying this for many years unsuccessfully. He wanted to be healed. Jesus instantly healed him. Jesus then told him to pick up his mat and go and without waiting, moved on his way back up the steps to go on this way. The man

[117] See the final days of Jesus Shimon Gibson p 74

collected his few possessions including his rolled up make shift bed and was on his way out of the temple site carrying it, when he was rebuked by the temple employees who kept the gate. It was the Sabbath when no-one should do any work, and carrying mats were regarded as work. It was especially offensive to break the law so near to the temple itself, and an ugly scene rapidly developed. His defence was that the person who healed him told him to pick it up. They naturally asked who had done this and at the time he did not know. They let him go. Later during the evening sacrifice in the court of Israel, Jesus saw the man and recognized him. He went up to him and told him not to sin. Jesus knew that in this man's case his past life had given the enemy the doorway he wanted to bring the infirmity upon him. Whether the man was grateful for this pastoral advice or not, he went out and told the temple authorities it was Jesus who had healed him. This caused Jesus had a lot of trouble (John 5:16) and indeed some wanted to kill him. Jesus returned to Capernaum.

Chapter 33

The Fourth Teaching Gathering December/January 32AD (Matthew 13:2; Mark 3:20)

Jesus now had a house to live in outside Capernaum in Gennesaret. Jesus and the twelve arrived at his house (Matthew 13:36) to be ready for the gathering. The gathering again over several days, marked an important moment for the twelve. Up to now they had been with Jesus everywhere he had been, but after this gathering they would be sent out. Just as Jesus had made sure his choosing of the twelve was in the public setting of his disciples so would also be this important sending them out on mission. Jesus had split Galilee into six parts and two disciples sent to each one. They would spend two months in their region before returning to Magdala where their return from mission would be welcomed by all the disciples at the next Gathering.

At this time of Dedication and New Year there were many days of Celebration that made a gathering lasting a few days possible. Jesus disciples came from all over Galilee and even beyond and gathered on the shore at Gennesaret in even greater numbers than ever before (Mark 3:20). Some had come from even farther south than Jerusalem – in fact from the deserts of Idumea (at the southern edge of Israel while others were from the east beyond the Jordan (mostly from Perea which was one of the territories of Herod Antipas the tetrarch). There were also those who had come from beyond the borders of Israel in the north- from the region of Tyre and Sidon. The journeys Jesus had undertaken with the twelve had just increased the number of disciples and a great multitude (Mark 3:8)came : many more than the last gathering. When Jesus and the twelve arrived amongst them it was chaos. Many had come because they wanted to be healed and Jesus and the twelve immediately set to work. Jesus quickly discovered that this teaching gathering would be different from the others. As soon as some were healed the large crowd pushed towards Jesus with such force that he knew he could be crushed if this continued. He turned to Peter and James and asked them to arrange quickly for a small boat to be made ready for him, so he could avoid injury (Mark 3:9). This was something they decided afterwards that they would always have available from now on. As they got this ready, the crowd continued to press forward seeking healing as they touched Jesus. Demons shouted in dismay as they saw him (Mark 3:11), their victims falling down on the beach in terror. In the chaos that ensued, many were healed and delivered.

Jesus was grateful for the boat which was now ready. Any exit was looking increasingly impossible along the path they had come. Jesus did not teach from the boat on this day. He remained on the beach because he needed to be able to be close to pray for those who wanted to be healed. Most healings were done with laying on of hands. But the numbers who had come for healing prohibited a one to one encounter even though it was not Jesus on his own doing the ministry but the twelve as well. Those who were ill were urgent to be healed and pushed forward to touch Jesus, so they could be healed (Mark 3:10). Many were healed in this way. There would be so many stories from this afternoon of healings in this way, that from now on whenever Jesus went into towns or villages the sick would be laid out in the market place in the hope that they might touch him and be healed. But as the crowd surged forward they stood on one another and there were shouts of protest and arguments amongst the people (Luke12:1). There was also risk of serious injury. Teaching was impossible, Jesus was overwhelmed so it seemed by the demands for healing. The twelve were involved with Jesus in the healing ministry and they had no opportunity to even eat. About 4pm it was clear that evening was on its way, so he dismissed them until the following day.

Chapter 34

Opposition December 31AD (Mark 3:22, 31 Matthew 12:24ff)

As in the last gathering, some who came were not disciples but rather questioned Jesus and were suspicious of him. This gathering was no different. The appointing of the twelve at the last gathering had been a very significant moment, and it was perhaps to be expected that opposition in some form would follow on its heels. The religious in Capernaum (Luke 5:17ff) had continued to develop their reservations about Jesus. The call of Matthew and especially Jesus staying with him in a house which the religious should avoid had unsettled them. Jesus' subsequent healing on the Sabbath in the synagogue soon afterwards strengthened the voices of opposition. Now into this mix came respected teachers of the law from Jerusalem who were regarded as experts (Mark 3:22). The Pharisees, who were bible believing and valued the network they had and the people they knew[118], were more closely attached to the scribes than the Sadducees or Essenes. The Pharisees had said Jesus was demonized: that His undeniable power was not from God but from the Devil, and wanted the respected teachers to strengthen their case. This argument was given legs when the previous day on the beach a troubled individual who was also blind and dumb had been brought to Jesus who cast out at least one demon from him, and the man had begun to see and speak. Everyone saw it and were amazed and told the local Pharisees whose anxiety grew when they realized many were asking the question, "Could this be the Son of David" (Matthew 12:23)- an alternative name for the Messiah. The Pharisees reaction when they heard it was to reaffirm their belief that Jesus far from being the son of David had power which came from Satan. (Matthew 12:22-24). Jesus decided to deal with this directly

---

[118] Josephus Wars 2.8.14

when he heard what was being said behind his back. He called the Pharisees with the respected teachers from Jerusalem to meet him (Mark 3:23) in his house at Gennesaret to discuss this face to face. Early in the day after the sun had risen, the Pharisees made their way to the house where Jesus and the twelve were staying. Away from the crowds they were able to have a close discussion. Jesus spoke directly to his guests, addressing their concerns by showing their basic premise had to be wrong. Satan cannot cast out Satan, for that would mean he was fighting against himself. He urged them to recognize it was in fact God at work and the importance of not calling what God the Holy Spirit does as satanic. This meeting had only a limited effect on his accusers. What they had said about his power being of the devil continued to spread and Jesus would face this issue in the cities towns and villages again and again during his ministry (Luke 11:14, John 8:48). The Pharisees began to speak openly against Jesus and this would increase to the ;point where they would cross examine him trying to catch him out about anything he did or said (Luke 11:53). They would continue do this especially whenever they could catch Jesus off guard (Luke 11:54). It would not be long before others, including the religious experts from Jerusalem he had just met, would also dog his steps (Mark 7:1; Matthew 15:1) and even threaten his life in Jerusalem.

The meeting in the house had followed Jesus' normal teaching pattern with which the disciples were familiar. It was interactive. Jesus taught the disciples who came from the controversy raised by the Pharisees. During this Jesus was asked by the expert teachers with the local Pharisees to give a sign (Matthew 12:38ff) to prove the truth of his position. This was not the first time Jesus has heard this (he had had such a request in the wilderness from Satan), and it would not be the last (see John 6:30) Jesus again refused and then continued to teach about the activity of the demonic.

The house where Jesus was already full of disciples and others by the time his family arrived. They had made the journey to see him. The "holiday" period gave Mary and her children an opportunity to travel and catch up with Jesus. She wanted to see her oldest son, and her children arranged for her to travel to Capernaum to see him. They had stayed with Salome in the town and had walked the mile or two to Gennesaret to see him. They had concerns in their hearts. The previous day they had noticed straight away the demands and the strains put on Jesus by those wanting healing and were not a little disturbed to see the order (or as they saw it lack order) in Jesus' life. They had become worried about his mental health when they saw his chaotic lifestyle - for there was not even time to eat (Mark 3:20). His brothers had decided to take him in hand as someone who was insane (Mark 3:21), and take him, by force if necessary, back to Nazareth. (Mark 3:20,21) It was – so they argued- "for his own good". (see Matthew 10:46). They had had no opportunity to do so. They had arrived as early as they could, but they were staying with Salome in Capernaum and by the time they got to the house where Jesus lived, the meeting he was holding with the Pharisees was already underway, and the crowd was large. They were forced to sit outside and wait for a moment. There were respected bible teachers – famous scribes- from Jerusalem in the house and they could not intervene. They waited until the meeting was about to be abandoned which was marked by some leaving the house. Jesus still taught the disciples in the house which was so full they could not get in. One of Jesus' disciples who they knew was nearby, and they approached him. They asked him to go into the meeting with a message that the family were there wanting to speak with him. He agreed and did so. Jesus would often teach on the back of a question or comment. When the disciple stood up and said the message, Jesus responded publicly saying his family were those who obeyed God. His mother and brothers waited outside and realised Jesus was not going to come. They watched as Jesus left and joined the crowd who followed as they went down behind him to the seashore where many more disciples had already gathered. They would eventually return to Nazareth without having the opportunity to meet Jesus but knowing Jesus and the twelve would visit them at Nazareth to spend the Sabbath with them in a few days' time.

Chapter 35

Fourth Gathering continued: Teaching at Sower's Cove
December 31AD - January 32AD
(Matthew 13:1, Mark 4:1ff; Luke 8:1-22)

Jesus held the gathering at the usual place which today is called "Sowers Cove". It was full of people. Crowds stretched further down the beach than they had ever done before and up onto the cliffs above them. Jesus could not be seen and heard by everyone because of the proximity of the large number of people pressing upon him. He took the boat that was now always prepared for him in the sea secured by a rope to the shore. Jesus loosed the rope and got into the boat. This time he was not on the beach being pushed by people wanting healing. Instead he spoke from a boat teaching about the kingdom. Jesus sat down and sailed it a few yards out in the sea so he to teach from the boat. Jesus preferred to sit in a place where he could be seen by those listening to him, and in the boat, he could be seen as well as heard by those on the shore and on the cliffs above This would be the last teaching gathering at this place. No gathering would be held in the Capernaum area after this one. During the gathering (Matthew 13, Mark 4) he spoke many parables of the kingdom including the parable of the sower from which the cove now gets its name. Everyone heard Jesus clearly as he spoke because of the natural amphitheatre created by the shape of the cliffs which rose from the beach at this part of the coast. Jesus when he had finished dismissed the crowd and then made his way with the twelve and other disciples (Mark 4:10) to the house nearby (Matthew 13:36, Mark 4:34). There was still quite a crowd of disciples, who filled the house, and Jesus' family again were unable to see him (Luke 8:19-21).

During the meal Jesus was asked by one of the disciples about his teaching and he explained his teaching in more depth to them. That day they ate freely. They had been too busy to eat anything the day before.

During the lunchtime Joanna and Mary Magdalene who were chief amongst those who provided the logistics for such major events in the ministry of Jesus raised an issue with him. They had noticed last time they met how cramped the site was and the numbers were not decreasing. In fact, they predicted even larger numbers when they met again. If there was over a thousand now it would be several thousand next time. They suggested Magdala. It was the home area for both Joanna and Mary (and therefore easier to organise). In addition, there was a lot more available space for Jesus to teach outside the town. They would also provide a boat for him to use so he could speak as at "Sowers Cove". They also argued that because Magdala was larger than Capernaum, there were more markets where people could buy their food whilst they stayed. Hospitality also would be arranged for Jesus and the twelve and there was plenty of additional homes where other disciples could stay. It was decided that this should be the next venue and everyone there would be told. Joanna ended the arrangement she had made with the owners of the house where Jesus was staying. Jesus and the twelve would be starting their itinerant ministry and would not require the house at Gennesaret any longer. They would have somewhere to stay in the Magdala region when he needed it.

The following day Jesus resumed his teaching on the kingdom from the boat, after which he brought the boat to shore so he could pray for the sick (Matthew 8:16-18). The demand was as great as usual, and Jesus turned to one of the twelve to say he intended to leave and go to the other side. The boat was already made ready, the twelve and Jesus turned to go. The crowd did not want him to go, but he told them would be back again the following day at the same place, during which there would be the formal sending out of the six teams from the twelve on mission. With the meeting (and healing time over) it was often the moment when disciples would approach Jesus about other issues. Sometimes Jesus had been standing talking with some before moving off, but this time he was moving towards the boat where already some of the twelve were sitting. Jesus would be the last one in the boat and there was room at the front of the boat. As Jesus went to the boat a scribe – one of the bible teachers there at the gathering- came and said he would follow him wherever he was going. Jesus said he had nowhere to live. This was true. Jesus now had no house to go back to. His staying at the house at Gennesaret had ended. Jesus and the twelve would spend the night on the boat. In every gathering Jesus did more than just relate to those who came healing or teaching. At the end of meetings he would be involved in conversations with some who came forward to talk with him. Sometimes it was further issues around the theme that Jesus had been saying and he would continue to teach them and others who were there at the time, but on other occasions the people he spoke to with a pastoral heart. The gathering was always an opportunity for disciples who came to deepen their commitment to Jesus. He would sometimes invite a person to join his disciples, not as one of the twelve but to follow him in a similar way that he had first asked the first disciples -that is to join in when they could and learn from him at the same time. Jesus did ask one of the crowd to follow him, but he turned it down because of other commitments (Matthew 8:18-22). As different conversations happened Jesus made his way towards the boat and he was soon walking through the waves until he drew himself into the boat which was lying parallel to the shore. The boat was twenty-seven-foot-long and there were four disciples at the oars. As soon as Jesus was in, the two oarsmen on the shoreside pulled their oars with all their might turning the boat towards the open sea before all four oars hit the water in a strong rhythm.

Chapter 36

The storm at sea January 32AD
(Matthew 8:23-24 Mark 4:39ff; Luke 8:22-25)

The boat had a flat bottom allowing it to get close to shore [119], with a single sail affixed midships so it could be rowed or sailed, so they were quickly away from the shore. Even so some tried to follow them (Mark 4:36). They were in smaller boats so there was less pulling power. The four staggered rowers pulled away from the shore with ease and in the dim evening light the other boats and the shore itself soon disappeared from view.

Jesus with the twelve had travelled by boat together before. What was different on this day was that Jesus asked them to go over to the eastern shore of the lake of Galilee. – a journey of over five miles. The place was outside Galilee linked to the Decapolis. It was deserted and there was a burial ground there which were not uncommon around the Sea of Galilee. (Tiberias for example on the western shore was built on an old Jewish cemetery.).

Jesus found some space in the crowded boat right at the front. It would be cold on the lake especially as evening was falling but there was no chance to go back for a coat. In winter the nights were cold and the weather unstable in night as in day. Jesus had had to get in the boat "just as he was" (Mark4:36). They could do nothing about this, so they kept firmly to their route and pushed out ahead of through the darkness. Whilst the strong fisherman took charge of the boat, Jesus took the opportunity to sleep recharging his energies for whatever might be next. Jesus was in a deep sleep as a cold wind from the east

---

[119] A boat of this type and size dating from the first century has been found in 1986 in the sea of Galilee. It had four oars.

came over the warmer air of the lake whipping up a fierce storm which suddenly stirred up the waves to such a degree that the water started to come into the boat. The disciples tried their best to bail out what they could, but the water was coming in faster than they could get it out. Jesus was still asleep unaware of the water lapping around him. The boat was at risk of sinking. They woke Jesus up. He spoke to the wind and the waves to stop and they did. The wind dropped, and the lake became as calm as a millpond, so no more water could come in the boat. The disciples were amazed as they continued to bail out the remaining water. They had seen wind suddenly stop, but never the waves immediately stop as well. They asked the question to each other Who is this that even the wind and waves obey Him?". They continued to push their oars through the still waters to arrive at the country of the Gergesenes.

Chapter 37

Gadarene demoniac January 32AD
(Matthew 8:28-34; Mark 5:1-20 Luke 8:26ff [120])

The land opposite Galilee was the land where the Gergesenes lived. They were a displaced people group coming long ago there either because of religious persecution or war[121].Few people went there. None of the disciples had ever been. The only people they ever heard about only went there to take the bodies of their relatives. The tombs were caves dug into the sharp cliffs which were just visible as they got nearer the shore. They did not normally sail this close. Some of the disciples had fished the waters in the past but had had no cause to land there. Their main fishing was further to the north where the fish were always very abundant. They rowed towards a harbour of stones built out in a short line into the lake. The harbour was linked to Gadara six miles

---

[120] The NU-text reads Gerasenes instead of Gadarenes in Mark and Luke but Gadarenes instead of Gergesenes in Matthew. Assuming in this narrative Gerasene and Gadarene were interchangeable from the earliest times the gospels were written , the reason is as follows. The people who lived in the region were Gergesenes (the name given to the locals in the region) but two Decapolis cities Gerasa (in the first century it was called by its Greek form rather than its original Semitic name of Garshu – later called Jerash-)and Gadara had an interest in pigs in this region. Gerasa was a large Decapolis city thirty miles south of Sea of Galilee in the deserts near the Jordan valley far to the south near the Dead Sea whilst Gadara was a Decapolis city much nearer being just south of the Sea of Galilee. It could be the two cities Gerasa and Gadara had come together to invest and develop large pig farming using as labourers the indigenous peoples. Two thousand pigs were a significant investment and the land and location was suitable. The pigs when reared were transported to both cities for slaughter. The pigs could have been transported for slaughter by boat to the harbour we know existed at the nearest point to Gadara on the Sea of Galilee and then the few miles overland to Gadara and then some taken to Gerasa.

The man who was delivered from demons is sent home to a city not in the region (as he as well as Jesus had been told to leave the region) which is probably Gadara as Gerasa was so much further away. He could have come from the city because of the pig farming before his behaviour declined. It is probable that he only became ill when in this area as the demons want to remain in the area. (Their power and character stem from the local deeds and culture in that area.)

[121] Gergesenes means "those who are from pilgrimage or fight" Smiths Bible Dictionary

away facilitating transport across the lake to the harbour of Gadara in the southernmost part of the lake[122]. In winter the harbour was empty. No boats were kept here. Most were at Tiberius on the opposite side of the lake. It was completely deserted. At Gadara -which was the nearest city to them- and the cities beyond there were many Gentiles with Roman/ Greek values. They were rich freedmen or ex-military living in the neighbourhood supported by a slave economy. The famous baths at Ahmar Gadara was just five miles south of the Sea of Galilee near Sussita (the largest city on the west side of the lake). The Roman road around the south part of the lake connected Sussita with Scythopolis (Beth Shean) which was a source of Roman cultural influence on the border of Judea and Galilee.

Jesus could see the tall cliffs against the sky getting larger as the boat neared the shore. The disciples behind him just kept rowing to bring the boat ever nearer to the deserted harbour. It was first light but unknown to the thirteen on the boat, there was two restless souls who could not sleep any night or day watching them. They had a clear view of the boat as it approached the shore. They were sitting in a cave tomb that was their temporary dwelling. For years they had made it their job to frighten people away for people had only made matters worse – chaining and imprisoning (Luke 8:29) when they could but the man, who history would know as the demoniac, had escaped every time. He had broken the bonds. He was always on the move. His restlessness providing temporary respite from the war which waged within. Although he had managed to free himself of the chains, he was still tormented: he was sometimes heard when the pain within made them cry out amongst the tombs. Since his escape the restless man had found a companion who was useful to him in a practical sort of way. There

[122] Harbour discovered in 1989. see 2008 Biblical Archaeology Society The Galilee Jesus knew p23. Sixteen harbours have been discovered around the lake. (see https://www.ritmeyer.com)

was no love lost between them. The other man had his own issues, so he thought but two were better than one (Matthew 8:28a) and was controlled as a slave by his demonized master. As long as he was useful he would allow this companion to be near him, for he drove everyone else away (Matthew 8:28c). Not that he had to do this often. He lived in a place few came. It was a cemetery (Luke 8:27) and the tombs in the cliffs overlooking the sea provided some shelter from the wind and shade from the sun. The storm had made sure they were in one of his hiding places away from the wind and rain. The storm had suddenly finished and as the light grew he watched from his caves as Jesus and his disciples disembarked. It was a lonely deserted place. Long ago this man had left his home town in Decapolis. He had had a house then (Luke 8:39), but he had travelled northwards going from place to place until finding this cemetery he had stayed by the sea of Galilee for some time. He was known and feared by the local population who had unsuccessfully tried to help control his bizarre behaviour with ropes and chains and had now frankly given up on him. They did not disturb the pigs who grazed nearby so no further action was taken towards them. They lived in the cliff using the caves most of which were tombs. They were sometimes seen by others when they were in the surrounding region hunting for food. There had been no burials there for some time since they had started to live there (Matthew 8:28c).

On Jesus' arrival the restless man got up quickly to his feet and ran down the track towards the newcomers whilst they were still on the beach, his companion managing to keep up with him (Matthew 8:28) Naked and threatening violence they were fierce (Matthew 8:28) and a fearsome sight. In this deserted place there was no-one to impede the men as they ran towards them, but Jesus just stood where he was. When he did not run, they both cried out one after the other "What have we to do with you Jesus, You Son of God? Have you come here to torment us before the time?" (Matthew 8:29). The men cried out as if they were linked in some way as they spoke. They seemed to know what the other was thinking. It just added to the horror of the situation. Jesus however confronted them. The principle demon was in the restless man in charge. The other man was under the total control of his loud and dominant partner. Dealing with that dominant man would release them both. The servant demons would have to depart with the others. The companion in some turmoil at the unexpected events wandered around unclear as to what was happening while Jesus addressed the demon within his friend directly. "Come out of the man unclean spirit" but it made no difference (Mark 5:8) – just a begging from the man not to torment him (Mark 5:7). Jesus could see the demons were hiding behind the identity of the man – now it was "me" not "us" Even before Jesus had said anything the demon had spoken to Jesus through the voice of the man "Why do you torment us" Matthew 8:29). Initially those who heard this might have thought the "us" referred to the two demonized men before them but it soon became clear that the "us" referred to the demons themselves. Jesus again addressed the demons within the man "What is your name" Jesus said. The demons replied, "Legion for we are many" (Mark 5:9). This accounted for the lack of deliverance. The unclean spirits of anger, destruction, and many others were of different characters, but their identity lay in their unity. As Jesus spoke, the demons seemed to be affected but there was no change in the man. The demons would be about to leave and then something would hold them back. Now Jesus understood the nature of what he was dealing with. Just as a Roman fighting unit sticks together, the demons were marshalling their power together to stop going from their dwelling wishing instead to continue to remain in the wounds and torment of the men which they had an interest in making worse. The demons however also knew there was a superior power at work in Jesus which they could not stand up to forever. They came up with a suggestion to go into the pigs. They hoped they would by that means not go to the abyss (Luke 8:31)– the eternal prison for spirits (Revelation 20:3)- but rather continue to live on the earth in the region where they had power. They were closely allied to if not the demonic principality of the region. They wanted at least to be in same area in which they derived power. After all, if they could stay, one day they might be able to find another suitable life in which to dwell. Anything was better than the abyss. Meanwhile Jesus could see the man before him and knew a quick release from the demons which were at war within him was far more preferable than a long drawn out battle. So, on hearing the demons request Jesus sent them into the pigs. The demons however had underestimated the results of them going into the pigs. A Legion was normally made up of a thousand men and there were two thousand pigs on the hillside – enough for one demon a pig and plenty left over. Their sudden entry into the animals, however, caused such disturbance within them that the pigs stated to run to get away mistaking their internal turmoil as something from where they were. They were behaving as the restless man had done when he was tormented by them. He had spent years trying to manage their destructive powers within him by self-harm, constant movement and withdrawal. The pigs had no such coping mechanisms so instead they just ran straight over the cliff and perished. The demons were unable to return in the death of the pigs and so were consigned to the abyss that they had so tried to avoid, and their old victim were now set free. The disciples got them clothed and sent them on their way, but the restless man remained talking with them finding out more about all that had happened just a few minutes ago. He was not a local. His background was not Gergesene, but he came from Gadara in the Decapolis. He had come to the area to work and become ill. As they talked many local people came from nearby. Amongst them were people who also originated from the Decapolis which was using the area to cultivate pigs. Slaves and the poor looked after pigs for their masters. They worked for their masters and were worried that the presence of Jesus and the disciples might inflame the situation. Two thousand pigs were a big investment to lose and they felt it easier to explain this to their masters if Jesus and the one he had made well was out of their territory. They could not understand what had happened or explain it to their masters. They preferred to blame the pigs demise on natural causes like the storm or plead ignorance rather than try to tell the truth. They needed to act quickly, or they might be judged as thieves and punished. So, they urged Jesus and his disciples to go. Jesus agreed, and they went back to their boat on the shore. The healed man followed them to the beach. They were his friends – in fact the only friends he had. He therefore asked Jesus if he could come with them, but Jesus knew this man had a purpose. He was to prepare Decapolis for the coming of the gospel. He therefore told him to return to his own home city of Gadara. A year later Jesus would visit parts of Decapolis and so this man's testimony might have played a part in preparing for his visit then. For now, no-one knew the future. They said their farewells and Jesus and the disciples got into the boat and sailed over towards Capernaum on the other side of the lake.

Chapter 38

Fourth Gathering continued– Sending out of the 12
(Matthew 13:53; Mark 5:21)

Jesus returned to Gennesaret (Mark 5:21). It was morning and many disciples had already gathered waiting for Jesus to arrive. The crowd knew that the moment had come for the twelve to go on their apostolic mission, and they had gathered in their hundreds (Luke 8:40) to see them off. Jesus announced they would return to Magdala at the conclusion of the mission just before Passover, and then taught the crowd on the beach in his usual interactive way. Some disciples of John who had not become disciples of Jesus asked questions on eating as the Pharisees had done earlier in the week (Matthew 9:14)– this time on the lack of fasting of the disciples of Jesus. It had been the fast of Tebet (January 13th) the previous day when both they and the Pharisees had fasted. The disciples had not, for they had seen them eating. This may not have been the first time that this issue had been raised (Mark2:18). Jesus or some of the twelve may have known some of John's disciples from the start and knew that they had stayed loyal to their master even when he had been imprisoned. Though not disciples, John's disciples regarded themselves as allies of Jesus. John the Baptist had affirmed Jesus and so they mingled easily with the disciples of Jesus. They noticed, however, many differences between their master and Jesus. When John was active, he was in the deserts away from people whereas Jesus was in the towns. The question they asked was concerning the difference in lifestyle of Jesus disciples from their own. They fasted whilst Jesus disciples never did. Jesus answered this by saying there is a new day and therefore there's a fundamental difference between the behaviour of the two sets of disciples (Matthew 9:15-17). His teaching was ended when someone in the crowd asked Jesus to come to heal his daughter (Matthew 9:18). Family and friends said their "goodbyes" to the twelve as they made their way behind Jesus as he walked towards Capernaum with Jairus the synagogue ruler, the man in the crowd who had asked Jesus to heal his daughter.

Chapter 39

Raising of Jairus' daughter January 32AD
(Matthew 9:18ff, Mark 5:21ff Luke 8:41)

Jesus may have expected to be teaching longer before setting off with the twelve, but he now knew that the Father had other plans. The ruler of the synagogue at Capernaum had been looking out for Jesus to return. He had heard about the large gathering and the numbers Jesus had healed whilst his daughter's health was deteriorating. She had been ill for some days and was not getting better – in fact all the signs were that this young frail girl was at death's door. (Luke 9:42). Jairus was known by many as the ruler of the synagogue. He spoke up from the crowd "My daughter lies at the point of death. Come lay your hands on her that she may be healed" (Mark 5:23). Despite the recent controversy amongst some of the Jews in his synagogue and beyond, he had set out to find Jesus. He was desperate. When he heard Jesus was with his disciples by the sea in his usual place, he immediately made his way to find Jesus – a journey of a mile or two - to plead for Jesus to come to heal his daughter. He had joined the crowd and as soon as he made his plea. When he found that Jesus immediately went with him, he was heartened. Behind them many of the crowd that had been with Jesus followed on. The crowd attracted others as they went into the city. It was around mid-day. The streets were not wide and there was some pushing and shoving in the narrow streets. It was at this point that Jesus stopped, turned and said who touched me. Silent bewilderment accompanied Jesus' request. Simon Peter spoke up saying everyone nearby would have touched Jesus. Jesus remained stationery. From the crowd emerged a woman who stepped forward in front of Jesus. She told her story in the hearing of all those nearby. She had decided to join the crowd seeking to reach and touch his garment for healing. She knew in herself she had been instantly healed and she told the whole story.

Others would hear this and decide to also touch Jesus for healing in the days ahead. (Mark 6:56)

As Jesus talked with the woman, some man came from the direction they were heading and spoke quietly to Jairus. At that moment Jesus sent the woman away and turned to find out what the news was that Jairus had heard. He was a strong man processing the devastating news he had heard of the death of his daughter without any outward cry or exclamation. Inside he was in turmoil thinking all his effort had been for nothing. Jesus said to him "don't worry only believe" and they continued walking the relatively short distance to his house. When they arrived, Jesus told the disciples to wait with the crowd except Peter James and John and they accompanied Jairus as they went in the house. They came into grief and mourning. Jairus' wife had had much support from the synagogue members in caring for her daughter and there were many already in the house when she died. Jesus needed to change the atmosphere so first of all said, "She is not dead but sleeping". In the atmosphere of grief what Jesus said seemed ridiculous and they laughed at his words. Jesus told Jairus to put them out of the house. This he did, not dwelling on any possible negative consequences if Jesus was wrong. His daughter being healed was all that mattered. Jesus met Jairus' wife and asked them to show him the girl. They led Jesus to the room where she was lying. When the three disciples Jesus had asked to come with him were in as well as the parents Jesus closed the door. On the bed was a young girl lying still. Jesus took her hand and told her to get up and the parents noticed how she did not stir but opened her eyes and so Jesus helped her to get up. He then told her mum to make sure she had plenty to eat. He recognized the weakness she had was because she had not eaten for some hours. The parents knew that in the hours before her death because of her illness they had had difficulty even getting water down her. Food had been out of the question. Now seeing their daughter restored to life there was great rejoicing as they got food for her. Jesus and the twelve were offered some food which they accepted.

It was well into the afternoon when they left Capernaum behind and made their way to Magdala where they would stay overnight. The twelve were looking forward to the opportunity to sleep. They had had no opportunity to do so the previous night. Magdala was on the route to Nazareth, which was the last home town to visit before the twelve went out in different directions all over Galilee. Magdala was the place they would return to after their mission was complete in a few weeks' time. They were to stay in the same place as they would at the end of the mission , so on their return they knew where to come. They would then journey onto Nazareth from there in the following morning.

Chapter 40

2 Blind Men. January 32AD (Matthew 9:27)

Jesus went from Jairus' house outside the town on towards Magdala on the road to Nazareth (Mark 6:1) - the next place on the ministry to visit all the towns they were linked to. They were followed by two blind men who helped each other with their limited vision to follow where Jesus was going. They were not totally blind but did have severe loss of sight. Jesus went south on the road five miles until he entered a small fishing town called Dalmanutha which was on the outskirts of the large town of Magdala. He went towards the house where it had been already arranged that they would stay. The blind men followed as Jesus went into the house. They sat down by the road and waited. Whilst it was still light, the disciples who had accompanied Jesus and the twelve started to go back to their homes. The disciples from Capernaum turned back whilst those from the local area dispersed to their homes, and the blind men recognized that this was where Jesus was stopping for the night. The darker it got, the more difficult they would be able to see. Now was their chance. Jesus was no longer on the move surrounded by lots of people. Their need drove them to approach the house. They knocked loudly on the door and asked to see Jesus. Jesus met them, and they asked him to heal them. Jesus did so and told them to keep quiet about it. The crowds though large were not unmanageable. If they spread the news of their healing back in Capernaum it could seriously impede Jesus' ministry in the area (Matthew 9:31c) as the leper's testimony had already done in that town. Capernaum had many people living there and such a testimony would be untimely just at this delicate time where he was starting to develop the twelve as ministers of the gospel. He had no wish for the team duo from the twelve who were going back to Capernaum area in a day or so to have the same problem Jesus had following the healing of the leper.

Healing of someone with a mute spirit January 32AD (Matthew 9:32)

As the blind men left, a local man was brought in. This was not unusual. There was often one needy person followed by another coming to see Jesus. The man who came in was accompanied by others. It was these who asked Jesus to help him. The man could not speak and there was evidence even as he came in of disturbance in the way he acted. Jesus started to pray for him. After a little while the demon was cast out and the dumb man was able to speak. Jesus did not ask the witnesses to keep quiet about this. They were locals. It would make little difference to the immediate mission. Those who witnessed and heard about it were many (Matthew 9:33) and all were amazed.

SECTION 8

From the "Twelve" to the "Seventy"

Jesus preaching the Gospel of the Kingdom in cities and villages around (Matthew 9:35, Mark 6:56)

In the next eight weeks or so Jesus and the twelve would have either together or in teams have proclaimed the kingdom at least once in every place in Galilee, and in some other parts of Israel. This was no small task, as Galilee in Jesus day was highly populated (Josephus wars 3.3.2). Jesus had from the start of his ministry intended to visit every community in Galilee (Matthew 4:23) and Josephus mentions that in Galilee there were when he lived (just after the death and resurrection of Jesus) 240 towns which if you included the immediate villages in the area of each town had at least 15,000 residents.[123]

Jesus wanted to reach all of ancient Israel of which Galilee was just the start. The harvest of souls for the Kingdom of God everywhere was very important to him. He sent out seventy to prepare the ground when he came so that the maximum number of Jews who lived in the ancient land of Israel would hear the gospel of the Kingdom in the shortest possible time. Although the gospels do not detail the routes he took, the roads of the first century were where most of the communities were both in Galilee and in Judea,(as well as Perea and Decapolis whose lands had been part of the promised land of Joshua and Moses) so it has been possible to give the general route Jesus would have taken at this time.

Alongside the strategy for harvesting of souls in Israel, Jesus began to share with the twelve revelation about his future death. About the same time as the return of the twelve, Jesus learnt about John the Baptist's execution and he knew this event of the forerunner also heralded his own death.

---

[123] The Comparative Geography of Palestine and the Sinaitic Peninsula Vol 1 page 342 by Carl Ritter

Chapter 41

Jesus visits Nazareth, January 32AD
(Mark 6:1-6 Matthew 13:54)

It was less than a week from the end of the gathering when Jesus arrived at Nazareth with the twelve. On the last occasion Jesus had been "home" he had nearly lost his life, but a lot of water had gone under the bridge since then and any past negative reaction to Jesus was no longer there. He and those with him were welcomed, and at first this was encouraging. They stayed a few days until the Sabbath. Jesus caught up with his family who had been unable to have any meaningful meeting with him during the recent gathering. They all gathered together in the evening to celebrate the Sabbath at his home. On the Sabbath day morning Jesus and his disciples made their way to the small local synagogue. Although of different sizes, each synagogue was the same design. Jesus and his disciples took their seats, and at the appropriate time Jesus was asked to step forward, and from the middle of the synagogue, he taught them (Mark 6:2). It was a contrast being in the synagogue that Jesus had known since a boy with the scenes they had recently witnessed on the beach at Gennesaret. The response from the people was negligible, and so only a few were healed. During Jesus stay there were so few opportunities to bring the kingdom. Why? In short there was no thirst. Jesus soon discovered that apathy was now the problem in Nazareth and the visit did far less than they had hoped. The problem was they knew Jesus as the local boy, and they thought they knew him. They had no expectation of God making a difference to them. They were at best slow to ask for healing and Jesus was amazed at their unbelief.

The 12 anointed and sent out (Matthew 10:1, Mark 6:7ff)

When they left Nazareth the first phase had been concluded. The twelve were now released to go throughout Galilee without Jesus. They were instructed to stay within the same ministry calling of Jesus by going "only to the lost sheep of the house of Israel". They were not to visit Samaria and not to respond to anything except a Jewish call (Matthew 10:5). They were not to focus on the Gentile cities or Roman watchtowers. It was the communities where Jews lived where they were to go, and there were plenty of them -in fact too many of them to visit them all. They could not stay in any one place for any length of time (Matthew 10:23). They each went and preached a message of repentance, cast out demons when they manifested as the word was preached and anointed the sick with oil who were healed. It was a wonderful time that none would forget.

The most densely populated areas were in Lower Galilee so there were plenty of places which had not been visited and there were also towns in Upper Galilee still to visit. They would be gone for about two months and they would be inviting those they met back to the gathering at Magdala just before Passover. It meant that many would be able to "drop in" for the teaching gathering on their way to Jerusalem. Jesus wanted to visit every place in Galilee to be visited before reaching the rest of Israel. Whilst the disciples were on mission, Jesus remained in the Nazareth area walking a circular route through neighbouring villages. Jesus visited the villages in a circuit (Mark 6:6). His region was the part of Galilee which stretched towards Mount Carmel in the south west where it bordered an area which used to be part of Galilee but now belonged to people from Tyre (Josephus Wars 3.3.1). Jesus went to the Jewish communities which were a day's journey south of Nazareth and up towards Cana which was the base of Nathanael who was reaching communities in Upper Galilee. As his instructions to the twelve, Jesus did not stay long in any village but taught in each one as he went. The six teams of two went gradually over the next few days after Nazareth (Mark 6:7) to their designated region and began immediately to visit the communities in the area. Each team of two reflected the relationships which pre- existed Jesus' call, so in that sense the teams were already formed well before the time came to be sent. The brothers Peter and Andrew, and of course James and John were two such pairs but there were also the father son duos – Simon the Canaanite and Judas Iscariot, and James (son of Alphaeus) with his son Thaddeus. Philip and Bartholomew (Nathanael) were long established friends. This only left two others. Matthew and Thomas who are named together in the order of the 12, who formed the other team. The twelve wherever they went spoke a similar message to the one John the Baptist preached. It was a message about repentance to prepare for the kingdom (Mark 6:12). In addition they healed the sick, mainly by anointing with oil (Mark 6:13) and casting out demons, as well as proclaiming the kingdom They signposted those interested to Magdala at Passover.

When the twelve left, other disciples continued with Jesus. It was similar days that Jesus had known at the start of his ministry before the twelve were formed, and he had to adjust back to what it used to be like. Wherever Jesus went there were disciples and new ones would be added after every place he visited. For the next few weeks, Jesus visited the communities in the Nazareth area. Jesus was doing on his own in the area around his home town what the others were doing in the areas around their home towns and places they went to. Without the support of the twelve he stayed within low population areas where there was less possibility of the problems which came with large crowds which had already started to accompany Jesus. He taught in the villages, and he visited them more than once during this time. (Mark 6:6). The ministry since the choosing of the twelve had been evolving away from a synagogue based ministry to an everyday ministry with no link to the synagogue. This was now fully in place. Jesus no longer was restricted to communities where there was a synagogue. He went everywhere he could. He visited each village at least twice before making his way towards Dalmanutha, the village just outside Magdala. He arrived a day or so before the twelve and other disciples started to arrive as arranged to prepare for the next gathering where many thousands were expected. Jesus walked the roads well before disciples took to them for the gathering. He needed to be ready at Magdala. The fields of sheep grazing on the gentle slopes near the town showed the variety of places Jesus could choose to teach the crowds who were coming. It was now the end of March and in a few days the roads to Magdala would be full. Before Passover there were always more people using the roads on their way to Jerusalem but this year many of those travelling were going to see Jesus. Thousands were travelling in their family groups. The main road from Tiberias to Capernaum and the north passed through Magdala as did the road from the west which went through Cana. These roads made Magdala reachable from every part of Galilee.

Chapter 42

Return of Twelve April 32AD (Luke 9:10)

As March opened into April the cold of winter was passing into the warmth of spring. Days in April were very pleasant with day time temperatures between 66 -70 F and though still needing to make up fires at night the nights were less cold. It was an ideal month to all gather together after the ministry of the 12 around Israel. He was at Dalmanutha near Magdala[124].John 6:1[125] Passover was approaching (John 6:4) when the 12 finally all returned (Mark 6:30) and there were already many disciples gathering. It was early April, a week or so before Passover which was that year on April 15th. The numbers that came for the gathering needed some serious logistics. The mission of the twelve had added many hundreds to the thousands of disciples that came to this gathering which was there to welcome the twelve back from mission as well as hear Jesus teaching. The gathering was held just north of Tiberias, the capital city of Galilee. It was at this time that news about Jesus first reached the ears of Herod Antipas. Joanna the wife of Chuza Herod's steward, who lived at the royal court in Tiberias just south of Magdala, had been healed before by Jesus (Luke 8:3) and had been central in arranging the hospitality and food for the gathering at Magdala. As we have seen she had supported Jesus in his ministry (Luke 8:3). Mary from Magdala was a wealthy woman also supported the ministry so Magdala. It had made sense to hold the gathering. Magdala was a larger town than Capernaum and had the capacity to look after

---

[124] See note 46

[125] John 6:1 says Jesus took the boat to where the feeding of the 5000 took place over the Sea of Tiberius. The Sea of Galilee was divided into various sections. The Sea of Gennesaret defined the area of sea near Gennesaret just south of Capernaum. The sea of Tiberius was further south in the same sea of Galilee

thousands of people. (in the wars against Rome Josephus states there were many thousands there).[126]

The twelve had completed their assignments and over a period of a few days they all arrived in Dalmanutha, the smaller village which lay just north of the large town of Magdala. (compare Mark 8:10 with Matthew 15:39). As the 12 returned Jesus listened to them relating what had happened and what they had said. But they had no time to do this fully because so many came for healing (Mark 6:31). The amount of people who came swamped them (Mark 6:30). There were thousands. They came [127] (see Matthew 13:2) to be taught but the ministry demands meant Jesus had less time to teach and there was so much coming and going that even when the crowds were eating, Jesus and the twelve were healing those who asked them. So, Jesus and the disciples as in the last gathering had no time to even eat (Mark 6:30).

---

[126] The land around Magdala and its town could accommodate large numbers. Josephus mentions during the Jewish revolt , of thousands being there (Josephus Wars 3.10). After the defeat of Magdala by the Romans during the revolt, as well as those killed, thirty thousand were sold as slaves and 6,500 were additionally captured who had fled by sea from the city.

[127] The feeding of the 5000 follows which were from those who gathered at Magdala

Chapter 43

Herod executes John the Baptist Spring 32AD
(Matthew 14: 1-12 Mark 6: 16-29 Luke 9:9)

Whilst Jesus was at Magdala, he heard the unexpected news of the execution of John the Baptist (Matthew 14:13) While the mission of the twelve was in full swing, Herod had executed John. He had been imprisoned for two years and Herod had every intention of keeping him there. In prison he could not excite his followers against him, and yet whilst alive he could not be a martyr. Herod Antipas wanted public discussion to move away from his personal life. The situation with his first wife was still a potential problem for him. Aretas his ex-father in law was the King of Nabatean people – an important trading partner who reigned over the region which bordered Perea - Antipas' domain east of the Jordan. He was more concerned about any internal sedition fuelled by zeal stirred up by John the Baptist's condemnation of his marriage to Herodias. Any disturbances would cause difficulties which could be heard in Rome undermining Herod's attempt to increase his influence as a useful friend and important agent for peace in the region. On the Eastern border of the empire was the enemy of Rome called the Parthians and Antipas had had some success in brokering a deal between Parthia and Rome, but his success upset the Roman general in charge of the Syrian province and he did not want any excuse for any negative narrative about him to come to Rome.

It was Herod's party. He had returned to his palace in Machaerus from Jerusalem where he had been attending the feast of Purim which had been held on March 16th and 17th. The end of another Jewish royal year was over. (April was when kings and other officials started their year.) Passover was still a fortnight away so there was a space in the diary in which to hold this lavish celebration at the start of his royal year. Although he usually lived in his capital Tiberias, he gathered the great and the good to his palace at Machaerus which was more suitable for a celebration. It had after all been built and adapted by Herod with such occasions in mind. Tables were laden with food were put in the paved courtyard with its impressive Doric columns. It was also only sixteen miles from Jerusalem so was well placed, and Antipas stayed there for the three weeks between the end of Purim and the beginning of Passover. (Tiberias in Galilee was near one hundred miles to the north from Jerusalem – more from Machaerus).

The feasting was good as usual. The wine flowed freely. Salome, now a teenager of 17or 18 years old, danced. The king was at first amazed, then delighted by the provocative dance and at the rapturous response of his party. He was also personally delighted with the dance. It made the party even more special. He felt flattered and responded with the rash promise which would open the door to John's execution. He spoke the words of Xerxes to Esther "I will give you what you desire up to half the kingdom". In his wine dominated head, his tongue spoke the words of King Xerxes in the book of Esther which a short time before were read as they were every year at the feast of Purim. (The party held by Xerxes at the beginning of Esther and the dinner party requested by Esther for Xerxes to attend are turning points in the book) Herod enjoyed the thought of Salome dancing a special dance for him as Esther had thrown a special party for Xerxes -and compared himself to the greatest leader of the known world in thre days of the Persian empire.

Salome left to the applause of the audience ringing in her ears, surprised at the offer Herod had given. She did not know how best to respond. She went to her mother to discuss what she should ask for. The bitterness against John's word stored up in Herodias' soul spilled out and she told Salome to ask for the head of John the Baptist- but to make sure it was fulfilled it was to be given to her in front of the guests. This prevented Herod going against his word once the drink and emotion of the occasion had worn off. Herodias had obviously been there before! She remembered the many delays to his promises of divorcing his first wife, so they could marry. His promise then had not been kept for over twenty years until she put pressure on him to wed. She was fed up with Antipas' decisions based on politics which affected her life. John the Baptist was the latest cause of problems which in her view Herod was not dealing with had to go now! The political storm that Herod had dreaded creating by marrying Herodias had become a reality through the words of John the Baptists and it had affected the relationship between her and her husband. She needed John dead! Herod's rash vow allowed his wife to now remove the thorn in her flesh. John the Baptist had spoken hurtful words which had made things difficult for her in public life and also privately. Her husband did not want to inflame the religious zealots of Judea by making John a martyr especially over the issue of his marriage, but Herodias forced his hand because of his public vow.

There was no room to wriggle for she told Salome to ask for the head of John the Baptist to be delivered immediately. [128] Herod had to comply, and so reluctantly gave the order. John's head was brought, and Salome took it from her step father in front of them all and gave it to her mother. In the morning in the political cold light of day, Antipas had to act swiftly to minimize any political fallout. One thing he could not risk with his Roman masters was creating a problem through his own personal life or actions. He risked everything if Roman favour was withdrawn from him. He had some quick decision to make to minimize any possible problems that might arise. Part of the price Salome must

---

[128] Since the divorce of his first wife, Herod had been concerned about war with her father Aretas. He needed the support of Philip to prevent a pincer movement against him in one of his domains Perea. (Philip to north, Nabatean kingdom to south). Philip was also popular with his subjects who were Jewish and agreed with John the Baptists re Herodias. Antipas in my view made sure Philip married Salome to help secure his reign.

pay to secure Herod politically and minimize any risk from the death of John was to be married to Philip the tetrarch (an old man of Herod Antipas' generation). Salome was young and attractive but had, as a woman of that age, to do what her step father said. Herod saw Philip as a useful ally who could help keep Aretas quiet. Aretas needed a good relationship with Philip for his economic prosperity. The important trading city Damascus was one of the cities of the Decapolis that Philip ruled, and so Aretas did not declare war with Antipas over his daughter's divorce. In addition, if there was any war declared, Antipas needed to have Philip as an ally at his back if Aretas invaded Perea the part of Antipas' domain which bordered the north of the Nabatean Kingdom. if Philip were allied to Aretas, Antipas as he defended his territory would be caught in a pincer movement from Philip to the north as well as Aretas from the south.

Some disciples of John the Baptist got permission to remove John's headless body for burial, and it was these men who came to Jesus to tell the sad news, so there could be no mistake John was dead. Jesus thanked them for coming, but he knew he would have to leave immediately to process what he had heard. Jesus saw John as the forerunner. Where he went Jesus would follow. What happened to John prepared the way. So, John's death meant a new phase in Jesus' ministry which like John would end in death. He needed time to process with His Father the implications of what he had just heard. It was therefore imperative to be away from the ministry demands that were present in Magdala. So, Jesus said to his disciples "Let us go to a deserted place" (Mark 6:31). Jesus would go first, and they would follow a few hours later

Chapter 44

Jesus to Bethsaida (Mathew 14:13ff)

Having got the `agreement of the twelve, Jesus left them as soon as he could. Jesus got into the small boat which had been organized for his use and sailed northwards. (Matthew 14:13 "by Himself"). Jesus rowed the ten miles across the Sea of Galilee to Bethsaida. Jesus knew the lake well and soon recognized the inlet which he needed to sail up to reach the city of Bethsaida (Luke 9:10). It had been rebuilt in 3BC after its destruction during the Hellenistic period. Although now no longer in Galilee, its people still had close ties with Galilee. Under Philip the city was being expanded into his capital and renamed Julias in honour of the mother of the Roman Emperor Tiberias, who had died two years before. The city, however, was still known to most ordinary folk as Bethsaida. There had been some clearances for new buildings as well as additional streets added so the town was gradually taking on a fresh and new appearance. Jesus took the boat up the river and landed near the city and made his way around the outskirts(Matthew 14:14). Bethsaida was built on a hill which in time long past had touched the sea, but now the water was quite a distance away. The city lay to the north where the river Jordan entered the sea of Galilee, and it was in Jesus' day over a mile upstream. Over the years the lake of Galilee had retreated southwards leaving a large flood plain. The mud and sand had now changed into a grassy plateau overlooking the lake, and although no - one lived there, it was part of Bethsaida, and formed one of the largest strips of plateau around the lake. Jesus skirted around the city and soon felt the grass under his feet. The disciples were to join him later in the day (Matthew 14:15). Jesus intended to go into the hills that lay eastwards of Bethsaida and to walk through the hills before joining the disciples. They had agreed to meet on the flat grass near the shore because it was easy to find each other. Wherever they landed, they would see Jesus, and they would be seen by Him. For now, Jesus intended to be alone for a few hours. The grassy plain was easy walking (Luke 9:16) as he headed for the mountains beyond.

Feeding of 5,000 April 32AD
(John 6, Luke 9:10, Matthew 14:14-21)

All the land he was walking on including the mountains were under the jurisdiction of Bethsaida. It was a safe place. it was not the territory further round the coast under the jurisdiction of Hippos or Gadara where they might be less sympathetic to a Galilean Jew. Jesus intention was to pray as he walked, and he hoped to find a suitable place where he could be undisturbed to sit and pray. He was grateful for the time and space. He had not long started to head out when he caught his first sight behind him of the crowds coming to find him. There were thousands of his disciples who had made their way overland. It was with some surprise that Jesus saw them. He greeted them and found out they already knew of the arrangements Jesus had made with his disciples. They had walked and ridden the 12 miles from Magdala in the time it took Jesus to row to Bethsaida, moor the boat upstream and walk down through the town. Jesus realized his prayer time with the Father had to be postponed. He saw they had come because they were spiritually hungry. They wanted the words of life and he had not been able to teach them at Magdala because of the sheer volume of those wanting healing. The people who were here were the well active disciples and their need was not for physical healing but for spiritual truth. Jesus led the crowd to the place he had arranged to meet the disciples. When he arrived there, he sat down and taught. He continued all day as more and more people arrived.

Back at Magdala, after the crowd had melted away, the 12 got into their boat as arranged. They could see where they were to go. It appeared as a green line near the shoreline from quite a way off. It was an area a few miles east of Bethsaida known to Peter and some of the others. When "the twelve" arrived, they discovered that Jesus had already been teaching a crowd of many thousands for some hours. The disciples were used to surprises with Jesus. They walked through the gathered throng to Jesus whilst he continued to teach. The first reaction the twelve had was to suggest to Jesus he send them away as it was a deserted place and there was no chance of food. They had already had experience over the last few days of not having time to eat because of ministry demands and enough was enough! Jesus instead of responding as they hoped, asked them to find out how much food there was already amongst them. The response was not encouraging. Andrew was the only one to find anyone with any food at all... a young man who had with him two loaves and a few fish.

Jesus commanded them to tell the crowd to sit down in groups of fifty. There were, so they later found out, one hundred groups which sat on the green grass at the instructions of the twelve. Each group had about fifty men in them though most had families with them, so the actual numbers were swelled with women and children. The forming of groups created aisles along which they could distribute the food. Jesus blessed the food he had and gave it to the disciples to distribute. Each one had found a basket and Jesus put broken pieces of both fish and bread into each basket. They then went throughout the groups giving the food away. They found as they gave it away the pieces in their baskets did not diminish. They went to each group in turn and kept going until all had had enough to eat. They then returned to Jesus with baskets full of the fish and bread scraps which had been too small to give away.[129]

---

[129] The "leftover fragments "Luke 9:17 are what is left in the baskets after everyone had been fed.

Chapter 45

The miracle of the loaves and fish was immediately evident to the crowd and they were filled with amazement. Nothing like this had ever happened before. Soon Jesus and the 12 heard that there was a movement to take Jesus and declare him king. The twelve believed it was credible and so Jesus had to get away before anything could happen. Jesus made some quick decisions. He wanted to continue the original plan of going into the mountains east of where they were in order to pray. He told the disciples to take the baskets food and return to their boat which they had berthed , and to sail towards Bethsaida (Mark 6:45). Bethsaida was situated on the other side of the flood plain inland from where they were, and the plan was that Jesus would join them there, so they could travel together to Capernaum. All decisions were made very quickly as Jesus still wanted to spend time alone with His Father. The implications of John the Baptist's death were important for the future. He explained to the twelve that once they had left, he was less of a target because he was on his own and so could hide more easily.

Jesus continued to finish the teaching. There would be no attempt to make him king whilst this continued. After he finished he made a surprise rapid departure hiding as he had done so many times before in the crowd. Then Jesus went up a mountain in the fading light to pray and the Father started to reveal more about the death Jesus would face in a future time of Passover.

As the afternoon moved towards the evening the disciples quickly packed up and got into the boat. There was a strong wind blowing from the north-west, but they immediately began to make for Bethsaida. (Mark 6:45) hoping that the wind would soon die down. They anticipated it would not be too much a problem to sail along near the shore to Bethsaida. It was early in the evening. They were used to fishing at night, so it was no difficulty sailing in the dim light of night.

It was only three hours or so since they had got out of the boat, but so much had happened during the short time they were there that it seemed a longer period of time. They set off from the shore, their thoughts quickly turned from the events of the day to the present. It was cold, and very windy. They knew although they may be seen on the lake in the fading light no-one could stop them. They set out to return to Bethsaida (Mark 6:45). They sailed out into the lake away from the crowds hoping that away from the shore the wind might be easier. It wasn't. This wind had all the characteristics of an Etesian wind (known to the Greeks and Turks as Meltemi) which flows from a high pressure over the Balkans towards in this case a heat trough in the deserts beyond the mountains of Israel. Peter and the others had seen these before and they normally died down at the end of an afternoon. They could remember once or twice such a wind lasting for days but that was uncommon. Today the wind did not die down at all. The strength of the wind was blowing from the same direction they wanted to go. It was impossible to sail to Bethsaida, and it was with great difficulty that they were able to maintain any course against the strength of the wind. They kept rowing, but their little boat kept being blown southwards as they rowed, and they soon found they were quite a way from the shore, unable to row back towards it. They decided the only option was to make for Capernaum, which had been their final destination – Capernaum (Mark 6:45, Matthew 14:22,34.)- and continued to row in the face of the wind. (Mark 6:48). The north wind continued to blow directly at them without abating and they struggled to make much headway.

Jesus walking on water April 32AD
(Matthew 14: 24ff Mark 6:45-53, John 6:16-21)

No event on the Sea of Galilee was greater than what would now unfold. The only one who could ride the waves was the one who spread out the heavens (Job 9:8). In the past Jesus had ordered the waves to stop as well as the wind and they had obeyed him, but on this night, he rode the waves.

It was after 3am and still dark. In April the sun would be over the horizon at 6am, and over an hour before that the first rays heralded dawn over the yellowy brown hills to the east but at this time they were still obscured by the darkness. Twelve men were crammed into the fishing boat sitting where they could. They each had a basket with the bread and fish remaining from the miracle earlier that day. The fisherman amongst them took the oars. There were only two oars, but they would not row for too long before handing over to one of the others. The rowers strong as they were made very slow progress against the wind. The sail was furled up unable to help them and it took them over five hours to row just three or four miles (John 6:19). They had left the shoreline some hours ago (John 6:17) and now the land they had left was forming a darker line just discernable against the night sky. They looked ahead, but whatever distance they had sailed, was only at most half the distance they needed to cover before reaching Gennesaret. They all knew that in normal conditions they should have been possible for them to have got over the water and be safe in bed by now, but not tonight – the strength of the wind mightily hindered their progress. They knew the only solution was to continue on until they arrived at the shore.

The howl of the wind made talking impossible though one would shout to another when needed. For the moment they hoped to hear the shout from the front of the boat that the shore was near, but nothing was said.

Land was still afar. The rowers kept their heads down and listened to the creaking of the oars as they pulled with all their might to cut through the waves.

Jesus had spent some time in prayer on one of the hills which overlooked the sea. The Father had begun to download elements of his future death as he prayed. Much of what he heard he had to process in the weeks ahead, but the Father had confirmed to him something he had thought when praying before choosing the twelve (John 6:64) – namely that one of the twelve would be the path Satan would use to betray Jesus. (John 6:70,71). Jesus was still praying as he turned to descend towards the shore. Jesus needed to be out of the region before first light in case anyone of the crowd who was still in the vicinity saw him. Jesus looked towards the lake. He could make out in the silvery moonlight the disciples boat far off in the middle of the lake (Mark 6:47). He could not make out any detail in the restricted light, but he knew that the rowers were finding it difficult to make any progress at all. Jesus stepped out from the shore onto the water to go towards it. He was unaffected by the wind and the waves for he was moving in the presence of the Father. During Jesus earthly ministry this was rare. Jesus was walking in another dimension of creation affected somewhat by gravity but not by other forces of nature. In this dimension he could walk over water as if it were solid. For Jesus, now was not the time to analyze how this was happening for to do so would have caused his mind to drift away from his relationship with the Father and the purpose before Him, causing him to sink as Peter would do. Jesus knew he had to stay in the Father's presence: in that child heart relationship with the Father. He just focused on walking to reach them. He heard the oars before they saw him in the darkness. The rowers spotted him emerging out of the dark still some way from the boat. As the others turned they all looked in horror and agreed "it's a ghost". Jesus was still too far away for them to see his features. From what they could see, they could recognize a human form in silhouette walking on the water and they were afraid. This was increased when they saw this "ghost" was making straight for them (John 6:19b) Jesus knew they had seen him because he heard the cry and the commotion in the boat and so he immediately shouted "Be of good cheer. It is I. do not be afraid". Peter stood up in the boat – he was amazed alongside all the others in the boat, but he spoke back to Jesus "if it is you, bid me to come to you". What drove Peter to say such a thing was deep within him. His focus was on Jesus and he wanted to make sure it really was him and not a ghost. He got out of the boat readily enough. He had done this many times when fishing to sort nets out, but this time he was getting out of the boat to walk on the water. He started to walk a few steps. He was walking on the waves. This lasted under a minute. He looked down at the waves amazed at what he was doing and at that point the movement of the waves jogged him out of that initial focus and relational place which had allowed him to walk to Jesus and he was now sinking. He cried out to Jesus for help and Jesus was now only a few steps away, so he reached out and lifted him up and they both immediately entered the boat. The presence of the Father which Jesus had been walking in now enveloped the whole boat that Jesus was in. They no longer heard the wind and without any delay they were at the shore of Gennesaret where they had intended to go. They quickly anchored the boat (Mark 6:53) and stepped out into the shallow waves wading to shore. They had no time to consider how they had travelled so far in so little time or why there was no wind, for their minds and hearts were amazed at what they had just experienced. No one asked him, and Jesus was moving onto land. When dawn came they were immediately recognized (Mark 6:54). There was a new day of demands of the kingdom which Jesus was being called to fulfil. The supernatural presence of God affecting the things on the earth that they had witnessed during the night would not continue. There were a few moments of respite before the crowd found Jesus again and before the day was out he would be immersed into controversy once again.

Chapter 46

Jesus at Gennesaret and Capernaum April 32AD
(Matthew 14:34, Mark 6:53-56, John 6 :41ff)

The boat that Jesus travelled in was anchored just off shore at the usual place at Gennesaret (John 6:17, Mark 6:53). Jesus and the twelve made their way through the waves to the shore. When he was recognized, news of his arrival went in every direction in the local area, and so it was not long before the first arrived bringing their sick on beds which were laid out in front of him to heal. Jesus then went on to Capernaum where he would stay with Peter[130]. Jesus was also invited to teach at the synagogue. Jesus accepted. Jesus would not stay long in Capernaum. He was still continuing his mission to visit all the towns in Galilee, and he would be going into Upper Galilee to visit remote towns in the central hills towards Tyre.

Outside Bethsaida, the thousands who had slept on the grassy plain where the previous day they had all been fed with just five loaves and two fish. They awoke wondering if Jesus would greet them. They knew Jesus had not sailed away with "the twelve". When Jesus did not come they sought to leave also. Wishing to make the journey quickly, they managed to board boats from the south of the sea of Galilee (Tiberias John 6:23). They sailed from a different place than where they had seen the twelve leave – in fact the fishing boats picked them up where they were- not far from where the feeding of the 5,000 had occurred (John 6:23). The boats from Tiberias were in this location because fish were numerous at this part of the lake. Seeing the crowd (some of whom were from Tiberias and therefore known to the fishermen), the fishermen saw a business opportunity ferrying instead of fishing. Such a

---

[130] Jesus did stay with Peter on the following time he was in Capernaum so he probably did so this time also. Jesus now had no home of his own at Gennesaret.

crowd in the boats would bring in additional money. So, it was that the men with their families started to arrive in a ferry shuttle service to Capernaum during the morning. The fishermen made several trips to bring all those that wanted to go, before returning to fish the northern part of the lake.

They were surprised to find Jesus back at Capernaum already (John 6:25). They asked was how Jesus got there. Jesus questioned their motive in seeking him because he wanted them to see Jesus was more than a provider of food. The teaching Jesus gave to these disciples puzzled, disturbed and divided them. In a few days some would not follow him anymore.

Jesus paused for a few days in the area. (John 6:26) They had been away from home for over a month and most of the twelve were able to catch up with their families. There were a few days before the Sabbath, so Jesus went to neighbouring villages (Mark6:56).The effect of the feeding of 5000 plus the stories of healing caused large numbers to be wherever Jesus went.

There were close ties from Capernaum with Jerusalem built up through trade and reputation in a way that was not the same in some other Galilean towns. Capernaum was growing in size and status during Jesus' lifetime and had begun to be highly regarded in Israel (Matthew 11:23). News of the miracles Jesus had done spread quickly to Jerusalem, and they also found out that Jesus was definitely in Capernaum on that Sabbath because it had been arranged for him to speak at the synagogue. Some religious leaders from Jerusalem immediately set off to find Jesus. Hearing about the miracles Jesus was doing made them curious, and they also felt a responsibility to assess the accuracy of his teaching. After all Jesus was untrained and a Galilean of obscure roots. Some Pharisees and teachers of the law (scribes) made their way north to Galilee.

Whilst they were on their way, as we have seen Jesus travelled with the twelve to some small towns and villages in the locality of Capernaum.[131] Whenever Jesus came to a village or a town, he discovered sick lying on beds in the market place. Their family and friends had carried the sick there when they heard Jesus was coming. What had happened at Gennesaret was also occurring everywhere he went. The sick reached out to touch Jesus as he passed through hoping to be healed (Mark 6:56; Matthew 14:35-36), and family members would also beg Jesus to heal their relative. Jesus had initially been ready to respond as he had in the past to requests and pray for the sick, but those who brought the sick to Jesus asked him just to be able to touch the hem of his garment. Those who touched Jesus' hem were healed. (Matthew 14:36). For Jesus and the twelve, the healing ministry had changed because of the increase of demand. The twelve with Jesus instead of stopping to pray for the sick, kept walking only stopping occasionally when the Father directed Jesus to do so. As in the past he had listened to the faith of the centurion when he said not to proceed to his house but to just say the word, so now he listened to those who asked him to let them touch his garment. Jesus recognized their faith in what was being said and so complied with their wishes, walking close to the beds of the sick so they could touch his robe as he passed. There were so many people that not everyone managed to touch Jesus but those who did were made well. Wherever Jesus went there was great rejoicing and many testimonies followed his visit.

---

[131] This could have been planned but it is more likely that as Jesus recognized the need, he decided to go to the towns and villages rather than have them travel to Capernaum. Matthew 14:35, Mark 6:56)

Chapter 47

Controversy at Capernaum (with the Pharisees from Jerusalem) April 32AD (Matthew 15:1, John 6)

When the Sabbath arrived, Jesus continued the conversations he had had with those who had been part of the miraculous feeding of the 5000. He wanted them to look beyond the provision to the signpost it was to the identity of Jesus, so their discipleship would be properly grounded. He faced those who challenged him to do "better" miracles like Moses did who did not just produce ordinary bread but bread from heaven (manna) by saying "I am the bread of life. He who comes to me shall not hunger and he who believes in me shall never be thirsty" (John 6:35). Now in the synagogue he taught on the theme (John 6:59) of the commitment necessary to receive him as the true bread of life. Everyone in the synagogue had either been there or heard about the miracle and so Jesus took the opportunity to try to help his hearers see the miracle as a sign which would then increase their faith. The teaching however was difficult for the disciples to understand and was not well received (John 6:61). They had been enthusiastic at the start but were disillusioned at the end.

Jesus knew of their complaints about the teaching only after disciples had begun to drift away. These who had rejoiced at the healing and parables they had heard were now finding what Jesus was saying far too extreme (John 6:52). Jesus attempted to give them the right approach, so they could receive the teaching (John 6:61-64) but he also knew that it was not hitting the mark (John 6:64b). Arguments over this teaching began among the disciples (John 6:52) which did not subside by Jesus' attempts to clarify his doctrine. So, lots of disciples no longer followed Jesus as they had done previously. Some of them had been well known accompanying them from town to town, indeed some had been travelling with Jesus as whole families. Many of those who left had known Jesus and his background (John 6:41), and Jesus had even grown up with some of them. These were now absent and Jesus as well as the twelve missed them. Thousands of disciples were reduced to hundreds overnight. When it was clear that so many had decided to leave, Jesus asked the twelve if any of them also wanted to leave. He did not want to hold them into an agreement they had made at the sermon on the plain against their will. Peter spoke for them all when he said, "Where can we go, for you have the words of eternal life.". They were with him as strong as ever.

After the synagogue service, Jesus and the twelve were invited to one of the local houses for a meal. He was a Pharisee and one of the leading lights in the synagogue who had also invited the scribes and Pharisees from Jerusalem. After the last gathering at Capernaum the scribes from Jerusalem had returned and talked with some of the Pharisees they knew at Jerusalem. As a result they had come up again when they knew Jesus was again in Capernaum. They were not slow to contrast the differences the disciples of Jesus behaved compared to strict ritual cleansing rituals they observed in Jerusalem. They asked Jesus about the lack of ritual washing of his disciples. This question came, as we have seen, just at the time when there was already disturbance among the disciples over Jesus teaching. It was a difficult question for Jesus to answer because it was probably true that his disciples had eaten without properly washing their hands as the law demanded. It was sad that the wonderful healings or teaching that Jesus gave was not what interested the bible teachers (scribes) and Pharisees from Jerusalem. Their specific accusation came from their legal expertise: "Why do your disciples transgress the traditions of the elders?" seeking to undermine and attack Jesus' values and his management of the disciples at the same time. Far from putting Jesus on the back foot however, he replied by challenging the laws they held as transgressing the command of God. Jesus as He often did, taught publicly on the theme introduced by those in the crowd and the Pharisees question was no exception. He taught how it was the inside heart that mattered rather than outward observance. In so doing Jesus attacked their traditions and his words offended them (Matthew 15:10-12). They had long been disturbed by Jesus practice of healing on the Sabbath and concerned about his teaching. Now Jesus had attacked and offended them in a way they would never forget. The twelve knew this and were worried (Matthew 15:12). The Pharisees that Jesus had upset, were powerful men in Jerusalem and beyond and the disciples (and Jesus) recognised that Jesus life would now definitely be endangered if he was on their territory. They were men who exercised some influence in the villages near where they lived and Jesus would from now on have to exercise great caution not just in Jerusalem but in the neighbouring communities in Judea. For the time being Jesus would stay in Galilee.

Chapter 48

Jesus no longer goes openly to Jerusalem and Judea (John 7:1) Based in Galilee (John 7:9)

There had been for some time murderous intent amongst elements of the Pharisees against Jesus (Mark 3:6) Now it had had spread to powerful groups of religious Jews in Jerusalem and Judea who now thought that God wanted them to assassinate Jesus, and their voice was growing in acceptance. The leaders however had not gone that far in their thinking yet. It would need revelation from Caiaphas before the leaders themselves would talk about conspiracy to kill Jesus (John 11:49ff). For now, they were negotiating with the secular authorities for the best way forward hoping that possibly Herod would arrest Jesus as he had done to John the Baptist. Jesus continued as before visiting the towns of Galilee. He and the twelve left Capernaum. They had a mission to complete.

Mission to Upper Galilee May 32AD

Jesus wanted to reach the remote towns of Upper Galilee. These were the last communities still to visit in Galilee – and the most remote. After this they would go to other parts of the territory of ancient Israel starting in Decapolis. So, after the Sabbath, they set off for the remote mountain towns of Upper Galilee.

They were accompanied for a short way by other disciples, but they turned back as Jesus and the twelve walked further away from Capernaum. They followed the road until they came to where the river Jordan emptied into the lake. They turned northwards a few miles to a village called Thella which was not far from the Jordan (Josephus wars 3.3.) from where they took the road which connected the cities and other remote communities high in the mountains. These Jews were strong, independent survivors who were used to living in comparably

224

isolated places. Deep canyons and high mountains restricted the roads to two both which ran north/ south, and then connected both at the north and south of the area forming a circular route. Part of this circle of roads Jesus and the twelve had taken earlier when they had visited some of the towns in the region, but they had never been around the full circle and there were many towns where Jesus had not yet been. Jesus and later during the mission of the twelve when based in Cana, had been able to visit towns in the south western part of the region, even as far as the port of Galilee which was Ptolemais on the Mediterranean coast[132], but those towns near Tyre were untouched and Jesus wanted to go through every village and town in Galilee (Matthew 4:23) before branching out further into all Israel. They first headed south to Acharabe after which they could strike west towards the towns located there. After visiting many small communities, they came to a junction. The road southwards towards Mount Carmel and Ptolemais went through towns towards the Upper/Lower Galilee border where they had visited before from Cana. They turned northwards walking on the road as it swung north west weaving its way through the mountains towards Tyre. (Matthew 15:21). They travelled through Sepph (Safed) which was located at an elevation of 2,953 feet and was the highest city in Israel before visiting Gischala[133] a fortified border town of Galilee. This was the last large community Jesus visited until he entered the region of Tyre at Capar Ganaeoi. There they joined the road that went west to the city of Tyre. They stayed for a few days recovering from what had been quite an arduous trip plan before getting ready to return from Tyre. They would be taking the road they had come to Tyre due east visiting other mountain towns like Gadasa, and Daphne, before making their way to Danos – the ancient city of Dan - on the border

---

[132] There was a route westward from Cana to Ptolemais used by traders in the first century

[133] Josephus mentions this as the most northerly city of Galilee before Tyre (Herod Antipas by Harold W. Hoehner page 282)

between Israel (Judges 20:1) sited in a strategic location at the meeting of ways through the mountains. From there the road would bring them to Caesarea Philippi. Once they arrived there, they would go onto Decapolis.

They had planned with one of the disciples they knew to stay for a couple of days near Tyre before passing through the other northern towns of Upper Galilee near its border. Everywhere Jesus went he taught and healed any who asked. There were disciples wherever they went. So, they always had a local welcome.

The climate was colder and wetter in that part of the country than Jesus and the twelve were used to in Lower Galilee... The people they visited were strong independent people (Josephus Wars 3.3.2) and good farmers. The terrain meant they did not have the followers who in recent month had accompanied them as they went from town to town in Lower Galilee There were also no late callers asking for healing or followers crowding around as they walked during the day. Jesus and the twelve had time to eat and talk together without any interruptions. They did not have to walk many miles between towns. The disciples could tell when they were getting near a town because of the number of terraces cut out of the hillsides where trees were planted, and crops grown. Some towns were fortified with walls whilst others were villages tucked into the hillsides.

Chapter 49

They came to the region of Tyre and Sidon (Matthew 15:21) where they were relatively unknown. Tyre with its important port had been comparatively recently been rebuilt under the Romans and was a flourishing city at the time and Sidon was about 25 miles north on the coast road. The distance direct from Capernaum to Tyre was 35 miles but they had walked about twice that distance to arrive at Tyre visiting the towns in Upper Galilee. In the countryside ruled by Tyre a Jewish family had offered them hospitality. Jesus had met them in Gennesaret and Capernaum as they had come for the gatherings. Jesus and the twelve stayed a few days. Although their hosts were Jews there were less links with Galilee and the language was more Greek than Aramaic. News about Jesus had reached there but they were not the crowds of Galilee. The Jews in the Greek dominated cultures were isolated as a minority amongst Gentiles. There would not be the sick brought openly into the pagan marketplaces of Tyre as they had been in the villages of Galilee.

Jesus meets a Syro-Phoenician woman June 32AD (Matthew 15:21-29 Mark 7:25-30)

Jesus and the twelve had left the crowds far behind, and they welcomed the space. They deepened as a team. It is one thing to be together in the business of what they had known in Israel; it was another to be together in these unfamiliar surroundings with no demands upon them.

Their stay in seclusion only lasted a few days. A woman of Canaan (Matthew 15:22) lived in that area. She shared a similar ancestry to one of the twelve, but not the same beliefs. She was a pagan and for some time Jesus just kept walking whilst the woman cried her cries for mercy behind them (Matthew 15:22). Jesus had heard her from the first time she asked for help but had delayed responding to the woman knowing his call of the Father was to minister to Jews. The disciples found the woman a nuisance and their concern allowed the woman the chance to talk directly with Jesus. Jesus for his part stated clearly to the twelve why he had not responded to her because he had a call to "the lost sheep" of Israel and this woman was not part of Israel. When the woman directly threw herself at his feet (Matthew 15:25) and asked for help, Jesus followed up his earlier comments to the twelve with a sentence which she would understand. Instead of talking about lost sheep he spoke about dogs "It is not good to take the children's bread and throw it to the little dogs" (Matthew 15:26). The woman replied, "Yes Lord". She agreed with him, but then she said, "even the little dogs eat the crumbs which fall from their masters table." Jesus recognized the wisdom of the woman's reply and knew it was from the Father. He spoke her daughter's healing by saying she was well, and then she departed back to her home and found her totally healed. Jesus and the twelve continued on their way. Whilst Jesus was called to Israel – and nothing could change that (see John 12:20ff), Jesus also knew that healing of Gentiles was right in the Father's eyes. There would be no delay in responding when non-Jews asked for healing. This would be very significant as Jesus and the 12 moved out of Galilee into Decapolis.

Chapter 50

Ministry in Decapolis June 32AD (Mark 7:31ff)

Jesus and the twelve had to leave Tyre suddenly. Once the healing of the Syrophoenician daughter became known, there would be others seeking him. Jesus was not called to minister there. Tyre and Sidon were a bolt hole from ministry not a place for ministry. Jesus and the twelve left eastwards through the mountain passes of Upper Galilee until they reached Caesarea Philippi. They then joined the road which went from Damascus all the way to Egypt, but they followed it just a few miles to the sea of Galilee before taking the minor road as it weaved its way around the eastern shore of the Sea of Galilee (see Matthew 15:29) until they reached Hippos (Sussita) which was the northernmost of the major cities of the Decapolis.

This was the most northern city of the Decapolis region Like most of the cities in Decapolis Hippos was outside Israel but built on territory given to the Israelites after they came out of Egypt as part of their promised land. The Father was sending His Son into every part of the territory given to the Israelites of old. In Jesus' day Hippos was on the rise as an important city, and it would become even more so after the Jewish rebellions. Each city of the Decapolis had a Jewish quarter within it. Hippos had a significant Jewish population, but they were fiercely independent from those of Galilee. In the past the Roman general Pompey when he started to establish the Decapolis, had chosen Hippos as one of its cities. Some still remembered their parents' sense of loss in the years that followed when they were forced away from Decapolis to be part of Herod the Great's Kingdom and also their joy at being reinstated within the Decapolis again after his death. The populace of Jesus' day whether Jew or Greek were opposed to Antipas and his new capital city Tiberias built on the opposite shore of the lake. Hippos culture and city plan with its architecture was Graeco-Roman. This was not in itself radically new for Jesus. It was like Autocratoris or Tiberias. Jesus had also been through Beth Shean (now called Scythopolis) several times in his life and this was a Decapolis city (the only one in Israel). Decapolis was a league of cities influenced by the city states of Greece with an organization of mutual benefit formed by Rome rather than Israel, and the foreign traits he had seen in the other cities he had visited previously were greater emphasized in these. His brief visit to Tyre and Sidon had been helpful preparation for this. Decapolis was made up of several regions centred on cities which had a Greek model of self-rule. The Jewish way of life was there also but as a minority. Decapolis bordered the eastern boundary of Galilee and northern Samaria before stretching eastwards south of the sea of Galilee and forming a territory in the eastern deserts from the Golan heights in the north to Amman the capital of Jordan in the south. It was a political and cultural buffer zone between the Roman empire and the countries beyond its domain. Decapolis was an alliance of city states through common trade with each other and agreed values of the Roman Empire. It was this autonomy which helped Jesus to be safe away from the religious leader's threats in Judea and the ministry demands in Galilee. Hippos was a "city on a hill which could not be hidden" about a thousand feet above the Sea of Galilee. The deep blue of the lake was clearly visible just a mile away from the city and there were various vantage points around the city where the lake could be seen. They continued their journey over and around the mountains and hills that Jesus and the 12 had seen most days they were in Capernaum on the other side of the lake. The green hills of spring around the lake had changed to the brown hills of summer. Decapolis had mountains like Upper Galilee though they were not wooded, and no streams flowed as frequently. The mountains of Decapolis were higher than those of Galilee and were set in a dry and deserted landscape. They went south eastwards through Abila to join the main Roman road called the Kings Highways at Capitolis. This ancient major trading route was used to transport luxury goods northwards to Damascus. But Jesus and the disciples took the road which went westwards "through the midst of Decapolis" (Mark 7:31). They went to Gadara[134]. This was a flourishing city where Jesus knew at least one of its citizens. It was a city where the elite were either retired Roman soldiers or well-connected freedmen. There were Jews who helped with finance, administration or buildings and there were many slaves also. Some of the buildings there were of black basalt and there were many monuments made of marble. For Galileans this was foreign unknown territory, but Jews existed together whatever city they were in, and so Jesus and the twelve had some familiar Jewish base, however strange the culture might be. The Romans in Decapolis were few, but they were rich. The language was Greek, (though Aramaic was also spoken.[135]). Gadara had been given to Herod the Great along with Hippos when he started to rule, but Gadara had been quickly moved away from his authority in 20BC It was a strong walled city with the usual accompaniments of a Graeco Roman city – baths, forum etc. Whilst still in the province of Syria they had autonomy as a Decapolis city to be a city state with lands stretching northwards to the Sea of Galilee, yet they knew they could call upon the Roman legion just based outside the area if they were ever needed as with every Decapolis city, Jesus headed for the Jewish quarter within the city where he would stay.

Decapolis healing of deaf and dumb July 32AD (Mark 7:31)

Jesus had arrived in the middle (Mark 7:31) of Decapolis[136]. Jesus was surrounded with many people as he arrived at Gadara. This was an impressive fortified city perched on a hilltop (1,240ft) overlooking the

[134] If Jesus had gone south to Gerasa returning towards the Jordan valley would be on the southern border of Perea rather than "in the midst".
[135] Bi lingual shows in name of the city: Hippos was the Greek name it was also called Sussita an Aramaic. both mean horse
[136] Probably Gadara as this is situated in the middle of the Decapolis

Sea of Galilee and the Yarmouk River gorge. No-one who came there could ignore the aqueduct which was built from Syria and brought water right into the city through well-constructed channels including the longest tunnel known to Classical antiquity. As usual Jesus went to the Jewish sector of the city, and surprised that not long after his arrival the citizens of the city brought Jesus a man who was deaf and could not speak clearly. Because they were citizens who held rights in the city rather than visitors or slaves that were asking him, it made it much less complicated for Jesus to respond to their request. Jesus reached out and took him by the hand and led him away from the people until It was just Jesus, him and a caring relative and friends [137]. The man looked at Jesus. There was no-one else to distract his attention. As he looked, Jesus stretched his arms and he felt his fingers in his ears. Then he saw Jesus put one of his hands to his mouth, spat on his fingers and put the spittle onto his tongue. He had no time to think about intrusion and hygiene. Jesus looked up to heaven. The deaf man knew Jesus was praying. Jesus said, "Be opened" and immediately the silent world he had known became full of sound. He was healed and as he spoke what he had just experienced, he also discovered his speech was normal. There was no hindrance at all. There was amazement and great rejoicing.

Jesus tried to keep this quiet, but to no avail and so the crowds and demands for ministry threatened to swamp them as it had done before in Galilee. They did what they had done before in their ministry trips. They decided to hold a gathering and signpost everyone there who wanted healing. The place they chose was in the south west corner not far from the Sea of Galilee. After the gathering they would go by boat across the lake to just north of Tiberias (Magdala) and then sail from there to Bethsaida. In this way they not only created a helpful way to

[137] Note "they" Mark 7:36 indicates some others witnessed the miracle

respond to the increasing demands, but also had an exit strategy should it be necessary.

Feeding of 4000 July 32AD (Matthew 15:29ff Mark 8:1-9)

Jesus and the twelve left the city of Gadara and went northwards crossing the shallow and narrow Yarmouk river which is the largest tributary of the Jordan river when it flows southwards from the Sea of Galilee. Its path created a line of green vegetation through a deep valley between the mountains. They came to the desert road which comes from Hippos (Sussita) in the north and goes westwards towards Galilee via the Jordan valley. The publicised gathering was just off this road overlooking the sea. Jesus stopped and waited for the sick to come. They came in their hundreds along this road to find Jesus and the crowd quickly grew to thousands.

This was the first gathering outside Galilee and formed the precursor of many others that Jesus would hold throughout Israel in thre coming weeks. Many – not just from Gadara- but from other parts of Decapolis as well as from some other places came. The blind, mute or maimed came long distances to beg for healing at the feet of Jesus. Decapolis had major cities but the communities between were sparse. So those who came from cities or villages in other parts of the Decapolis came from far, far away. Some sick were carried and laid as near as they could to Jesus (Matthew 15:30). They came in such numbers that it took three days of constant ministry. Jesus healed them one by one. As each healing happened a new respect and wonder grew amongst those who gathered (Matthew 15:31). Towards the end of their time together, Jesus miraculously provided for them all. He split them into similar groupings that they had found worked well with the feeding of the 5000, so this time they only needed to find seven baskets to distribute the food. Whereas the earlier feeding of the 5,000 was after just one day teaching, here the miraculous provision came after three days. During these days, they saw the lame began to walk, the dumb to speak, the blind to see, and the maimed had their limbs restored (Matthew 15:31) It was an amazing time. There was water to drink in rivers but there were no villages nearby [138]. It was a wilderness (Matthew 15:33). Food was scarce after three days

These who came were not all Jews – in fact the majority were not. But they glorified not their own gods but the God of Israel (Matthew 15:31). Jesus knew he had been sent to the lost sheep of the house of Israel, but he now found himself in Gentile territory and there were needs to be met. What His Father had taught him through the Syrophoenician woman, he continued to put into practice. He now healed those who were not part of the lost sheep of the house of Israel. He had seen his heavenly Father's revelation in the reply the woman had given him, so he was now healing without any questioning or delay anyone whether Jew or Gentile.

The miraculous provision happened in the same way with this Gentile group as with the earlier Jewish feeding of the 5000 except the reaction was different. There was no attempt to make Jesus king. This Gentile group did not share the Messianic king doctrines of the Jews. Jesus dismissed the crowds who, when they saw there was nothing else to stay for, departed. Jesus and his disciples got into a boat they had recently bought from one of those who lived nearby. They used this boat to get to Magdala and then to sail onto Bethsaida). A boat was the quickest way they had found to avoid the crowd and move on. They sailed from the harbour built and owned by Gadara and sailed past Tiberias , avoided the busy harbour at Magdala before coming to the shore of the ancient village of Dalmanutha.

---

[138] Contrast the feeding of the 5000 where the disciples suggested the crowd go and buy bread from surrounding towns. No such request possible here

Chapter 51

Magdala July 32AD (Matthew 15:39 Mark 8:10)

Jesus and the twelve pulled their boat onto the pebbles of the beach. It was only weeks before that Jesus had sailed from here towards Bethsaida where there had been the first miraculous feeding of thousands. Now they were returning from Decapolis after another miraculous provision. Jesus and his disciples stayed for a few days. Hospitality was again organized well in the small fishing village [139]. (In fact, its southern boundary is only 500 feet from the ancient city of Magdala).

Magdala was a prosperous busy fishing town with a bigger harbour than Capernaum. More salted fish were processed here for export than its northern neighbour. It had other industries there e.g. glass making. In recent years it had been eclipsed by the large capital city of Tiberius a mile or so to its south, whose buildings were clearly visible on the slopes along the coastline to those who lived in Magdala. Tiberius was where Antipas and his entourage (including Joanna, the wife of his steward) lived. Magdala, however, still maintained its ancient life. It lived a separate life, and though some travelled by boat to Tiberias, many Jews never went there because it was built on an ancient Jewish cemetery. Some Jews because of financial incentives lived at Tiberias, but many who lived there were non-Jews.

[139] Dark Palestine Exploration Quarterly Summer 2013

Controversy in Magdala from The Pharisees and Sadducees July 32AD (Matthew 16 :1-6; Mark 8:11)

The controversy Jesus had known at Capernaum had not come to Magdala until now. Pharisees and Sadducees came out from Magdala [140] – who were normally opposed to each other came together to catch Jesus out. They wanted Jesus to provide a sign from heaven to prove he was who he said he was. Jesus refused. He saw there was no benefit in further debate, and left Magdala. He had a schedule and the next step was to go to Caesarea Philippi. Whilst at Magdala Jesus had started to discuss the sending out of teams to prepare the way for him around every part of Israel which he had not yet visited. They had identified about seventy including the twelve, and Jesus had sent instructions for the teams to gather at Capernaum in a months' time from which teams would be formed who would work out any further details whilst they travelled to Jerusalem for the Feast of Tabernacles. Jesus had no time to spend time in controversy.

Jesus needed to be away with the twelve for another reason. He needed to start to introduce them to some of the details of his death. He decided to take them to Caesarea Philippi. He knew the town as they had passed through it on their way from Tyre and he had identified it as the best place to be.

Jesus got into the boat that had brought him there from Decapolis and with the twelve sailed out onto the lake. They left behind the eastern foothills of Mount Arbel which dominated the skyline over Magdala and headed out northwards towards Bethsaida to the north and on the other side of the Sea of Galilee (Matthew 16:5) - the same route the twelve had taken before feeding the 5000 (matthew14:13) four months

[140] Mark 8:11 "came out" from Magdala rather than Jerusalem. Magdala being so near the capital had stronger representations from Sadducees and Herodians mark 8:15, Matthew 16:1

previous. They landed in a deserted place to the north east corner of the Sea of Galilee, so they could access the road northwards to Caesarea. When they arrived, they found no-one had brought any bread with them which they would need to take on the desert road in front of them. So, there was a delay while they had to go back a mile or so into Bethsaida to buy bread (see Matthew 16:5-7, Mark 10:13-22). Just as they were becoming aware of this, Jesus told them to beware of the leaven of the Pharisees and Sadducees. Jesus would usually teach as he walked with them. They did not understand Jesus. They thought at first, he was also talking in some way about the bread. Jesus quickly addressed their concern about the bread by reminding them of the remarkable provision of bread and fish for thousands – they were after all walking over the very place where the miracle of the feeding of 5000 had taken place- and reaffirmed his message to be cautious with those who appeared strongly religious because they could influence and distort the kingdom seed within them. They entered Bethsaida, now called Julias, and under the rule of Philip the tetrarch.

Bethsaida healing of blind man July 32AD (Mark 8:22)

In the short time Jesus was at Bethsaida (Mark 8:22) he healed a blind man. They were on their way out of the city with food for their journey when some came up to Jesus with a man who was blind. Jesus welcomed them to join them and he led him out of the city and when outside the city healed him. Jesus had no desire to be swamped again with crowds or people following them on what was to be a very important time for Jesus and the disciples away from the crowds. He therefore told the blind man not to return to the town (for people would see the difference) and not to tell anyone. He wanted this kept quiet for the time being until at least some days had passed after they had left Bethsaida. He trusted this man would obey the instruction despite being badly let down by the leper earlier when the results had brought difficulties in Capernaum. It seems that the blind man obeyed

Jesus' instruction, so Jesus and the 12 were able to leave the area without any difficulty or delay.

They left Bethsaida walking northwards on the main trading road from Capernaum to Damascus which took them through Seleucia a town which although destroyed by earlier conflicts and so although not the large town it had been, was at an important cross road and so there were still people living there. It was the last town they would go through until they reached Caesarea Philippi. It was a desert road, but they got more provisions, and then arrived at their destination without further incident.

Chapter 52

Caesarea Philippi July 32AD
(Matthew 16 Luke 9:18 Mark 8:27)

Caesarea was the main city in a self-governing area of Philip's territories called Batanaea paying 100 talents tribute to Philip each year. After the death of Augustus Caesar, it had become a walled city (Josephus Wars 2.9.1). The area where Caesarea Philippi was being mentioned in the bible as the "hills of Basan" and stood on the foothills of Mount Hermon which on a clear day Jesus as a boy had seen from Nazareth over 30 miles away. The peak, which was snow-capped at other times of the year, stood 9,232 feet above sea level. On the south western base of this famous mountain there was Caesarea Philippi where Herod the Great had built his white marble palace which dominated the skyline of the city. There was also a pagan temple he had built near a cave long associated with the god Pan at the source of the river Jordan. Visitors came from other countries because of it, as they did to Apollo's shrine in Delphi or the shrine of Artemis in Ephesus. When Philip became tetrarch, the new city became known as Caesarea Philippi and had become the capital city for Philip until recently when Bethsaida was changed to Julias. Caesarea Philippi was not a large city. It was more of an administrative centre than a place with a vast population. The people who worked there lived in surrounding towns (Mark 8:27). The city itself was built on terrace 1,150 feet high overlooking a fertile valley enriched by the river which flowed from the mountain down the Jordan valley to the sea of Galilee. Here was the largest of the springs which sourced the Jordan. It was a fertile place with fruit trees and waterfalls. There were many groves of trees and green grass in abundance, and an ideal place for Jesus to spend time away from Galilee with the twelve.

Philip had already put his mark on this city. It had been his only major city (until he was given Bethsaida). From the start of his reign as tetrarch over 33 years before Philip had been expanding and building Caesarea Philippi into a notable Graeco-Roman city. When they arrived, they found that Caesarea Philippi was still celebrating Philip's reign and marriage to Herodias.[141] Special coins had been issued as part of the celebration in the thirty fourth year.[142] [143]For now this more Graeco-Roman than Jewish environment provided for Jesus and his disciples necessary refuge from the conflicts they were facing in the more Jewish areas of old Israel. They spent six days in the city and surrounding area unknown, with no crowds accompanying them. This was a welcome change for all of them and they spent time together as friends. Jesus waited for the right moment to introduce them the revelation about his future death. They had already been there 5 days. This may have been the Sabbath and so they may have planned to go to Mount Hermon on the next day. Jesus knew this was the day to reveal what the Father had been teaching him ever since he had heard of John the Baptist's execution.

---

[141] Salome did marry Philip the tetrarch who lives only one year after Jesus death and resurrection. She must have been married after the dance she gave at the party of Herod. It would have been a scandal for a married woman to have done so. The date of the coins fits perfectly with a celebration of his marriage tp Herodias as well as his building of Julias.
[142] See Bethsaida to Julias by Heinz Wulfgang Kuhn Page 65
[143] Coins were made to commemorate special moments. Herod the Great issued coins at the start of his reign marked three because although proclaimed king in 40BC he finally defeated all rivals by 37BC and he wanted to state he was undisputed king. Archelaus issued coins and Antipas did when he had established Tiberius as his capital. Philip the tetrarch issued coins periodically. His first dated five (2 AD) and his last 37 (the year he died 34AD or the year before 33AD) In the thirty fourth year of his reign (31AD) He issued a unique set of coins because of their variety and in which on one he calls himself "founder". This was in the thirty fourth year of his reign Herod the Great died in 4BC and there was a little delay before Philip and the others were named as his successors. The most likely date for his becoming king was Spring 3BC which was regarded as the start of the royal year and when high priest, and other officals were also appointed.

Jesus and the twelve went to the villages around Caesarea Philippi. It was a hub attracting people from many parts of the empire Jesus blended in amongst the many visitors there. It had many temples and around it had grown towns benefiting from the trade that Caesarea brought. They were there so it appeared at first to start the planning for the teams for the mission of the seventy which Jesus began to share. He had mentioned it before and the disciples were gathering in Capernaum. But Jesus had a greater task to share.

This was the time and place that would provide necessary space for Jesus to introduce the twelve to the truths about his future death on a cross. Over the past few weeks since they had returned from mission, Jesus had been praying about and receiving revelation about this from His Heavenly Father. The twelve needed to know first before the rest of the disciples, so Jesus took them away from the crowds, so this could be done (e.g. Matthew 16:21). When they had been to Tyre a few weeks before, on the return journey they had come through Caesarea Philippi. It was as they journeyed Jesus realized this would be good place to come to get away to be with the twelve away from the ministry demands that accompanied them wherever else they went. They walked from place to place in the immediate area discussing as they went. After they had been there some days during one of these journeys that he asked the disciples (Mark 8:27) "Who do men say that I am? Behind the controversy in Magdala was the question "who Jesus is?". It was now the commonest question amongst the religious folk at that time (see John 7:40). Not for the first time Jesus heard repeated what they had heard from others. Within the synagogues and family relationships the true news of Jesus deeds and words were mixed with false judgements and questions which was heard by all. There were various theories including that Jesus was John the Baptist or one of the prophets resurrected to life. One of the sources for this was an "off the cuff" remark Antipas himself had made when he heard about the impact

Jesus and the twelve were having in Galilee. Back in Tiberias what Joanna knew about Jesus stayed in her family for some months, but when Jesus was becoming talked about simultaneously in different parts of Galilee because of the increase of healings and deliverances following the mission of the twelve into every part of Galilee, Herod had started to ask questions about Jesus and Chuza his old tutor who he had known since his teenage years in Rome recounted stories he had heard from his wife. Antipas with a mixture of astonishment and guilt exclaimed Jesus was John the Baptist raised from the dead.

Amidst the current theories which were being mentioned, Peter stood up and said with deep conviction that Jesus was indeed the Messiah. This moved the conversation onto a whole new level. Jesus recognized the Father had revealed this to Peter and it provided the doorway to start to explain the old testament teaching about the suffering of the Messiah (e.g. Isaiah 53), preparing them for the news of Jesus' future execution. There was much to say to prepare them for what Jesus knew was coming and they found the teaching deeply disturbing. Peter took Jesus aside to advise him that this was not right to talk about this. It surely would not happen. Jesus first rebuked Satan who he could see was behind the thought that had stirred Peter to speak and then exposed the doorway through which the enemy had worked "you think as men think not as God thinks". Jesus continued to teach the disciples the theme of suffering (Matthew 16:24) but they found difficulty understanding or receiving what Jesus said.

Transfiguration July 32AD
(Luke 9:28 Matthew 17:1 Mark 9 1)

On the next day Jesus and the twelve walked towards Mount Hermon called the holy mountain (2 Peter 1:18). Around Mount Hermon were many Ituraean settlements who were non-Jews. They were an ancient people who had lived as semi nomadic tribes until settling from

Lebanon into the region for many generations. They were settled with a distinct culture and pottery and still preserved some of their ancient traditions and beliefs. Caesarea Philippi was on the foothills of Hermon which lay fourteen miles to the North East, so it was under a full day's journey to reach it. They passed flocks of sheep and goats as well as herds of cows who were grazing freely near the road they took. The hot temperatures of summer cooled as they climbed up the foothills onto the mountain to a pleasant 70F in the sun. Jesus intention was to go there to pray (Luke 9:28) so the twelve accompanied him as they now did every day. When they got nearer the mountain, Jesus identified where he was going to pray and he with only Peter, James and John climbed the steep mountain itself. The other disciples found a place to stay (Mark 9:28) nearby. They knew Jesus and the others would be gone for a time – in fact they would not return until the next day (Luke 9:37). It was not unusual for Jesus to spend nights in prayer. In fact, amid ministry demands, night time had been the only time Jesus could meet with his Heavenly Father in extended prayer. Jesus and his three companions made steady progress up the mountain. It is the highest in Israel standing over 11,000 feet from the Jordan valley and can be seen from the Dead Sea more than 100 miles away. Jesus led the way (Matthew 17:1) and when he knew where he should pray he stopped told his companions that this was the place and went forward from them just a few yards and knelt and prayed. The disciples who were with Jesus sat down nearby and felt "heavy with sleep" (Luke 9:32). They were just drifting into sleep when something strange happened. Simon woke up fully first[144], and then immediately woke the others. They were immediately fully awake because the wonder of what they could see was only a few yards away. As Jesus was praying, something

---

[144] Whilst all the gospels talk about Elijah and Moses appearing, only Mark talks about seeing Elijah first. Mark is by tradition the memoirs of Peter and so Peter saw it first because of the way the vision unfolds.

had happened. Jesus' clothes had become dazzling white sparkling like snow does when it is below 20 degrees (Mark 9:3). They could tell the shining did not come from the clothes, but from Jesus himself. His head and body were shining. His face became what could only be described by a mortal as angelic as it shone like the sun (Luke 9:29; Matthew 17:1). He was transfigured before them (Mark 9:2). They were in a new dimension. They saw first Elijah and then Moses (Mark 9:4) and as they watched they saw them both talking with Jesus. They could not tell what was being said but found out later that the conversation was about the death that Jesus would suffer (Luke 9:31). They watched open mouthed and silent until Elijah and Moses started to get up to go. Simon Peter caught up in the moment offered to build offered to build places where they could rest. There was no take up of his offer or even reply. A cloud came around them, so they could see nothing at all. Out of the cloud came a voice which all three disciples heard "This is my beloved Son. Listen to Him". Almost straightaway after this they saw Jesus approaching them alone through the cloud as it started to lift. He told them to tell no-one about what they had seen until after he was raised from the dead. They did not understand what he meant but continued to find the best route to descend, and they came down the mountain without any delay.

Healing of a demonized boy. July 32AD (Luke 9:37)

It was well into the day by the time Jesus and the three with him reached the bottom of the mountain. They were amazed to see a crowd already there (Mark 9:14). The nine disciples who were staying at the bottom of the mountain had talked about their exploits with Jesus, and so a father with a demonized boy had decided to come to ask for healing. He was someone from the local synagogue and some of his friends came with him. They had arrived from the earliest moment – such was the desire to be healed. The disciples had tried to heal the boy without success. Their commands to the evil spirit to leave had gone

244

unheeded(Mark9:14). The argument started when the scribes who had come with the father tried to suggest why there was no success as the disciples were obviously not bringing to healing to the child (Mark 916,17). The crowd that Jesus saw had first come together when they heard the commotion and arguments following the screams of the boy. The mixture of suggestions for alternative ways to heal and doctrinal posturing alongside others who had pastoral concerns for the father and his child provided enough interest to hold the crowd there. It was all very embarrassing for the disciples who had not experienced this before. Demons had always left at their command. The crowd was large and were voicing their opinions as they engaged with disciples who were not having a good day. The disciples were too busy talking to the scribes to notice Jesus as he approached the crowd to join them (Mark 9:14). Those at the back of the crowd spotted Jesus first. They were not expecting him to come (Mark 9:15) and the crowd turned around and moved towards Jesus. Leaving the disciples behind they greeted him. Jesus was not sure what the cause of the problem was and so he spoke not to the disciples who looked deflated at the back of the newly assembled crowd but to the scribes (Mark 9;16). Before they could answer a man in the crowd unexpectedly spoke. The scribes were normally those who spoke for they were the respected leaders well taught and used to arguments. But the ordinary man immediately identified himself as the father of the ill boy and how the healing had not happened so far. Jesus immediately responded. He asked the boy to be brought. Some went back to the home where the boy had been taken after the disciples' unsuccessful attempt. He was being looked after there and his carers with the support of others brought him to Jesus. By the time the boy came the crowd had dispersed (Mark 9:25). The discussions were over, and the tension had subsided so most went back to their tasks. When the boy eventually came he had a fit falling on the ground wallowing and foaming at the mouth. Jesus did not respond to this immediately but asked his father how long this had been happening and found out it had been throughout his growing years since he was a baby (Mark 9:21). The father accurately diagnosed the cause as an evil spirit (Mark 9:22,20). The child had no normal intention of self-harm, but he had witnessed sudden drives of energy driving him to drown himself in water or be burnt in fire. Jesus listened and understood, but he replied to the man's closing comment of "Please help us if you can" (Mark 9:22) by making a statement of truth "All things are possible to him who believes". The father then cried out with deep emotion and tears "Lord I believe help my unbelief". He so wanted his boy well. The sudden cry made the people turn their heads and begin to move quickly towards Jesus and the boy. They were not interested in the boy, why they came was to see if Jesus would fail like the disciples had done. Before there was any change or distraction, Jesus rebuked the deaf and dumb spirit. Its deafness was its defence. Disciples had failed because their commands it could not hear. Jesus brought the power of the spirit in prayer to dislodge it so before Jesus spoke, it knew it had to obey. Its defences had gone. It heard the command of Jesus and it cried out in dismay (Mark 9:26). Its dumbness had also gone with his deafness. The spirit convulsed him as it now had to go leaving the body it had lived in. It came out of him unable to return (Mark 9;25). It had spent years dwelling in the boy's body growing as he grew. Now the demon had to leave. After it left, the boy just lay there not moving so that some said he was dead, but Jesus reached down took him by the hand and helped him to stand which he did of his own accord. A grateful father returned with his son back to his home.

The disciples showed Jesus where they were staying and arranged for them to eat something. Peter James and John as well as Jesus had not eaten anything yet that day. When they were eating they asked the question which had been at the root of the discussion with the scribes and which remained on their hearts. "Why could we not cast the demon out? Jesus simply said it was to do with the nature of the demon "This kind only come out with prayer". Jesus had dislodged the demon by prayer. Instead of addressing the demon directly in the first instance he had been praying even while still talking to the boy's father. It was the prayer which emptied the demon of its power to stay before Jesus spoke the words it had to adhere to and so leave the boy for good.

Chapter 53

To Galilee August 32AD
(Matthew 17:22 [see Matthew 19:1] Mark 9:30)

The miraculous deliverance ended the time of seclusion for them. Jesus knew they could no longer stay in the region. It was approaching the end of August as they journeyed from Caesarea Philippi back into Galilee where they stayed (Matthew 17:22) a few days but Jesus did not want anyone to know (Mark 9:30) because he wanted to remain crowd free for the time being. He and the twelve had been without the hundreds of disciples accompanying them they had experienced every day before going to Caesarea Philippi and he had no desire to go back to that place just yet. He wanted time to build up the twelve and prepare them for the future. The "twelve" by contrast were to a man full of awe at the recent demonic deliverance they had witnessed of the young boy, so as they journeyed, Jesus took the opportunity to speak into their wonder with a message of his future betrayal (Luke 9:43,44). The twelve were very upset at what they heard.

They travelled onto Capernaum which was just a stop on their way to Jerusalem. (Luke 9:51) The Summer was almost over, and the autumn equinox was near. Jesus wanted to get to the Feast of Tabernacles which officially marked the start of autumn which stretched from the equinox to the shortest day of the year which marked the start of winter. For Jesus it would be his last opportunity to attend this festival. They travelled by the main road from Caesarea Philippi by the main road which ran from Damascus to Egypt. It was paved and so easier walking. There started through a wilderness devoid of any villages or towns until they reached Seleucia which was about half way on their journey to Capernaum. Jesus walked on ahead of them at a great pace (Luke 9:51), much to the surprise of the disciples who were used to Jesus walking and talking with them as they went. With Jesus ahead of them, the disciples held a discussion amongst themselves as to who would be the best to lead. What they had just heard of Jesus' betrayal and death provided the context. Jesus overheard their discussion but chose not to address the issue until later. There was a journey to complete. They would be staying with Simon Peter. They continued onto Bethsaida and walked the familiar road to Capernaum.

Peter went on ahead to make sure that all was ready for their arrival. Peter's house was near the synagogue in the middle of the town just a few houses down on the same street which led to the sea. It was like other houses in Capernaum with several rooms built around a courtyard. The outside walls had no windows, so the courtyard had maximum shade from the sun and security. All windows that there were, faced into the interior courtyard. Once inside, the house felt private and secure. It had been extended when Peter was betrothed, and so there was room for Jesus to stay.

Jesus with his small band of followers opened the heavy outside door which led into the courtyard and from there into the house where a meal was being prepared. Jesus and the disciples were ushered into a room whilst the women prepared the meal elsewhere in the house. The room was the communal area for all the family. Those who wanted could see courtyard from the room. There were chickens walking amongst some fishing tackle and various storage jars. The guests filled the room and they settled down to wait for the meal. A neighbour was helping Peter's wife and mother in law. She had responded quickly when the news came of Jesus' imminent arrival at the house and she was a good pair of hands. She had come with her young boy, and so he was put in the room with Jesus and the disciples. Peter probably knew the child but did not know the boy by name. When they were all seated Jesus took the opportunity to ask the question to his disciples "What were you discussing?" They looked sheepishly at each other uncertain how or who should respond as they had been arguing about which disciple was the greatest. He picked up the small child and placed the boy in the middle of the group for all to see. The child was a little concerned to be amidst strangers, so Jesus then picked the child up in his arms, reassured him and said, "whoever receives one of these little children receives me" (Mark 9:37)

John who lived not far away from the house introduced a different subject. For some time, they had exercised freedom of choice and Jesus had been ignorant of some of the decisions made. In the light of the discussion about children, he was not sure whether some of their decisions had been accurate for they had not been made from a childlike perspective at all. They had seen someone casting out a demon who were not part of the band of disciples. This stranger had not been commissioned as they had been by Jesus and so they forbade him. Jesus said, "Do not forbid him." In so doing he does not attach blame – he does not say "you should have not forbidden him"- but instead points to the future. "If you see him doing this again do not stop him" , and gives them the reason why they can do this: "For no-one who works a miracle in my name can soon afterward speak evil of me" Mark 9:39.

The child was still present, and Jesus had not finished the subject before John interrupted. Jesus returned to his theme of welcoming still with the child nearby. The child may have been given a drink to settle him down and Jesus says "Whoever gives a cup of water to drink in my name because you belong to Christ assuredly I say to he will be by means lose his reward, but whoever causes one of these little ones who believe in me to stumble

Chapter 54

Jesus family in Capernaum September 32AD
(Matthew 17:24-27)

They had arrived back in the town in September[145], and Jesus waited for the seventy and his family to join him as they were visiting him at Capernaum and then would journey together for the feast of Tabernacles in Jerusalem. His mother was being brought from Nazareth by his brothers and they would stay with Salome for a few days. The Feast of Tabernacles started that year on October 9th. Salome and Joanna had both used their extensive contacts to organize some hospitality in Jerusalem.

Jesus mother arrived at Capernaum on September 24th, so they could celebrate the New Year (Rosh Hashanah) with the family on the following day. They spent the Sabbath (September 26th) together before getting ready to leave for Jerusalem at the end of the following week.

Jesus was staying at Peter's house. One morning there was a knock on the front door of the house. Peter got up and opened it. Outside were some local men who were calling to collect the temple tax which was the way the building of the temple was being funded. Peter tried to get rid of them. But they must have noticed Jesus in the house because one asked Peter whether Jesus paid or not. "Yes" lied Peter and Jesus heard. When Peter came back through the courtyard into the house, Jesus explained why he did not pay the temple tax. It was a worldly system and the rule that worldly systems had was the insiders do not pay. Regarding the temple Jesus and his disciples were the true insiders, and

---

[145] Jesus walks to Jerusalem for the Feast of Tabernacles when he healed a man born blind (John 9) The same year he was at the Dedication festival at the end of December (John 10:22)

so by the rules of those who introduced the tax, they were not obliged to pay. However, Jesus knew those receiving the tax would never have understood this argument for they did not know who Jesus really was, so in order not to offend them he told Peter to fish with a hook and line rather than a net because he only needed to catch one fish. The fish he would catch would have a coin in its mouth which would be enough to pay the tax for both Peter and Jesus. Peter went down to the sea and the first fish he caught had indeed a coin in his mouth. He grasped the coin and went to the house of one of the men who had called and gave him the coin to pay for Jesus and Peter.

When Jesus family arrived, Jesus went to eat with them at Salome's house. The upcoming visit to Jerusalem came up naturally in the conversation. Jesus' brothers were surprised when Jesus said that whilst he would be going with them towards Jerusalem he would not be joining them for the feast itself. (John 7:2,3) The reason was the policy he had adopted that year which was to avoid the religious authorities in Jerusalem and Judea. They questioned his wisdom. "Hiding", they said "is no way to become properly known".

John records they did not believe in him. When they said, "if you do these things, show yourself to the world" (7:4) they were implying Jesus and others were making up the stories and hiding, so others would not be able to discover the truth. Jesus refused to defend himself. He simply replied, "My time had not yet come." and the conversation changed as they turned their attention to the words they spoke over the special Sabbath meal which Jesus shared with his family.

Travel to Jerusalem for the Feast of Tabernacles October 32AD (Luke 9)

The day soon came to go and when everyone had assembled, they left Capernaum for Jerusalem (Luke 9:51). They went with adequate supplies for their journey and stay. The wealthy Zebedee family wished to support their sons James and John and many others also gave money to assist Jesus and his disciples to eat and have somewhere to sleep. Jesus and his disciples had often slept under the open sky, but it was more usual for Jewish families to put them up at basic cost. As well as the twelve, Jesus was accompanied by many disciples, both men and women.[146] The feast started on this year on October 9th which was a Thursday. Because the earliest they could set off was Sunday (after the Sabbath) and the large group would take longer to cover the distance, Jesus and the twelve had suggested they go through Samaria– the same route they had taken when they had stayed at Sychar (see John 4). It would take them less time, be less hot and they would avoid the steep walk from Jericho to Jerusalem. They all agreed. It was safer to travel through Samaria because they thought they had somewhere to stop in Sychar. The elders of the city had welcomed Jesus previously and there was an open invitation to him and those with him. They had been very hospitable, and they had no doubt they would be willing to put up all the disciples and his family because they were travelling with Jesus and the twelve. It was an opportunity to again meet those they first met at the start of Jesus' ministry, and introduce the many with him to the Samaritans they counted as friends, and a great chance to cross a cultural divide.

Jesus sent two of his disciples to walk on ahead to get things ready for their arrival. A few hours later the two disciples Jesus had sent surprisingly returned. They explained that the Samaritans would only welcome Jesus and those with him if they were only coming to meet

---

[146] It is during this trip Jesus organises and send out seventy. To do this they must have been present. There is no reason to assume the seventy were all male. Women were present at the cross and resurrection as well as Pentecost. Why not before then? Also, there was by the time of Jesus' death a developed relationship between his mother, Salome and Mary Magdalene and other female disciples so they were almost family (so they accompany Mary & Salome to the tomb of Jesus),.The relationships needed time to develop. This would have happened if they shared the same ministry experiences together.

them. They were not willing to play second fiddle. If Jesus was going to Jerusalem, they were not interested in showing hospitality. This was disappointing to say the least. They had to change their plans and it affected everyone including his family and friends. They would now be possibly forced to sleep in the open. (Luke 9:57). The nights were getting cold. In addition, they had at least thirty miles more to walk, and what made it worse was that all had witnessed his rebuttal from the Samaritans. James and John considered a curse on the village, but Jesus rebuked them. They returned on the path they had come and then struck eastwards towards the Jordan valley to find the usual route to Jerusalem where hospitality was assured. This meant at least one day's extra walking.

The surprise and the extra difficulties caused by the Samaritans refusal to give hospitality (Luke 9:54) was an affirmation Jesus was right about sending out the seventy (or seventy-two). Never again would they arrive in a village or town unprepared. As Jesus walked along, around him were disappointed disciples, annoyed at the extra miles they would have to cover to get to Jerusalem. Their recent experience was still biting them. Someone picked up the disappointment at the detour. He said to Jesus "I will go wherever you go" (Luke 9:57) but Jesus had nowhere to stay so he said, "Foxes have holes, and birds of the air have nests, but the Son of Man has nowhere to lay his head" (Luke 9:58)

They journeyed down towards the Jordan where there were many communities. Local disciples swelled the numbers whenever Jesus came into a town. In one of the towns they passed through Jesus did meet someone else who he felt should join them, and so he said, "follow me". When this man replied about first burying his father Jesus remembered a similar conversation around the time he was sending out the 12. Although not identical, the conversation did include parts which echoed the earlier conversation a year or so before. Jesus knew this was not a coincidence. It was a repeated pattern because it reflected a similar climate in the heavenlies. The sending out of the "seventy" had some close similarities in the Father's purpose to the sending out of the twelve because it was for the harvest of souls (Luke 10:1,2). Jesus knew he was in the Father's will.

In the week before they had left Capernaum Jesus had encouraged the twelve to form their teams and plan their routes before arriving in Jerusalem where they would then fully divide into their teams. Each team was led by two of the twelve in the same duo when the twelve were sent out. To each duo was added another ten disciples. The twelve were reproducing six teams after their likeness. The teams were made up of male and female. Jesus' mother had come to Capernaum to join a team and Salome also was included as well as other female disciples of Jesus.[147] All the disciples who were part of the seventy were known had demonstrated their commitment over most of the time when Jesus had ministered and formed the core of disciples around the twelve.

Jesus wanted to visit every part of Israel. He gave instructions which were similar to those he had given the twelve. They were not to take nothing with them, and to bring peace to nay place that offered them hospitality. They were however to remain focused in where they were going so Jesus told them not to greet anyone on the road (Luke 10:4). Their call also reflected Jesus' ministry as it had developed since the call of the twelve, so the instruction to the twelve to go only to the lost sheep of the house of Israel was omitted (see Matthew 10:6) The areas still to be visited were identified into six areas and a team assigned to

[147] Mary and Salome are integrally part of the disciples by the time of the passion of Christ in a way that was not earlier in Jesus' Galilean ministry where she is only mentioned when with Jesus' brothers, she is outside the circle of his disciples (see Mark 3:32-33). It will be seen that Salome (and therefore Mary also) were still within the orbit of disciples and in close proximity to Jesus at more times than previously (see Matthew 20:20). This lasted until his death. The sending of the seventy falls within this period so they must have been part of this.

visit each one.[148] By the time they attended the Feast of Tabernacles in Jerusalem they had to be ready to go. Their task was to prepare for Jesus' coming into their region. He would visit them all in the new year.

---

[148] The probable areas were :- Israel West Coast' South Judea, Idumea, North Judea, Perea, West Jerusalem

Chapter 55

Jesus in Jerusalem for the Feast of Tabernacles October 9-15 32AD (John 7:2ff)

When the time came His brothers and other members of his family as well as his disciples went onto Jerusalem without him. Whilst they turned westwards towards Jericho and onto Jerusalem, Jesus turned eastwards to go beyond the Jordan. This was where his ministry had started, and he knew places where he could stay. The twelve went with friends and families to Jerusalem, but Jesus remained alone.

He remained for the Sabbath October 10th/11th before setting off for Jerusalem to arrive on Monday October 14th – about half way through the feast - as a late pilgrim to the feast (John 7:14). Before Jesus arrival, Jesus' reticence to come openly to the festival had proved wise. Jews who knew the family of Jesus asked where he was and were told he was not coming. There was also a lot of discussion amongst the Jews during the feast about who Jesus really was. When the talk was heard by those who wanted him dead, it just increased their anxiety and determination that this was the right course of action.

Meanwhile Jesus walked up the steep road to the top of the Mount of Olives and made a quick descent into Jerusalem. He could see the lights from the 75-foot-tall Menorah's in the courtyard of the women which had been lit on the opening evening of the feast. Like the temple itself, they were tall enough to be seen from every direction. Jesus needed to plan his stay. He went into the city secretly for a short time that day just so that his disciples would know he would be teaching in the temple on the morrow. Jesus was safe in crowds, but vulnerable in public places without them.

Jesus did not seek hospitality in Jerusalem. It was too dangerous. If Jesus stayed anywhere in Jerusalem it would be known within the Jewish community in no time at all. When he had stayed within the walls of Jerusalem Nicodemus had found him (John 3). He could not risk members of the Sanhedrin or Pharisees knowing where he was and finding him now. So instead he chose to stay at night hidden away amongst the trees in the mount of Olives (John 8:1) where it was impossible to find anyone in the dark. The mount of Olives was a long ridge east of the temple mount separated from the city by the deep Kidron valley, but reachable even on the Sabbath from Jerusalem (acts 1:12) Here Jesus was safe. Since he was a boy Jesus had walked the road over the Mount of Olives which separates Jerusalem from the desert on the road from Jericho to Jerusalem. Many times, he had looked down on Jerusalem as he had walked past the mount. The view combined with the end of the uphill journey since Jericho always made the mount of Olives a welcome place. Now it was welcome for very different reasons. It provided a safe refuge from the authorities who wanted to arrest him or kill him.

Each evening Jesus was in Jerusalem when everyone went to their own home, Jesus made the lonely journey out of Jerusalem sometimes directly from the temple through the eastern gate of Susa, but often by the north gate past the pool of Bethesda which meant easier walking on the main road to the Garden of Gethsemane. (John 7:53). The Feast of Tabernacles was for families and his 12 disciples were with their family or team groups. But for Jesus this could not be. Jesus slept under the stars alone, hidden from view amongst olive trees which had been growing there for hundreds of years. The old trees were more than three feet in diameter and so provided shade and shelter during the day and a refuge at night. Each night he would return there to a place at the foothills of the mount of Olives, out of the sight of the main road to Jericho which went nearby. The "garden of Gethsemane" was a section of level ground on which the olive trees which gave the mount its name had been planted. It was situated between the pathway directly up the mount and the busy road to Jericho which took a longer but less steep incline over the hill. As his purpose and passion was to be in Jerusalem, He had no desire to venture further up the mount, and it became the usual place he stayed. It was during these times alone he communed with his Father – a practice and place he would return to at his darkest hour before his arrest. For now, he was relatively untroubled, and it was here he slept. The pattern developed over these days worked so well that Jesus continued this practice when in Jerusalem until his arrest.

Jesus awoke as the sun rose shining on the walls of the city and the eastern gate directly to the west of where Jesus was. Whilst they were still gleaming gold and white in the early morning sun, he crossed the Kidron valley towards the city and through the east gate which led directly to the temple site. Each day at every gate of the city, traders and servants with their carts and animals gathered outside waiting for the customs office to open where taxes on goods had to be paid on entry or exit of the city when the large gates could then be opened for the day to give access to the city. There would be greater crowds around the other gates because access to the other gates were from main routes, whereas this gate was accessed from a narrow winding track across the Kidron valley.

Each morning Jesus did not delay. He and others without goods could go through the smaller entrance adjacent to the large gate and made his way up the steep steps to the temple with many worshippers going for the morning sacrifice. Each day He walked the same familiar steps leading up the mount, he joined others whom he knew. They quickly past the Levite on duty at the gate and went through into the temple staying most of the time in the court of the women Jesus found a good space and sat down to teach. Some heard him briefly as they arrived for the morning sacrifice or as they left the temple, but others stayed all day. His disciples were there from the earliest hour so in the temple he was never alone. They arrived - sitting down on the steps in the courtyard of the women where the ordinary Israelite – whether male or female could go. Jesus could also be found in the outer court of the Gentiles teaching as he walked as well as seated within the temple itself. The numbers of those listening and discussing varied, but Jesus was never alone so the authorities found it impossible to arrest Him, and those who heard Jesus were astonished at what they heard and were deeply impressed. The numbers listening to him and the reaction of those who heard Jesus increased the alarm felt by the Pharisees. There was open discussion in the synagogues as to whether Jesus was the Christ or not. The Pharisees were even more convinced that Jesus was dangerous. His popularity meant they could not easily arrest him and this added to the discussion as they heard it being said by the pilgrims that because Jesus was able to continue to teach without being arrested, the authorities also must secretly recognize Jesus as the Messiah. The Pharisees knew something had to be done and there were some urgent discussions behind closed doors about this Galilean.

One of the tactics the authorities was to alert the temple guards that they wanted Jesus to be arrested. So, each day they looked for the opportunity to arrest him. Jesus did not break any rules and his teaching was so powerful that the temple guards did nothing. Jesus taught in the temple (John 7:14; John 8:2) for the remainder of the week. Jesus debated with his hearers and as a result some tried to arrest him but without success (John 7:30; 45-48)). Those who questioned Jesus had more to think about after the debates than before(see John 7:18-43). The concerns that were being raised reflected the question Jesus had asked the twelve in the summer "Who do men say that I am". The discussions Jesus was having, the numbers

The "eighth day" of the festival arrived. This was a special day after the Feast of Tabernacles and was the Sabbath of Sabbaths. It had its own rituals which included the pouring out of water gathered from the Siloam pool. During the feast Caiaphas the High Priest accompanied by various temple dignitaries and watched by many of the pilgrims went to the pool of Siloam at the southern edge of Jerusalem in formal procession. He took the golden pitcher used each year and dipped it into the pool, filled the special jar they were carrying with water and carried it back to the temple courtyard. In the inner court with the men looking on from the court of Israel he began to pour the water out as the crowd waved their Lula lot – the name given for the date palm frond, willow and three myrtle branches pilgrims made for the festival. As they waved they sang Psalm 118 "Save us we pray O Lord. Give us success. Blessed is he who comes in the name of the Lord. We bless you from the house of the Lord" Psalm 118:25,26). Jesus was in the court of Israel witnessing this as he had before in his life. He could see over the barrier wall what the high priest was doing and as he heard the words the anointing in Jesus was stirred to speak out. "If anyone thirsts let him come to me and drink". It was to many in the crowd a momentary shout which was not unusual and could be ignored, but for Jesus' disciples it was very important.

Woman caught in adultery brought to Jesus October 17th 32AD (John 8:1-12)

Jesus stayed in Jerusalem after the festival whilst the main crowds departed. The Sabbath this year started on the evening of the day after the eighth day and others also stayed to observe the Sabbath before starting their journey home. Jesus entered the city early (John 8::2) but the city already felt back to normal. All but a few stragglers had demolished their booths. It was now a workday until the Sabbath started that evening. The "holiday" was over, the crowds had lessened after the festivities the previous day: and the atmosphere was different.

Jesus arrived early in the temple. Most of his disciples had already gone, travelling with their teams to their designated regions to prepare for Jesus coming as part of the mission of the seventy, but others also had decided to stay for the Sabbath. They knew where to come. Jesus welcomed them and taught them in the treasury (John 8:20) – otherwise known as the courtyard of the women- which was his normal place to teach just below the Nicanor gate. He had scarcely started when a group of men came. In the midst held by two men was a woman. She was unable to escape. They explained before all that she had been caught red-handed in the very act of adultery. There was no doubt about her guilty. Her captors had taken her to the scribes and Pharisees in the southern porch of the temple site to see what should be done with her. One of the Pharisees there had suggested that it might be a good opportunity to put Jesus on the spot. They knew he was in the court of the women teaching, and so had dragged her across the outer court into the temple. Jesus was indeed there teaching with a crowd around him. They pushed through the crowd to get to the front, so everyone could see and immediately interrupted him. Jesus did not respond to them but seated as he was he just bent down and wrote in the dust on the floor. They came up close as if he was deaf invading his space to get his attention. They wanted this interview in full view of the crowds. Standing over him as Jesus sat on the steps with the woman in front of him who was forced to stand so everyone could see her, they told the sordid story of the woman's adultery. Jesus did not respond. He did not stand up or speak at all. He did not even look at the woman or her accusers. He just bent down and continued to doodle with his finger in the dust on the ground as if he had not heard them speak. So, they spoke louder and closer to Jesus speaking over him, raising their voices in case he was deaf. Jesus waited, and then stood up (John 8:7) so he could have some space from those who accused this woman and so all could see him and so that his voice would carry to the back of the crowd which had grown with curious bystanders standing to look at what would happen next. The stage was set – or so the Pharisees and scribes thought. Jesus then said one sentence: "He who is without sin among you, let him cast the first stone", and quickly sat back down returning to making doodles on the ground with his fingers. John the disciple was still there[149]. He was at the back of the crowd with other disciples of Jesus. He saw some of her accusers started to leave from the back of the group and noted it was the older ones who were leaving first. Jesus did not see this detail. He was just doodling and waiting. John had witnessed a spirit of conviction come upon his accusers. Some had left feeling uncomfortable and not knowing why; others had specific memories they had long since forgotten when they had broken the law, others felt the zeal to stand and accuse the woman drain away. Not many would be able to verbalize what was happening to them and those who knew their sin would not wish to admit it. They found it easier to just slip away. The numbers around the woman dwindled until the few who were left felt they could no longer press the point and they also reluctantly left the woman standing alone in front of Jesus and the crowd. Jesus looked up and saw the woman now no longer held. He stood up and looked around (John 8:10) and asked if there were any accusers. She said "No". Jesus said neither do I condemn you. Go and do not sin again". The woman turned and walked away. Jesus resumed his teaching. He felt now was the time to share some of his thoughts during his time at the feast. This same courtyard had four huge 75-foot-high lamp stands specially erected for the feast of Tabernacles each year. They towered above the walls of the temple courtyard. Jesus had seen them alight during the feast of Tabernacles. Their powerful light had

---

[149] I speculate that Peter and James had left already with their team for the West coast (as they were fisherman). It is probable that Peter developed a relationship with Simon the tanner from Joppa during this time. John was going to another area with Mary in his team (after all he developed a sufficiently quality relationship with her for Jesus to hand his mother to him from the cross). It was likely to be less distance to walk than other areas as his team included older women.

pierced the darkness over the temple mount all night long and it had been clearly visible as Jesus settled down to sleep on the Mount of Olives. As a boy Jesus was told the lights pointed back to the time when the Jews were led out of Egypt into the promised land, but every year on the eighth day the first chapter of Genesis 1 was read. As the words "let there be light" were read, they seemed more poignant set against the backdrop of the light from the lamps. This thought was in a moment the vehicle of revelation – connections between the creation narrative and Jesus as the light of the world began to fill Jesus' soul. He knew He was the light of the world sent by the Father. Much Jesus heard from the Father he spoke immediately, but other times he knew the disclosure of revelation was to wait for the right time. The time had come to say what the Father had placed on his heart a few days ago. So, he said. "I am the light of the world. He who follows me shall not walk in darkness but shall have the light of life" The Pharisees immediately reacted against this and they waited their moment where he was on his own and seized him and tried to stone Jesus. It was touch and go whether they would have succeeded. Jesus escaped and hid and then walked out the temple in the crowd, no-one realizing who he was. He saw His accusers (John 8:59) as He went but they did not see Him. Jesus then met up with his disciples to celebrate the Sabbath. In the morning Jesus was still on the move avoiding the authorities who had tried to kill him earlier (John 9:1). Jesus saw a man blind from birth and the disciples asked him whether the blindness was his fault. Jesus said it was for the glory of God and reached down and mixed some soil with his spittle put it on his eyes and told him to wash in the pool of Siloam – the very place the water had been taken on the eighth day earlier in the week. He did so and was healed. It was not long before the Jewish authorities heard of it.

The blind man who could now see was brought to the religious authorities. Jesus seemed a constant thorn in their side. At the start of the week Jesus remained unscathed after they had brought the woman accused of adultery. Next there was the unsuccessful attempt to stone Jesus for blasphemy and now Jesus had healed a blind man on the Sabbath. The result of this was that blind man was thrown out of the synagogue with all the privileges of belonging stopped. Jesus was still in Jerusalem as the final teams left for the mission of the seventy. Jesus heard about his plight and found him, and he became a disciple of Jesus (John 9:38).

Chapter 56

Jesus had visited every village and town in Galilee alongside bringing his disciples together to teach them more about the kingdom of God. Now the strategy changed. He wanted to bring the Kingdom to all Israel visiting many people as possible whilst focusing now on the end of his earthly ministry. He was on a journey which would end in Jerusalem , visiting cities and areas where people could gather (Luke 10:1 "cities and places"). Gatherings which had been so important in his mission to Galilee continued by more frequent gatherings organised by the teams of the seventy in the areas where he went. Great numbers accompanied Jesus during his journeys from place to place, and vast numbers attended the gatherings which were now arranged according to the schedule of his travels rather than according to religious festivals or "holidays". In Galilee, it had had to be at times when people were free to travel from all over Israel, but a gathering for the local area had no such restraints. As a result of what was sometimes daily gatherings hundreds more became disciples.

The areas left to visit were the people in Idumea (south Israel), southern Judea below Jerusalem, West of Jerusalem and people at the coast south of Galilee. There were also those who lived kin Judea north of Jerusalem as well as those cities and towns in the Jordan rift valley. Further east was Perea, a domain of Herod Antipas which Jesus had not yet visited. There were few cities in Perea (Julias (not the same city as Bethsaida) had been built by Antipas when Tiberius became emperor and there were two other large cities in Perea east of the Jordan). The cities Jesus visited therefore were mainly in the other areas. The cities of Galilee visited before when the twelve were sent out were not on the list. (Luke 10:10-15).

The seventy were deployed to prepare the way so that as Jesus passed through there could be the maximum harvesting of souls (Luke 10:2). His route would take him from Jerusalem and would end in Jerusalem.[150] The seventy would prepare the way and Jesus gave them a period of forty days. He arranged for a gathering of the seventy which was open to all at the Jordan after the feast of dedication in December. Jesus would spend this time away from the public gaze preparing for what was to come.

The seventy would demonstrate the kingdom (Luke 10:19) and prepare for the time that Jesus would visit them so that no-one would miss his coming. Wherever he went people could gather to meet him (e.g. Luke 12:1). The teams as part of their preparatory visit got to know who they could trust so that hospitality and help was available for them even in places where they were unfamiliar. This was made more important because of the growing number of enemies who wanted Jesus dead. The sending out of the seventy brought a further acceleration for the itinerant ministry of Jesus of Nazareth.

The Sending out of the "Seventy"
(Luke 10:1-24 [72 Luke 10:1NU text])

Known as the seventy –though it was 72- they were disciples who had followed Jesus for most of his ministry and as we have said earlier, were both male and female[151] The 70 were not like the 12. There was no public sending out before a gathering. The "twelve" was a core structure which once instituted remained at the core of disciples around Jesus and after Jesus' ascension remained as an identifiable

---

[150] The route that Jesus took is not recorded in the gospels, but assumes Jesus followed the main roads starting in North Judea going to the west then south and then east to cover all of Israel.

[151] Hippodotus' list of the seventy is all male and includes people who could not have been there (e.g. Trophimus a convert of Paul). Women were there in the 120 at Pentecost (e.g. Mary the mother of Jesus) so why not as part of the 70?

body to which only certain people belonged (Acts 1). The "twelve" exercised some leadership (see for example Mark 9:38). It was a structure around Jesus to serve the disciples as well as mission and so survived. The "Seventy", by contrast, was a temporary structure for mission. They had a specific task which was to prepare the way for Jesus' coming by healing the sick and getting to know the area. They had clear instructions. They found, just as the twelve had found when they were sent out, that they encountered the demonic. They had not been commissioned as the twelve had been and could not deal with these situations using their own words or faith. They found, however, that if they used the name of Jesus the demons went, (Luke 10:17). They had defeated the enemy by simply trying out ideas. No wonder Jesus rejoiced at the wisdom given to babes (Luke 10:11)

The seventy had been sent out in six teams by Jesus, (the NU text of the specific number 72 is probably correct[152]). He had a few months before sent the twelve out two by two, but these were now each duo was leading of a team of ten others. The team was very adaptable. It could be divided into two teams of six under one of the twelve when required. It was also possible to subdivide the team into threes or fours if needed. The team was highly flexible and functioned to get the job done quickly. They went out gradually, but most left immediately after the Feast of Tabernacles. Each team went to its designated area where they demonstrated the kingdom and arranged for Jesus coming to them.

Throughout November Jesus had been without the twelve as they led their teams. They would all be together again the feast he was to attend in Jerusalem. He had arranged to meet with them by the Jordan near where he had been baptised. If it had been just the twelve, the feast would have been a good time to meet but it had been agreed that

---

[152] Different early manuscripts differed – some reflecting the actual number whilst others reflecting the more general figure by which they were referred to in later years.

seventy excited disciples meeting Jesus on their return in Jerusalem was too dangerous. Jesus did not want to draw any more attention of the authorities towards him knowing that many wanted him dead.

He travelled alone towards Jerusalem without any accompanying disciples. The winter nights were cold, but the day was clear quickly warming the air. At this time of year, the maximum temperature would only be about 16C. He walked the familiar route he had taken since a boy by the Jordan until he turned west to ascend the hills of Judea to Jerusalem. When he got to the top of the mount of Olives the wind from the north west that blew most days at this time of year caught him in the face and he put his head down and walked towards the valley which would herald the ascent through the gates of the city.

Feast of Hanukkah December Thursday 17-24 32AD,[153] (John 10:22-40)

Jesus was in Jerusalem alone[154]. He was there incognito to celebrate the feast of Hanukkah (dedication) (John 10:22).

Once through the gates, Jesus headed towards the temple site. There was no incident until Jesus went from the temple onto the paved courtyard surrounding it (called the court of the Gentiles) and decided to walk through Solomon's porch – a double colonnade built on the east. This was the boundary of the temple which had remained unchanged since Solomon's time[155]. Solomon had laid the foundation raising the ground level from the Kidron valley to match the temple mount, and

---

[153] Two calendars published at *cgsf.org* are the calendars of the Western world and of the mainstream Jews

[154] There is no mention of the twelve on this occasion.

[155] These cloisters belonged to the outer court, and were situated in a deep valley, and had walls that reached four hundred cubits [in length], and were built of square and very white stones, the length of each of which stones was twenty cubits, and their height six cubits. This was the work of King Solomon, who first built the entire temple" (Josephus Flavius Ant. 20:9, section 7)

Herod had strengthened it. Jesus was walking through the colonnades built on these ancient walls looking at the view on the Mount of Olives which could be seen clearly from there.

Jesus was still the talk of the town especially after his healing of a man born blind last time he was in Jerusalem (John9). The main question which continued to be being whispered and debated in every synagogue in Jerusalem was whether Jesus was the Messiah or not (John 10:24). The debate had not got lessened since Tabernacles and the anxiety of the authorities was increasing. Because Jesus was not with anyone, it was far easier for him to be surrounded They lost no opportunity. He was recognized as he walked in the shade of the colonnades. Some went behind him while others blocked his path and closed in on Jesus until they surrounded him. Some had wanted to stone him before during the Feast of Tabernacles (John 8:59). They were not going to let him escape again especially now he was relatively vulnerable on his own. They questioned in an intimidating manner (John 10:24), directly asking "Are you the Christ?". They had a supply of stones to hand. Jesus was not intimidated. They had addressed this before, but it was obvious they had not moved forward in their thinking. Jesus gave them a resume of his teaching he had given previously (John 10:25-30) and it resulted in the same reaction as before. They picked up stones to throw at him. Last time Jesus had run away and hidden (John 8:59) but this time he continued to stand and said boldly "For which deed of My Father are you stoning me". His boldness caused some to hesitate. Caught off guard they answered their accusation of "blasphemy". Jesus confounded them with a bible exposition of Psalm 82, and the resolve of some weakened. Jesus was showing himself to be rabbi and they did not wish to harm revered teachers of Israel. Jesus took the opportunity their hesitation brought and was able to wriggle out of their grasp making his escape from the temple. Jesus left the city immediately. He could not stay. He cut short his time in Jerusalem and went to the Jordan to walk back to where he had already arranged to meet the 70 who were due to return before the following Sabbath.

Return of the "Seventy" December 32AD (Luke 10:17-22)

Jesus met them as arranged at the Jordan. The seventy came back and reported what had happened in the towns and places they had been. Many had been healed and demons cast out. When Jesus heard it, he rejoiced (Luke 10: 21). There was no time to wait. Jesus immediately started to visit the places where the 70 had prepared the way for him to go.

SECTION 9

Jesus' itinerant ministry to all Israel

Jesus travelled surrounded by crowds wherever he went. The twelve and the seventy were the main part of what could sometimes be a much larger group who accompanied Jesus wherever he went

Chapter 57

Jesus Ministry to the rest of Israel January 33AD (Luke 10:38-18:43)

The teams had successfully encouraged local disciples to organize events in different communities to maximize the blessing Jesus' visit would bring. Their earlier visit also had helped to break down any prejudice that might have existed in the community between Galilee and the rest of Israel.

Galilee had been part of the Northern Kingdom of Israel which had been separated from the southern Kingdom since the rule of King Solomon. The Galileans though as Jewish as those in Judea, had a different outlook then their southern neighbours, and Galileans were often despised by them. The individual places visited are too numerous to record in the gospel narratives, but his teaching and some events where they explain the context of the teaching is contained in Luke 10:25ff-17:10 and Matthew 17-18. Jesus taught both what he had taught elsewhere alongside fresh material which mainly came about through events or questions that happened during his journeys. Scores of disciples and on occasions hundreds of disciples were with him as he walked into each town during these weeks. Local disciples would welcome Jesus and the twelve and bring them into the town. Hospitality was already arranged, and a schedule already decided before they arrived.

Bethany (Luke 10:38-42)

The starting place for Jesus mission was Bethany. Jesus surrounded by the twelve and the rest of "the seventy "immediately set off back into Judea. They went to Jericho and took the familiar road to Bethany. The team which Simon and Judas had assembled were responsible for this section of the mission. Martha had specifically requested Jesus to stay with them so whilst the others stayed in the houses of Simon and some other disciples, Jesus had the luxury and challenge of being on his own[156]. He followed Martha in to her house and met Mary sitting as usual in the room. Jesus had met Mary before. She was the woman who had cried over his feet last time he was in Bethany. Many months had gone by since then. Mary, following the custom of the Jews, vacated the chair and sat down on the floor, so Jesus could sit down. Martha left the room to prepare the meal. Mary and Martha were two of Jesus' disciples – and Martha being part of Simon and Judas' team (Luke 10:39) had enabled her to suggest that Jesus stay with them. Jesus sat down in the chair vacated by Mary who now sat on the floor at his feet. There was nothing unusual about this. It was normal for men to sit on the seats whilst the younger or women sat on the floor. Jesus spoke with Mary and the presence of God filled the room as he spoke. As they talked Martha interrupted them. She was missing all that was being said because of cooking and needed help there so they could both listen. Jesus spoke to the anxiety in her soul. He called her name in a tone which was a combination of understanding and affection which provided the context for her to hear without shame the words which followed. Jesus knew that His Father had a purpose for this meeting with Mary and it should not be taken away from her. (Luke 10:42)

From the Judean Hills to the west coast January 33AD

The following morning, they assembled to set off. Bethany was not far from the road that went northwards towards Sychar. They set off towards the Judean Hills. They went through Anathoth and when they got to Capharsaiam took the road to Michmash and Ephraim before returning to take the road to Bethel. The cities were in the hills. Judea stretched up to the village of Anuath which lay on the border with

---

[156] It is probable that Martha was on Simon and Judas' team so was able to arrange for Jesus to stay in her house rather than with Simon and Judas as he had done previously

Samaria. Jesus soon completed the area Simon and Judas[157] had been given. He had proclaimed the kingdom in the cities of northern Judea. Next, they went towards Bethel. Jesus taught in the Ephraim[158] region where they stayed before following the road [159] to the coast which went through many cities and villages until they reached Apollonia on the military coastal road from where they went southwards to Joppa where they stayed for a night[160]. They went eastwards over mountains and hills until they came to the coast to visit more cities and villages of Judea (e.g., Lydda, Emmaus, Azotus) that lay west of Jerusalem. Jesus lost no time. He wanted to complete his visitation of all Israel. They did not stay in any town for longer than necessary except on the Sabbath. All the cities of Judea westwards of Jerusalem were visited very quickly. They were sited on major routes and it was not difficult to visit. (Unlike the northern section where some of the cities were in remote locations). The roads were better than the ones through the hills. They were comparatively level with a good stone surface so there was less mud to cope with as they walked, and it showed in their pace and the shorter time it took to cover the ground.

[157] Bethany was where Simon (and Judas) came from (John 12:4, Matthew 26:6) Bethany was a good starting point for the towns and villages in the hills to the north.

[158] After the resurrection of Lazarus and the media storm it created, Jesus and the 12 went to Ephraim. The only time Jesus could have been here before is during the mission arranged by the 70. It is probable that one of the seventy was from Ephraim and as part of the team of Simon and Judas had organized this stop over. It made possible this sudden escape from unexpected danger brought about by the miracle.

[159] The route which follows is the most likely route Jesus took based on where the main cities were and quick access via roads to them. Jesus did not go everywhere. He might have included Caesarea the provincial capital of Judea whose access was via the coast road, it was quite a bit out of their way. The other towns were all on circular routes.

[160] Simon Peter has a good well-established relationship with Simon the tanner in Joppa (Acts 10) in three or four years. This could have come about if Peter was a leader of the team that established the coastal area. It is not improbable that they stayed at Joppa on their travels.

From the west coast to the south January 33AD

From the coast, they travelled eastwards back through the valley of Elah (valley of Rephaim 2 Samuel 5:17-25) on the road to Jerusalem before heading south. Within each team were people who would be helpful in that region. Clopas and his wife Mary (John 19:25) who lived at Emmaus (Luke 24:18) were on the team for their area. Crowds followed Jesus wherever he went and more joined as they went. The gatherings on route had been well arranged but the numbers attending were greater than they anticipated and frequently outgrew their venues (see Luke 12:1-3). Jesus continued to proclaim the kingdom and teach to as many people as possible in these last months of his life on earth. His teaching was a combination of some he had taught before but there was always fresh teaching. [161]Jesus now turned his attention to southern Judea which was called at that time Idumea. Beersheba near the desert and Hebron in the hills were two of the major cities on the circular route Jesus took. They turned south from the road to Jerusalem walking about fifty miles to Beersheba visiting the many cities of Judea they went through on route. From Beersheba they took the road eastwards which weaved its way through what was called Idumea. It was still under the jurisdiction of Judea, but the Jews had been invaded in the past by people from Edom which gave Idumea its name. Disciples from here had followed Jesus from his earliest days (Mark 3:8) and so although Jesus had not visited here before, he was not unknown. Great crowds met him, listened to him and walked with him throughout. They went to the city of Hebron which lay high in the high mountains of Judea. Central Judea was mountainous bordered by a coastal plain on the west and the Jordan rift valley to the east. The roads took the best route through them and so Jesus and those with him kept walking until

---

[161] Luke records the teaching Jesus gave during the mission of the seventy. He therefore includes many parables not included by the other gospels because they were first spoken during this time.

they found a settlement of which there were several. The population of Judea was more numerous than Lower Galilee.

Travel in winter meant walking in the rainy season. It did not rain every day but when it did rain, it could be sufficient to cause streams to flood. In addition, as they climbed higher the colder it became. On the barren high hills of Judea there was always a risk of snow in December and January, and the start of 33AD in January was no different to previous years. Wherever Jesus went crowds of disciples gathered to hear Jesus. Amongst them were the curious and the seekers who were not yet disciples. The type of gatherings had different characteristics. Sometimes Jesus spoke and they all listened, but mostly his teaching flowed from questions because there was a lot of interaction between Jesus and the crowd. There was nothing new about this. It happened everywhere Jesus had been both in Galilee and in the temple in Jerusalem. Wherever he was, Jesus would try to be seated in a place where everyone could see him. It was like a Rabbi gathering his disciples around him except these gathered disciples were many more. The crowd sat around him, whilst onlookers often stood at the back of the crowd to listen. When someone wanted to ask a question, they would stand up (e.g. Luke 10:25) – (a synagogue practice which was now on the streets). This was not always the case especially when there were hundreds. Standing was not sufficient to be noticed to ask the question. So, people would then just shout out from the crowd (e.g. Luke 12:13), but Jesus answered them just the same. His teaching was sometimes directed at the disciples which were there (Luke 12:22 etc.) and at other times he addressed those who were not yet disciples (Luke 12:54,41). It was during these days that Jesus taught the disciples the Lord's prayer and also taught the parables recorded in Luke 14-17. Jesus and the twelve were constantly on the move except each Sabbath Jesus stayed in a town or village. Jesus as a good Jew observed the Sabbath restrictions of travel. There were still especially at the beginning of his mission when in the Judea just north of Jerusalem the old arguments with the religious authorities about Jesus (Luke 11:15 etc.) and his disciples (Luke 11:18ff). and any healing on the Sabbath especially in public in the synagogue was condemned and yet Jesus was at the same time the talk of the town (see Luke 13:11ff). The teaching Jesus gave during this time was a mixture of what the twelve had heard before and teaching that was fresh and new. Much of His new teaching was in response to events at meals he shared on the Sabbath (e.g. Luke 14:1) or as a response to questions from disciples or people in the crowd. Those who had been with Jesus for the last three years could see a new emphasis in Jesus' teaching, for He began to speak much more of the day of judgement and the end times in parables and directly. (Luke 14::14, 16:19-31;). The twelve noticed this and when they could they began to ask him questions about this (Mark 13). Whilst the synagogues in Jerusalem and elsewhere were disputing whether Jesus was the Christ, his disciples were already convinced. Their debate was how Jesus the Messiah would redeem Israel (see Luke 24:21).

The places where the crowds gathered to hear Jesus varied. Sometimes those who listened were very squashed together being in a place without any possibility of overflow. Those who came had to listen uncomfortably pushed up close to others. (Luke 11:29,12:1). Sometimes they were even unable to sit down or if they were sat down were trampled on by others who had not yet found a space to sit (Luke 12:1) All this caused some minor disruption from time to time, but in the main the disciples were buoyant, and excited that the Messiah had come. Testimonies of miracles and healings continued to result from every visit Jesus made. Hundreds were healed – some dramatically.

Jesus and those with him trusted God for their food. They went with no major provisions, and the Father always provided. In Jerusalem the religious rich were Sadducees, but in the villages and the cities the rich who were able to offer hospitality to Jesus and his disciples were usually Pharisees. At one of the towns they went through a Pharisee invited Jesus to eat with him (Luke 11:37-53. It was the Sabbath so like every other Jew Jesus did not travel. He rested for a day and became more vulnerable than when walking in a crowd or speaking to vast crowds. Each Sabbath had more of a familiarity to his time in Capernaum than any other day at that time. On one occasion Jesus arrived at the house where he had been invited, and he found a gathering of lawyers as well. Jesus was not intimidated and did not mince his words. He succeeded in upsetting them so much that it spilled out into the meetings on the streets (Luke 11:53). Complaints from the Pharisees would become a feature in Judea as it had been in Galilee. (see Luke 15:2,16:14)

The valley of Hebron they had walked through was rich and fertile. Fig trees and pomegranates were in great abundance intertwined with vines. From Hebron they left Idumean Judea walking a further thirty miles to reach Jericho. The road went through many towns and villages. To the left were the mountains of Judah and to their left the wilderness of Engedi. and they eventually arrived at the town of Etam in the low hill country of Judah and walking through the rich gardens abounding in rivulets of water past Herodium the royal palace complex three miles south east of Bethlehem before taking the dry desert road eastwards to Jericho.

Judea February 33AD (Luke 12)

Whilst on his travels in Judea Jesus heard about Pilate's defilement of sacrifices (Luke 13:1) by a cruel murder of Galileans that had happened during the winter months (Josephus Antiquities 18.3.1)[162] The back-

---

[162] This is the only incident Josephus mentions which could be referred to in Luke 13. Josephus describes those who dies as Jews rather than Galileans, but the incident is recorded in Antiquities 18.3.2. immediately followed by "about this time Jesus, a wise man,

story behind this was some time before in Caesarea Pilate had been forced to take away images he had placed in the temple as the only way to pacify a crowd who had not been intimidated by military force. He felt he had not been able to exercise his true authority because of the unexpected willingness of the crowd to be killed. He felt he risked losing respect and control if his authority was weakened in this way. He had determined not to be seen to be "soft" again. Later he faced another objection over the use of Corban – money given to God – to build another aqueduct to increase the water supply to the city He planned to draw water via the aqueduct from a river twenty-five miles away. This was not popular with the local Jews who benefited from the water where it was, and who objected to the secular ruler using sacred money. When the Jews who had gathered for a religious festival in Jerusalem, they came together as a mob to object to Pilate's plan in a similar way to how they had done in Caesarea. This time Pilate was prepared. He knew the crowd would shout abuse at him, so he ordered some soldiers to dress as Jews and at his signal to kill as many of the mob as possible to silence the crowd (Josephus Antiquities 18.3.2,3). Many were killed and many more wounded. It put an end to any voiced opposition, but the sense of horror at blood spilt during a festival was deeply felt. This news was mentioned to Jesus as he travelled in Judea as there were Galileans from his home area who had died. Jesus however chose to reply with another example of news of the eighteen local residents of Jerusalem who were killed by the collapse of the old tower of Siloam in the south of the city. He said the tragedy did not happen because they were worse sinners than anyone else, but the news was a warning to all to repent so they did not perish eternally. (Luke 13:3)

if it be lawful to call him a man, for he was a doer of wonderful works, - a teacher of such men as receive the truth with pleasure" Ant 18.3.3

Woman healed in synagogue February 33AD (Luke 13:10ff)

After the first few days the Sabbath approached and Jesus stayed in one of the towns of Judea teaching in their synagogue. At some point during his teaching, as Jesus faced the congregation, he noticed amongst the women at the back a woman who was bent double. Jesus called her to the front and she came walking as she had done for eighteen years with back bowed seeking to look up as she walked. Jesus said Woman you are freed from your infirmity. And he laid hands on her activating the word he had spoken over her. As he did so she began to straighten and as she realized the difference she gave glory to God.

The elder of the synagogue was responsible for proceedings and was concerned that this event might cause a stampede for other healings. He wanted the meeting to be dignified and without controversy. He had been content with Jesus teaching and would be very happy to return to this. So, he said to the crowd not to come forward for healing as it wa the Sabbath when no work should be done. Jesus turned to the elder and said would not he give his donkey a drink on the Sabbath. How much more should this woman, bound by Satan, receive healing on the Sabbath. The crowd loved it. The leaders did not like it but kept quiet and repressed their anger deep inside.

Perea February 33AD (Luke 13:23ff [see Luke 13:31])

Jesus went from southern Judah to the communities that lived East of the Jordan in Judea. For Jesus this felt more familiar territory for this is where it had all started with John the Baptist. The last town in Judea was Amathus. It was an important fortified town east of the Jordan. Ancient Heshbon was part of Judea and was on a road from Jericho. It was an ancient city conquered by the Israel of the Old Testament and by Herod the Great just before the New Testament. By Jesus' day it was a small Jewish town with a fort built by Herod the Great who had sought to strengthen the defence of his eastern border during his reign.[163]From there Jesus went to the cities in Perea. The latter was not as well populated as Judea. It lay east of the Jordan and the Dead Sea. Its northern border was south of Pella in the Decapolis and its southern border was Machaerus the fortified town built around a palace where John the Baptist was imprisoned and killed. Perea was under the rule of Herod (Luke 13:31). When Jesus visited these places in Herod's dominion (Luke 13:22,31) he was told to flee as Herod wanted to kill him. Jesus refused to be intimidated by the reports and continued his mission of proclaiming the kingdom in word and deed. Gadara of Perea (not the same as Gadara of the Decapolis) was the main city. A strong fortified city of at least two miles circumference built near the river Hieromax. It was six miles south east of the Sea of Galilee. Although larger than Galilee Perea was mainly rugged mountains set in a desert climate which made it difficult to grow anything, so communities were in specific regions where the soil was better and trees like the vine, olive and palm tree could be cultivated[164]. Where cities were built , mountain streams or springs allowed them to flourish, but in between these Jesus walked through wild wilderness. The visit to the cities in Perea took much less time than had been the case in Judea In Perea as there were less places to go. They travelled by roads which provided the easiest route and also the speed they required to cover the ground. They went from town to town avoiding nights in the desert. During this time the future church was forming. All the time Jesus was teaching and healing there had been a hidden development of the disciples to a place where 120 of them could be together with the same focus and values in the Upper Room at Pentecost. The twelve were part of a wider community many of whom they knew well and who knew them. This would be crucial after Jesus' departure.

[163] Josephus Antiquities 15.8.5
[164] See Josephus War 3.3.

Chapter 58

The Gathering East of the Jordan river February 33 AD
(Matthew 19:1,2; Mark 10:1, Luke 16:18)

Jesus returned to the Jordan river outside Herod's domain and safe from those in Jerusalem who wished to kill him. His mission with the seventy was not yet over, but they had by and large covered all the territory of Israel. The final task was to proclaim the kingdom in the cities in the Jordan valley before going to Jerusalem (Matthew 19:1). He had arranged before embarking on this latest mission for a gathering at the place where he was baptised by John. He knew that as in previous missions it was important to signpost both new and old disciples to a gathering where they could be nurtured in the kingdom and grow together relationally. Although what was talked about was the deeds of the kingdom that Jesus was doing, one of the most important features of these gatherings was the beginnings of the church of God. Jesus had publicised this gathering before sending out the seventy from Jerusalem. It was at a place where John the Baptist used to teach so well-known and accessible. Disciples came from every direction(Matthew 19:2; Mark 10:1). Jesus taught them many things including the parable of the dishonest servant (Luke 16:1ff) [165]As usual some came seeking healing, but religious leaders from Jerusalem took the opportunity to search him out (Matthew 19:3) with theological questions. The healings they could not dispute. It was the underlying concern about the orthodoxy of Jesus which concerned the Pharisees. The Pharisees came to see which theological school of thought Jesus agreed with on the issue of divorce. The house of Hillel taught divorce should be possible even for trivial offences whereas the stricter house

---

[165] This parable is spoken to his disciples in a different context to the earlier parables and Luke 16 contains the same teaching in Matthew 19 (see Luke 16:18)

of permitted divorce only for serious transgressions. Jesus cut through both by stating the original purpose in creation was for no divorce, but because life is not perfect, God introduced divorce out of mercy to those who had hard enough hearts to go through with divorce. This reply silenced them. Jesus then told for the first time the parable of rich man and Lazarus (Luke 16:19ff), but he also shared teaching he had given before in private to Peter and the twelve in Capernaum (see Luke 17:3 and Matthew 18:21,22 & 19:1). Jesus was a teacher of the kingdom who brought out treasures both new and old, (see Matthew 13:52), and the disciples listened with enthusiasm.

Meanwhile the healing ministry continued through both Jesus and the twelve. Laying on of hands was now common practice for healing. At this gathering there was a further development when families who had come asked if Jesus could lay hands on their children and pray. The parents realised that Jesus' prayer could not only change the past and bring healing in the present but also make things different in the future. This new idea of a prayer for a blessing for their children was at first opposed by the disciples until Jesus intervened (Matthew 19:13,14). He took each child up into his arms, laid his hands on them and blessed them (Mark 10:16) From now on prayer for blessing became more common.

The next day Jesus announced they were going to Bethany. The gathering was over. This was not only unexpected, but the twelve thought it dangerous. Thomas verbalized what they were all thinking "Let us also go and die with him" (John 11:16). To go to Bethany was to go less than two miles from Jerusalem. It was risky, and they recalled the last time they were in Jerusalem when the authorities attempted to stone Jesus (John 11:8). Jerusalem was a dangerous place. Two days before, a messenger had come from Bethany and given the news that Lazarus was dangerously ill, and that his sisters Mary and Martha requested Jesus to come to heal him (John 11:3, 21,32). The messenger had returned alone with the message from Jesus "This sickness is not unto death, but for the glory of God". By the time the messenger returned, Lazarus had died and so the sending to Jesus in the first place seemed futile to the sisters – too little too late. The message that Jesus had given the messenger seemed unusually inaccurate. His reputation as a prophet was not lessened by this because the grief of Lazarus' passing took up everyone's attention.

Now after two days Jesus said he was to go to wake Lazarus up from death. His disciples had seen the messenger go and had not anticipated going there at all. They were unaware that Jesus had already decided to go, waiting only for His Father to tell him when Lazarus was dead. The twelve and the others with Jesus got ready to go, and they left that same day arriving at Bethany in the afternoon. Jesus expected to find Lazarus only just dead perhaps the night before they had set out. He asked about him as he entered the village and was surprised that he had been buried four days. Burial happened very quickly – on the day of death or early the following day- so Jesus found Lazarus had been dead even whilst he had waited beyond the Jordan. As He questioned this timing to the Father, he received assurance that the timing was to bring even more glory. There could be no doubt about the power of God when Lazarus was raised to life after such a time in the tomb. No-one could doubt it.

Jesus waited at the outskirts of the village whilst a message was brought to Martha that Jesus was coming (John 11:20). There was a large assembly of friends and family gathered from Jerusalem as well as the small village where they loved (John 11:18). The shiva – as it is called- was the time when family and friends sought to comfort the deceased and remember the deceased well and help establish the future. It normally lasted up to seven days.

Fortunately for the messenger Martha was outside the house making sure all the preparations were in hand. When Martha knew where Jesus was, she was not content to wait for Jesus to arrive. She wanted to see him straight away. So, she left her tasks and slipped away with the messenger who then brought her to Jesus. Martha greeted Jesus and then said, "if you had been here my brother would not have died" – a phrase she and Mary had both heard said and spoken themselves (see John 11:32; 37). Martha then said two further things. One that she still had hope that Jesus could do anything though her mind was slow to grasp the idea that Jesus will raise her brother from the dead that afternoon. The other statement she made amidst all her confusion, she needed to say out loud what she knew: "You are the Christ, the Son of God who has come into the world". Jesus then asked after Mary and Martha said it would be better if Jesus stayed there and Mary came to him. He agreed, and she turned back up the hill towards the village to find Mary. Whereas Martha had been processing her loss by action, Mary was sitting in the house processing her grief by being in company and the attention of others. It was not unusual for Mary to be sitting whilst Martha was serving (Luke 10:38-41). Martha came in to the room where Mary was and whispered in her ear. Those in the room had taken little notice of this until Mary got up and went out the room without saying anything to anyone. They were concerned, and their immediate thought was that grief was the reason. They also got up and followed her , thinking if she was going to the tomb to weep, it would be good for them to be there as a support. They were all weeping (John 11:33). They discovered Mary and Martha just a few yards down the road to Jericho at the outskirts of the village meeting Jesus. t Jesus was at the same place he had been when Martha had left him about ten minutes before. Jesus saw the grief struck faces of those who followed the sisters and heard their cries. He asked where the tomb was. The grief was tangible. Jesus wept with them as they went off the main road down a steep path round a steep rock cliff face. As they came around onto more level ground Jesus soon saw a cave with a sizeable stone newly rolled over the entrance which Martha pointed out was the tomb of her brother. Jesus stood in front of the tomb and turned and said to some men nearby to take away the stone. Martha objected saying there would be a stink. Jesus reassured her, and the stone was taken away revealing a bandaged body lying on the ground. There was no smell. Jesus knew death was not here. He acknowledged this with a prayer "Father I thank you that you have heard me". He then continued with the crowd still in focus as he prayed "And I know that you always hear me, but because of the people standing by I said this, that they may believe that you sent me". Jesus finished praying, and standing where he was, he shouted "Lazarus, come forth". Lazarus heard him from the place of death, and his human soul and spirit returned into his body, and he discovered he could move its limbs. To the amazement of the people there, Lazarus sat up and rose to his feet. However, he found it difficult to see where to go because there was a cloth wrapped around his face, but he headed in the direction of Jesus' voice which had been replaced by the cries of astonishment from those near him as he walked towards the light that he could recognize through his bandages. Jesus remained where he was as Lazarus made his way out. It only took a few seconds. Jesus helped him as he reached the cave entrance. Walking was not easy bound as he was, and so Jesus said to his friends to unbind him, so he could go.

The response of the crowd was utter amazement. As a result, some finally recognized that Jesus was indeed the Christ and believed on him, but others would remain as they were before. With Lazarus now alive, there was no reason to stay and those who had been attending the shiva returned unexpectedly that day. They recounted what they had witnessed to their friends on their return. (John 11:46) So the Pharisees in Jerusalem heard the same day from those who had witnessed the event, and they quickly convened a high-level council meeting chaired by the High Priest to discuss its implications. (John 11:47) Their concern was that there were very significant numbers becoming his disciples which could threaten their authority which was important if they were to maintain a good relationship with the Roman authorities. Their answer was to kill him and Lazarus too. When Caiaphas suggested killing Jesus, everyone including the moderates fell into line. The council decided that Jesus should die as he could no longer be ignored or contained, but not in such a way that it created a popular uprising. So, they decided they should not do anything during the Passover. There were more ongoing meetings between the chief priests to discuss how they could kill him (John 11:53) in such a way as to avoid a riot. There was no denying the popularity of Jesus, and he always had a crowd around him. For the time being a joint command to the Jews from the chief priests' council and from the Pharisees stated that if anyone knew where He was that they should report it, so he could be arrested (John 11:57). During their discussions It became obvious to Caiaphas that they should bring Jesus before the Romans to be put to death. This would then stop any adverse fall out from Jesus' execution. If they executed him themselves as some suggested, there a protest riot ensued, their situation would be worse than it was now with the Romans.

Jesus disciples were everywhere, and it was not long before Jesus heard of this decision. (John 11:54) Jesus took evasive action. He no longer walked openly amongst the people and instead of returning to the Jordan (where many Pharisees had visited him, so he could be followed), he and his disciples vanished from public gaze. Lazarus was deemed to be safe in Bethany for the time being. It was Jesus the authorities really wanted. Jesus with the twelve and the others who had been with him throughout the mission of the seventy took the ancient road from Jerusalem northwards through the hills of Judea passing through famous old testament sites like Michmash. The road to Bethel from Jericho intersected their journey as they followed the road as it ascended through the thick wooded mountains and well-watered fertile valleys of Ephraim which stretched from Bethel to the valley of Jezreel. It was a journey Jesus had done before at the start of his ministry (see woman of Samaria). Today Jesus he and the twelve stopped and stayed in the town of the same name as the mountains - Ephraim near Bethel[166] and Jesus stayed there (John 11:54) now away from the crowds of recent weeks.

Ephraim February 33AD (John 11:53)

Ephraim was a border town – one of the last in Judea before crossing into Samaria. It was in a sparsely populated part of the country being on the edge of the wilderness. It was not very far from Shiloh – the ancient religious centre of Israel before the days of Samuel. Ephraim was in an area between Judea and Galilee sharing the same history as the rest of the northern kingdom of Israel but distinct from Galilee. It had been in border country between Judea in the south and the Northern Kingdom. In Jesus 'day it had a distinctive culture different from Jerusalem and from Galilee. Here Jesus was safe from the Jewish authorities in Jerusalem. Already as pilgrims arrived in good time for Passover, Jesus was the talk of the town (John 11:55-56 and there had been an edict issued by the chief priests and Pharisees that if anyone recognised him, they should tell them so that he could be arrested. Ephraim was to Jesus what Saxony was for Luther. It was a place of relative safety.

They stayed there for a few days, but Jesus was on a timescale. He wanted to be in Jerusalem for the Passover, and to complete the mission of the seventy by proclaiming the kingdom in the cities and towns of the Jordan valley which they had not yet visited because of the sudden change to their schedule brought about by the raising of

---

[166] Ephraim is mentioned in 2 Chron 13:19 with Bethel in the immediate context. Josephus also links it with Bethel (Wars iv,551))

Lazarus from the dead. They set off towards Sychar before going eastwards to the Jordan.

Samaria March 33AD

The road from Ephraim northwards went through Shiloh to Sychar where they hoped to meet those they knew from earlier days. They did not stay but went on the road they had been forced upon when the elders of the town had refused permission for them to stay a few months before when they were last in the area. The road brought them down into the heat of the Jordan valley and into Judea. Jesus and the twelve were again surrounded by crowds of disciples as they went down towards Jerusalem

Healing of 10 lepers March 33AD (Luke 17:12)

They left Samaria making towards the Jordan. On the borderland between Samaria and Israel they met a gang of men similar in numbers to the twelve. They discovered they were lepers and were together for mutual support because of the social exclusion leprosy brought. They asked for healing and Jesus sent them to Jerusalem with the promise of healing. They went on ahead whilst Jesus taught in the villages they went through. Jesus' progress was slow as he spent time in every town. As they went, the lepers discovered they were healed. One of them returned to say "thank you" to Jesus for he recognized the source of his healing. Jesus talked with him and discovered he was a Samaritan. There was something ironic sending a Samaritan to Jerusalem when for hundreds of years Samaritans had been replacing worship on the mount at Jerusalem for Mount Gerizim in Samaria. The leper now healed did not care about anything except the wonder of Jesus bringing him healing. He joined the disciples and walked with them on their way to Jerusalem where he would have his healing verified by the religious authorities[167]. The disciples of Jesus were now his companions. As Jesus went others joined the disciples swelling the numbers that followed him as he walked.

Rich young Ruler March 33AD
(Matthew 19:16ff Mark 10:17 Luke 18:18-30)

When they reached the Jordan, they went southwards past the mountain fortress of Alexandrium which was one of the many restored by Herod the Great. They went through important cities like Phaesalis[168] to Jericho. There were many important towns in the Jordan rift valley and Jesus had gone through them on his way to Jerusalem many times. This however was different. The seventy had prepared places for him to proclaim the kingdom. As Jesus was setting out to leave (Mark 10:17) one of these Israelite towns (large enough to have a synagogue), a young ruler of that synagogue came running to meet him as Jesus walked along the road. Out of breath, but able to speak he said, "Good Teacher what shall I do to inherit eternal life". Jesus answered his question and asked him to join them. He refused and went away sad. His possessions causing him to hold back from Jesus. Jesus said to those near him about how hard it is for those who are rich to enter the kingdom. The disciples said who can be saved? Peter took a slightly different line. He had got nothing now he had followed Jesus and asked what reward he could expect from following Jesus. Jesus then as his usual practice was turned to the crowd and used this to teach them.

---

[167] Samaritans were still excluded from the temple at some festivals especially at Passover when the doors of the temple were opened at midnight. This was in reaction to what they did when Coponius was procurator under Cyrenius in the first decade of the first century. (Josephus Ant. 18.2.2.). They could still go to the temple at other times.
[168] Josephus Wars 2.167 describes the city as containing Palm groves

SECTION 10

The final journey to the cross

Chapter 59

Jesus foretells his death March 33AD
(Luke 18:31, Mark 10:32-34, Matthew 20:17-19)

The seventy walked with Jesus as they had done throughout his mission around Israel, but there were many others also accompanying them. They were all journeying to Jerusalem for the Passover. When Peter had asked the question about the benefits of following him, Jesus knew he had to talk again with them about the imminent future to explain what would happen. This was not easy because of the sheer numbers of disciples to grab the time together with the twelve on their own. They were surrounded with people all the time every day. Jesus eventually managed to get the twelve on their own from the others. When they were all there Jesus started with something they had known for months "We are going to Jerusalem" he said. Their interest rose when Jesus then said, "All the things written by the prophets concerning the Son of man will be accomplished". They questioned in their hearts whether this the time when God finally redeems Israel out of the domination by other nations of the earth? Many thought so, for they already knew Jesus was the Christ (the Messiah). But Jesus went on to talk about the mockery, insults and death he would receive from the Gentiles. They listened but they could not make "head nor tail" of what Jesus was saying.

James and John make a bid for leadership recognition
(Mark 10:32-45)

Salome, the mother of James and John heard something of what Jesus had said from her sons about his possible suffering. Although neither she nor her sons knew what it meant, they decided that she would present a request to Jesus with her sons to bid for, clarify and obtain a good position with Jesus above the other disciples. She found a good time to do this and approached Jesus privately accompanied by James and John. The mother of James and John had been a supporter of Jesus and her sons throughout his ministry, and gradually her commitment as a disciple had increased. Jesus knew her well. She had journeyed with her sister Mary, Jesus' mother throughout the mission of the seventy. Face to face with Jesus she requested that he appoint her sons as his right hand and left-hand men. Jesus instead of replying to Salome directly, turned to James and John and what he said left the issue open. He said it was not up to him to choose. The Father had already got that in his plan. Jesus could not change that even if he wanted to. The incident would have been left there except news of what had happened leaked out to the other disciples who were not pleased. Jesus had to intervene to resolve the tension that now existed amongst the twelve. He called them together and talked with them about servanthood being the mark of leadership (Matthew 20:25-28) – a theme he would speak about in more depth to them at the Last Supper (John 13:1ff).

Bartimaeus March 33AD (Luke 18 :35-43)

There was no further incident until they approached the ancient city of Jericho. In the time of Jesus, Jericho was in two parts. As Jesus approached from the north he came to the ancient city known to the Old Testament and then after this he went a mile southward to the new city where he would join the road going towards the cliffs westwards onward to Jerusalem. Jericho was rich and had royal status. Beyond the city was the palace built by Herod the Great. It was situated on the high cliffs near the road that led up to the Judean desert and onto Jerusalem. The palace had been often used as the king's winter dwelling, and in fact the place Herod the Great had died. In its history Mark Anthony had given Jericho to Cleopatra queen of Egypt, but when they were defeated in the Rome's civil war, the victor Octavian (Augustus) had given Herod the Great rule over the area. Herod had wished to make his mark and so had embarked on ambitious building projects in the area. His palace complex became the place he entertained foreign dignitaries. During his reign Herod the Great had three attempts at building his palace – each time bigger and more luxurious. In Jesus' time it spanned both sides of the Wadi Qelt connected by a bridge and had stimulated the construction of many buildings nearby.

Jericho both old and new was built on a plain surrounded by mountainous country which sloped toward it. it was an ancient oasis in the desert situated 846 feet below sea level making it even today the lowest city in the world. Palm trees were everywhere, but there were all kinds of cultivated and fruitful trees. Notable amongst the trees was the balsams noted for their healing oil. Jesus passed the oasis near the old city and as he did so passed the famous spring – called Elisha's spring who since he had prayed (2 kings 2:19) had produced water to drink and so aided the development of much prosperous agriculture in this otherwise desert region. It was now marked by a Roman temple built close by. It was not the only water source. Jericho was a garden city using the water from many natural springs there. It had a desert climate with rich alluvial soil and abundant spring water. It had become a desirable place to live for the rich and famous.[169], who lived in fashionable new Jericho.

As Jesus was leaving the old city (Matthew 20:29) at the junction of the roads – one that came from the east met the one from the north where it was possible to go to Bethel in the north and the Dead Sea in the South west. Jesus ignored both these. He kept right on the road to Jerusalem which took him into New Jericho. It was just then he heard a cry "Son of David have mercy on me" (Mark 10:46). Jesus did not respond to everyone who shouted as he walked along, but he recognized that there was something in this. The blind man was calling

---

[169] Josephus Antiquities 5.1 mentions outside the old city as a spring which claimed to help fertility of woman and plant.

him "Son of David" – an unusual term used only before by the angels at Jesus' birth. He saw the Father in his request. He called him and the man by the roadside threw away the special cloak marked him out as a genuine beggar. He was led to Jesus by one of the disciples. When he got near, Jesus asked "what do you want me to do". Lord that I may see", was his clear reply Jesus prayed and Bartimaeus saw clearly. Jesus walked on. Bartimaeus had no life to go back to. The only way was forward and so he joined those following Jesus.

Zacchaeus March 33AD (Luke 19:1-10)

Jesus made his way into modern Jericho where the rich lived. One person who lived there -a tax collector called Zacchaeus- saw the crowd surrounding Jesus as he came and so took the opportunity to climb one of the trees for the best view of Jesus. As a tax collector in prosperous Jericho he was a very rich man. The wealthy attracted by the pleasant climate and abundant water escaped congested cities like Jerusalem to live there for large parts of the year. There were also people who became rich working in Jericho. Their wealth was generated through growing rare spices and plants which benefited from the combination of the climate and water. Chief amongst these was the opobalsamum plant whose oil was one of the costliest in the ancient world and so very profitable to the growers. It must have cost Zacchaeus quite a price to buy the tax rights of the area from the Romans and no doubt he was making a very good living as a tax collector. Jesus stopped as he got near the tree where Zacchaeus was perched. He looked up, called him by name and invited himself and his disciples to stay at his house. Zacchaeus was delighted. He had a large house- a palace by ordinary standards- and Jesus was very welcome. It was Friday and the Sabbath was due to start in the evening. Zacchaeus organized for them all to stay for the Sabbath after which early in the morning they went on to

Jerusalem. He was very happy that Jesus was in his house. It changed his life.[170]

[170] Tradition has it Zacchaeus became the first bishop of Caesarea before Cornelius

Chapter 60

The onward journey to Jerusalem (March 33AD)

They had stayed with Zacchaeus for the Sabbath. On the Sunday they said goodbye to Zacchaeus and the other disciples they had met in Jericho. Jesus set out with the twelve surrounded by many others and set off ahead of them towards Jerusalem (Luke 19:28). Jesus was walking with the same determination the disciples had first seen when Jesus had been going to Jerusalem from Capernaum in the autumn (Luke 9:51). He took the familiar road up past the royal palace/castle which lay to the south of the road as he continued up the steep ascent on the flaky limestone surface which characterized the major road to Jerusalem. There were a crowd of disciples with him. Five miles from Jericho they went through the steep mountain pass called "red" after the colour of the rocks and then walked the remaining thirteen miles to Jerusalem. They were not the only ones taking this route that day. Although many had arrived in the week before, crowds were converging on Jerusalem for the Passover. The chief priests had ensured everything was ready. Any bridges were repaired which had been damaged during the winter so that the pilgrims would not be hindered in any way, and tombs which were in every direction for over a mile around the outside of the city were painted white, so no-one would accidentally defile themselves by touching them. Each year this was a major undertaking. Jerusalem would be full of pilgrims travelling from all over Israel and beyond. Passover this year was on the following Sabbath (Friday evening April 3rd until Saturday April 4th). No-one would ever forget the events that would take place before the next Sabbath could begin. It was now six days before Passover (John 12:1).

Palm Sunday (Mark 11 Matthew 21:1-11; John 12:1)

They approached Bethany on their way to Jerusalem around midday. Whilst still a mile or so from Bethany, Jesus sent two of the disciples into the nearby village Bethphage, to get a donkey with its colt. They paused at Bethany before making the final part of the journey during which the proposed meal to celebrate Lazarus' being raised from the dead was arranged for the following evening. It was now afternoon by the time they were ready to travel. The disciples brought the donkey and colt to Jesus. They returned with them in hand telling Jesus it had happened just as He said it would. Jesus and the others with him left Bethany, the two disciples making sure the donkey and colt also came with them. Jesus however paused, stating his intention was to ride the donkey to Jerusalem. When this was clear some quickly got some clothes (Luke 19:35) to provide padding for Jesus to sit on and helped him onto the donkey[171] (Matthew 21:7), and in the early afternoon sun they set off to make the short trip together. They ascended the familiar path which rose steeply up the Mount of Olives to Bethphage where the terrain levelled out a little before then descending on the other side towards Jerusalem. They travelled to Jerusalem at a much slower pace than Jesus and the others had covered from Jericho to Bethany. The spring equinox was past and so the days were noticeably longer than even a few weeks before, and Jesus and the twelve would return to Bethany that evening. The afternoon sun was bright as they made their way down the mount of Olives. In the crowd were some of Jesus' relatives. Salome and his mother were with some of the other women who had supported his itinerant ministry from when it used to be just in Galilee – Joanna and well as Mary Magdalene. Joanna had many contacts and had arranged for many to stay in Jerusalem for the feast. Other disciples too had relatives who were attending the feast, and they would stay with them. Whilst they were safe to stay in the city, it was not safe for Jesus. The twelve would go wherever Jesus went and so also, they would not be staying with the other disciples in the city during this time.

---

[171] Jesus probably road both animals during the journey. (notice "them" in Matthew 21:7)

The crowd made up of men and women were rejoicing because of the miracles Jesus had done (Luke 19:37). The first part of the journey was as expected. It was only after they passed through Bethphage when Jerusalem came into view that it all changed. The whole crowd began to sing what they sang every year in the temple "Blessed is the King who comes in the name of the Lord (Psalm 118:26. This seemed inappropriate to some of Simon's friends who shouted from the crowd "Tell them to be quiet" (Luke 19:39) but Jesus recognized the Lord of the universe was behind this and so he said "I tell you if these should keep quiet the stones would immediately cry out". They continued the descent towards Jerusalem and as they did so the temple itself which had been obscured by the Mount of Olives came into view. Jesus began to weep as he interceded for the city (Luke 19:41-43), as its towering walls got ever closer. He rode the donkey down the steep winding track which took him across the valley Kidron to the east gate of the city.[172] Jesus arrived in Jerusalem early afternoon. The noise of the crowd shouting Hosanna and the accompanying disturbance through the narrow streets of the city caused quite a stir. Jesus arrived at the temple, left the donkey in safe hands and went into the temple. He knew by now it was too late to start anything. He just arranged to meet the disciples in the temple the following day and walked out of the city with the twelve and the donkey back to Bethany (Mark 11:11) [173]where they had been invited to a meal. The events of this day were enough for that day. Jesus knew there would need to be the cleansing of the temple, but that would wait for the following day.

---

[172] Susa Gate which was situated near the present day bricked up Golden Gate which was built in the middle ages.

[173] Matthew and Luke omit the detail of Jesus cleansing the temple on the following day. The meal at Bethany is mentioned by Matthew & Mark (not mentioned in Luke) in the context when Judas betrays Jesus because it was at the meal that the seeds of his betrayal were sown (see Matthew 26:6ff Mark 14,). Luke just mentions the betrayal to the chief priests by Judas in the same time as Mark and Matthew

Chapter 61

Return to Bethany—Sunday
(John 12:1ff Mark 11:11, Matthew 26:2, Mark 14:3-11 [174])

When they arrived at Bethany, there were many to greet them. The supper had been specially prepared for Jesus and those who were with him to celebrate the miracle of Lazarus' return to life. Some were relatives of Lazarus– some of whom had travelled from afar- coming to Jerusalem for the Passover as well as friends from Jerusalem and local villages around. Martha and Mary's house, though used to visitors, was not large enough to host such a gathering, and so they had arranged for the supper to be at the home of Simon who was sometimes referred to according to his religious party as Pharisee, sometimes as his medical condition a leper[175], Amongst the twelve when they wanted to talk to this Simon they needed to make a distinction between him and other Simons both in the twelve and in the wider group of disciples. They neither wanted to make his old allegiance to the Pharisees (especially as many enemies of Jesus were of this party) nor to make his past illness his identity so instead they referred to his ethnic background "Canaanite". It was a special meal to celebrate the raising of her brother Lazarus and she wanted to do it. Simon the Canaanite [176] and his son Judas were coming back to their home with Jesus. Just as Peter had hosted them at Capernaum so now it was Simon the Canaanite and his son Judas, the only difference `being Martha (and perhaps Mary) oversaw the meal arrangements. The preparation was done before 6pm

---

[174] The meal where Mary anoints is included in Mark and Matthew at the time Judas betrays Jesus to the chief priests as the supper provided the motivation for Judas.

[175] Simon must have been healed from his leprosy because it was unlawful to eat with lepers.

[176] John 12:4 "Judas Iscariot Son of Simon" – known as Simon the leper. "Son of Simon " was omitted from the Latin Vulgate, Syriac, Persian and Ethiopic versions (quoted in Gills exposition of the whole bible)and so is omitted in some English translations.

when they ate together. The sun set in early April around 7pm, so there was light enough as the meal began. Candles were placed on the tables to be lit when needed and a fire with its welcome heat cast its light against the walls into the room. They sat down on the floor to eat off the low tables laden with food. Martha was busy as usual putting dishes of delightful food on every table. The atmosphere was celebratory, and Jesus was the honoured guest alongside Lazarus who sat near Jesus (John 12:2). Such had been expected by Simon and Judas. What happened next was unexpected. Mary full of gratitude for her brother's life being restored remembered a time when she was grateful to Jesus for the deep well-being his words of forgiveness had brought dealing with many wounds of her past. Then she had tried to anoint Jesus but had been overcome as she got near and found herself unable to move, crying at his feet. This time she was determined to do it right. She took some very expensive perfume into the house and at the right moment broke it pouring the rich oil over Jesus' head. There was more oil than she had anticipated so she carried the broken container round to his feet and anointed them. She had in effect anointed Jesus from head to toe (Mark 14:3 John 12:3). Jesus recognized this was for his burial. The oil began to flow over Jesus' feet. Last time she had wiped her tears with her hair. She now did the same with the oil. Simon and Judas recalled the last time Mary had done this I their house and they were not impressed on either occasion. Mary was the sister of Lazarus and obviously delighted at the miracle they had all witnessed, so it was acceptable. Simon certainly was not going to think anything negative about this as on the last occasion Jesus had read his mind and told a parable at his expense. There was however this time some murmuring against her amongst the twelve (Mark 14:4). Judas was displeased with Mary's actions on the basis of waste and verbalized what the others were saying amongst themselves (John 12:4). Jesus however defended her actions calling her action "beautiful"[177]. Judas kept quiet as his father had done when rebuked by Jesus last time. Underneath though, he was concerned that the attention of this woman was turning his head, or he was becoming proud through the adulation of so many people following the miracle that had happened to Lazarus. Here were seeds of betrayal being sown in their midst, but no-one recognized it.

Return to Jerusalem—Monday
(Mark 11:11, Matthew21:12-14, John 12:12)

They had some breakfast of sorts before taking the road to Jerusalem. Martha and Lazarus were there to see them off. They were not coming to Jerusalem with them. It was now too dangerous a place for Lazarus as they knew the authorities there had wanted him dead to quash the talk of the amazing miracle that Jesus had brought him back to life.

Passover this year coincided with the following Sabbath so early on Monday Jesus left Bethany. He was hungry as he walked down the slopes and approached Jerusalem. He went aside from the path because he could see a fig tree with leaves on it. (figs and leaves grow together). Jesus went over to take a fig from the tree[178]. He looked amongst the leaves. Not a single fig was there. It was pointed out to Jesus that figs were unlikely to be on the tree as June was still some months away when figs would again be fully in season. This did not stop Jesus cursing the tree. As they approached the city, they passed the very large monuments to the prophets which had been built recently[179] and could be seen easily from either side of the valley.

---

[177] Zechariah 11:10-14 contain a foretelling of these events re. Jesus betrayal.
[178] Near the lake of Gennesaret figs and grapes hung from the trees for ten months of the year (Josephus wars 3.10.8 Whiston note)
[179] Tomb and monument which is today called the tomb of Zechariah was cut out of the rock during Jesus' lifetime

The disciples and others who had heard about all that had happened the previous day came out from Jerusalem (John 12:12) to meet them. As the previous afternoon they were shouting "Hosanna" as they went on across the Kidron valley and up the hill into the city. Jesus knew the full business from Palm Sunday had not been completed and the shouts echoing his triumphant entry into Jerusalem the previous day emphasized this. Jesus decided to sit on the donkey they had brought with them as they went on towards the eastern gate (John 12:12-13). Once in the city they went up the steps to the temple site and were soon onto the paved marble area of the outer court which was at its least 39m above the street level.

The outer court (Court of the Gentiles) was always a busy place with people walking through, buying and selling animals for sacrifice as well as temple business. With the approach of the feast it was much busier. The Court of the Gentiles was large (750-foot square[180]). Jesus went past one of the marble screens warning non-Jews of imminent death up the fourteen steps onto the fifteen-foot-wide terrace which surrounded the inner temple through the Beautiful gate which led into the temple itself accessing the first court called the Court of the Women. He saw money changers and sellers of pigeons there who should be outside on the paved area he had just passed through. They were encroaching into the temple building itself in the Court of the Women[181]. There had set up extra tables because of the increased demand at the festival and the purification rites which preceded the feast. For the second time in his

[180] According to Jewish tradition. The temple was levelled by the Romans in 70AD and then a temple to Jupiter was built on it. The Roman platform created for the Jupiter temple forms the site for the temple mount mosque today)
[181] Commentaries tend to state that Jesus cleansed the money changers etc. out of the court of the gentiles where they normally operated at least since the building of the second temple I the time of Haggai. But the bible text says "temple". Acts 3:1,2 references Peter and John going into the temple through "Gate Beautiful" which was the gate from the court of the gentiles into the court of the women. If temple refers just to the temple (rather than the whole site), Jesus cleanses the money changers etc. out of the court of women.

life (see John 2) Jesus rose up to drive them out. They knew they should not be there. The usual place was where they had bought and sold for centuries – the paved area which we know as the Court of the Gentiles. He made a whipcord and began to drive our those who bought and sold. People went quickly when they saw Jesus turning tables over. They risked losing their hard-earned money. They saw retreat as the better side of valour and it was not long before the temple was free, and the money changers and sellers reluctantly tried to find a place in the Court of the Gentiles somewhere underneath the colonnades knowing that now they would have less footfall and profit.

Jesus remained by the gate while he stopped everyone with anything which might be for sale from coming in. Things brought for sacrifice did not need to be taken through the court of the women – there were gates to the north or to the south to bring them into the temple. So, when they protested they were not selling anything but just carrying something through, Jesus would not let them do it. (Mark 11:16). Nothing should displace this area as a place of prayer. Those taking their recently bought doves for sacrifice could go directly to the Israelites courtyard via the north gate or to the altar via the south gate which was the place where larger animals were taken.

Just as clearing the mourners helped the miracle of the raising of Jairus' daughter, so the cleansing of the temple allowed a greater freedom to preach and teach, as well as provided more space for the crowds to gather to hear Jesus in the days ahead. People began to fill the place where the tables had been, and the true purpose of this temple began to be reflected in the atmosphere of religious devotion.

The commotion caused by religious zealotry in the temple was not unusual especially at times of religious feasts. Devotion sometimes brought about such events. But what was different was the blind and the lame who could get as far as the Court of the Women came over to

Jesus and he healed them (21:14). There was a lot of noise – whole families including the children witnessed the miracles Jesus did. Many were making emotional responses to the marvelous healings that were occurring. Children were always in the Court of the Women and so disturbance and noise from young babies was common. The noise on this occasion was excessive, was not caused by a child in distress and included older children who ought to know better than make a disturbance. It was not long before Jesus (rather than their mothers) who was approached to tell them to be quiet. He refused. This would be the last day that healing was a major part of Jesus' ministry. For the rest of the week Jesus would teach in the temple as he had done before, but on that day the blind could see, and the lame would walk after being healed. The chief priests and scribes were very angry (Matthew 21:15). They tried to find ways to get rid of Jesus (Mark 11:18), but they were thwarted by the popularity Jesus enjoyed combined with the astonishment at his teaching. Although Jesus had been throughout Israel, for many this was the first time they had heard him teach and the people loved it. (Mark 11:18). The chief priests decided to plant spies amongst the crowd and hoped to trip Jesus up in something he said when he was teaching there (Luke 20:20).

Chapter 62

Teaching in the temple
(Luke 20:1-38, Matthew 21:23-26:3, Mark 12:1-44)

They left the temple in the afternoon to go to Bethany for the final time (Matthew 21:17)) As they went they saw the fig tree they had passed in the morning now withered and dead. They were amazed to see it had withered so quickly and when they said so, Jesus just stated it showed the normal power of faith and prayer. They slept safely at Bethany before returning early to Jerusalem the following morning where they headed for the temple where Jesus would now be teaching. When he arrived, there were already many disciples eager to hear him.

Tuesday

It was now Tuesday and for three days Jesus would arrive in the temple early in the morning with the twelve to teach (Luke21:38). By the time Jesus arrived there was already many disciples gathered in the outer court waiting for him. He went through the outer court up the steps into the court of the women which was the usual place where Jesus spoke as it was accessible to every Jew. Here was the treasury. Jesus would sometimes teach here and sometimes he was seen elsewhere on the temple site. Jesus would vary where he was. On this day he told the parable of the two sons, and the parable of the marriage banquet amongst others (Matthew 21:28ff; 22:1fff) Throughout the day when disciples were there he would teach them, and when there were some bystanders who were not his disciples but just curious to hear what was being said, Jesus would preach the good news of the kingdom inviting them to come closer and join them. (Luke 20:1). The temple was open during daylight hours just before the morning sacrifice and closed after the evening sacrifice.

During the day Jesus had several encounters with the religious authorities. Whilst in the temple it would be unseemly for Caiaphas or Annas as high Priests[182] to dialogue directly with Jesus in such a setting, but they were monitoring the situation and engineering schemes behind the scenes. The scribes worked with the chief priests (Mark 11:18) and shared the same consternation about the actions of Jesus in the temple. The scribes were the lawyers of the day and the chief priests were the judges who were a constituted body (see John 18:35) able to hand people over to trial. The chief priests were the religious power behind the Sanhedrin which made and ruled according to the religious laws of the day. The scribes and chief priests for all their authority could not take on the people. The scribes accompanied by some of the chief priests to add weight to their request (Mark 11:27) approached the Pharisees who were more respected by the people and together they tried to catch Jesus out. They waited for their moment. Jesus was walking around the temple courts, (Mark 11:27) so he had less of an audience and asked him their question "What is the basis of your authority that you take it upon yourself to do what you do". This came directly from Jesus cleansing the temple the previous day. They hoped by their question to expose Jesus as unqualified or in his actions being above his station so that they could undermine his influence. Jesus had seen some of his questioners the previous day when they had approached him to try to keep the noise down from the children and young people who were shouting praise at the healings that were happening then. (Matthew 21:15) Jesus noted how they were not impressed by the unique actions of healing in the temple which no-one else had ever done and recognized the hate in their hearts[183]. He remained at peace (John 15:24). God the Father would give him what he

---

[182] Josephus states (Wars.1v,151,160)that once a high priest always a high priest. Annas had not been high priest for years. Members of his family had held the position. Caiaphas was his son in law who became high priest in 18AD

[183] "those who hate me without a cause" Psalm 69:4

needed to say. (John 12:49, John 5:19). Jesus pointed them to John the Baptist – a contentious figure to the authorities but a popular prophet in the eyes of the people. Jesus by doing so put them in a difficult position. Jesus was addressing their question. He knew His authority came from the One who had also called the forerunner, John the Baptist. He had known He was the Christ and had said so. The questioners however could not say whether John's authority was from God or man because of the crowd's reaction and so as they refused to answer, Jesus did not have to give an answer either. Jesus continued to teach whilst they were still there. He taught the parable about tenants killing the son to seize a vineyard. The Pharisees knew the parable was against them (Luke 20:19) but they could not say anything because they did not want to expose publicly their desire to arrest Jesus and get him out of the way. When they took their leave even more determined that Jesus had to die. They then asked those who appeared to be righteous but were spies in the crowd to see if they could catch Jesus out by what he said (Luke 20:20). They engineered an opportunity to try to trap Jesus. They were by the treasury, so it provided a good backdrop for the question "Should we pay taxes to Caesar". They hoped that whichever reply Jesus gave he would be condemned. If Jesus said "yes" it would offend some of the religious supporters and if he said "no" they could arrest him for treason against Rome. Jesus however asked to see a coin. And asked whose image is on it "Pay to Caesar what is Caesar's but you who are made in the image of God, so you are to give to God what is God's. They were dumbfounded and kept quiet (Luke 20:26.) Further questions followed. This time it was from the Sadducees. They were no friends of the Pharisees, but they thought they could ridicule the beliefs of the scripture-believing Jews of which Jesus was part. They gave a common story they had used in their schooling to ridicule the doctrine of the resurrection. The story they told was of a widow who married her dead husband's brother as the law states. There were seven brothers so as each brother died she married the next one. The punchline followed: -

In the resurrection "whose wife would she be? they asked. Jesus spoke directly to the issue, saying there is no marriage and no giving of marriage in heaven. The responsibilities around the creation of a marriage no longer exist in the new creation. He then addressed the doctrine of life after death. He quoted a verse when God introduced himself to Moses at the burning bush "I am God of Abraham, Isaac and Jacob". He is not the God of the dead but the living. The Sadducees were silenced. The teachers of the law were also there listening to this reply, and they were impressed. One of the teachers of the law asked a question of which the most important commandment is. Jesus said Love the Lord your God with all your heart soul mind and strength and your neighbour as yourself. Jesus then asked a question to the teachers of the law. "if David calls the Messiah "Lord" how can the Christ also be the "son of David". It was a question which could open debate within their hearts about who Jesus really was. Each thing Jesus said had an opportunity for them to find out the truth. Jesus Son of David after the flesh but was also the only begotten Son of God. None were that serious to seek the answer. Jesus then turned to his disciples and exposed the scribes' hypocrisy. This further incensed his enemies.

As we have seen, Jesus was in the court surrounded by both men and women near the place where people could bring their money gifts to God. The money given was used for the running of the temple. Jesus noticed a woman give two mites into one of the large treasure chests nearby. Jesus said to his disciples that she had given all. None of the disciples knew any more than that but it was not unusual for Jesus to arrange to give gifts to the poor. Only Judas as treasurer would know (see John 12:5[184]).

---

[184] John 12:5 shows Jesus regularly gave to the poor out of money given him.

Jesus and the twelve left the temple. Several disciples came up to Jesus intending to show him the buildings of the temple (Matthew 24:1). When they made comment about the beautiful building (Mark 13:1), Jesus said there would come a day when it would be thrown down. This was heard by others including the spies who would later stand and accuse Jesus of claiming to destroy the temple. Jesus had said he would destroy the temple and rebuild it in three days when at the start of his ministry (John 2). Witnesses would disagree about what they heard this afternoon when they spoke up in Annas's courtyard a few days hence, but the source of what was said, was this conversation overheard as Jesus left the temple.

The prophecy of the destruction of the temple birthed a discussion amongst the twelve about the end times after they had left the other disciples back in the city. Jesus left Jerusalem before nightfall when he could pass relatively undetected amongst the people. They went to the olive groves called the garden of Gethsemane just across the Kidron valley directly east from the temple and there, hidden by the trees, was safe from those who wanted him dead. Jesus stayed at the place he had found the previous year to be a safe refuge. Jesus knew once still and quiet amongst the olive trees at night it was almost impossible to be detected. In the evening before the sun went down Jesus sat down with Peter, James, John and Andrew (Mark 13:3) on a place overlooking the Kidron valley directly opposite the temple (Mark 13:3). Jesus explained in great depth about the future -both of the judgement of Jerusalem which would occur in under forty years' time , and also the end times. When the twelve joined them Jesus also spoke again about his betrayal and death before they each found a place to sleep so they would be ready for the following day.

Wednesday

The next day dawned. Its first silvery light made it just possible to pick out where the disciples were sleeping. The red sky to the east soon disappeared as the sun appeared above the Mount of Olives making the walls of Jerusalem shine pure white. They were up early. It was damp on the ground, as they got to their feet, but spring was always special. The cold of January and February were long over. The almond trees were blossoming pink in the spring sunshine and wild flowers were appearing everywhere you looked - even in the cracks of the roads. Though not every day would be free from rain, every spring day was wonderful. It was the best time to be in Jerusalem

Chapter 63

The Betrayal begins—Wednesday
(Matthew 26:2 Mark 14:3-11, John 12:2-11)

It was now two days before the Passover which start on Friday evening at 6pm. [185] Whilst Jesus had been teaching in the temple, Judas had been working out how to betray Jesus. Ever since Sunday night he had been unhappy. He had not liked the fact Jesus had defended Mary when she wasted the perfume on him at the meal. All the others had agreed with him until Jesus spoke, and whilst everyone had moved on, Judas could not. He thought Jesus should not be acting like a despot receiving expensive perfume when there was more pressing expenditure. The meal had been good in Bethany, but they were times when they lived a hand to mouth existence. Food was expensive to buy, and he was after all in charge of the money. He had to pay the bills. As he continued to think like this a thought emerged. He had seen the chief priests approach Jesus and challenge him about the cleansing of the temple. He could go to them and offer to betray him, but he had needed a plan that would work. He now knew where Jesus was staying at night, so by Wednesday morning he had a plan when and how he could betray Jesus. He determined that day to approach the chief priests. He told no-one of his plans. It was relatively easy to slip away from the others. He had done it many times before to buy food or for other reasons. He approached the chief priests with his plan unseen by any of the disciples. The chief priests saw this as a break through. Finally, one of the disciples of Jesus was coming to his senses and joining them rather than this religious upstart. They had already decided not to arrest Jesus during the feast because of the uproar, but Judas' offer of betrayal

---

[185] Mark 14:1,10 states the time when Judas went to the priests not the timing of the supper. The reason he mentions the supper was because it was as a result of his negative view of the anointing of Jesus by Mary (see John's gospel) that he went to betray Jesus

opened to them the possibility of a secret arrest and a quick trial before the Roman authorities which was the only way they could deal with it. The people would not – in fact could not- riot at the Romans in the same way as they could against the chief priests who were friends neither of Rome or of the people. The chief priests were delighted at what they saw as good fortune. They gave Judas thirty pieces of silver. After all, it was right, so they thought, that Judas should be paid for his service. Judas went back to Jesus and the twelve in the temple.

Thursday

The day (Mark 14:12) after Judas had been to the priests, was the day that everyone got their houses ready for the Passover [186]. Like the Israel of old preparing for the first Passover, they also got rid of all leavened bread and it was during this day that lambs were sacrificed in readiness for the Passover which would take place on the evening of the following day. Many did not want to leave the sacrifice of the lamb until Friday because there every family in Jerusalem wanted a lamb for the special Passover meal which needed to have been cooked before Passover started on Friday evening. The day before Passover was called "the day of preparation" (John 19:14) and it officially started on Thursday evening at sunset. (Mark 14:12). The Passover was the focus of the first two days of the feast of unleavened bread which continued for the week.

On Thursday morning Jesus and his disciples awoke amongst the olive trees and began to discuss the arrangements for the day. Because of Jesus' words (Matthew 26:2), they had decided to have the Passover on Thursday. Jesus and the twelve were a family and Jesus had said (Luke 22:15) they should hold a Passover meal together on the Thursday evening. He was really looking forward to this (Luke 22:15). The

---

[186] It formed an important part of the feast of unleavened bread like for us Christmas Eve does for Christmas

disciples would then be able on Friday night to eat the Passover with their families. Although Jesus spoke of his suffering, none could foresee how that would happen and so were content to stay with a plan which ignored the suffering hoping no doubt that what Jesus had said would not really happen. Jesus instructed Peter and John (Luke 22:8) to follow a man carrying a water pot. This was a job which women normally did, so they went through the Water gate and up to the pool at Siloam where so many filled their water pots each day and waited for a man to come. They then followed him up the steep streets and alleys of Jerusalem until he went into his house. They knocked on the door told them what Jesus had said and he showed them upstairs into a large room built which was the length and breadth of the whole house below. It had within it a big table and benches each side with cushions. There was plenty of space for thirteen men – the room could accommodate as many as one hundred (see Acts1:15). They thanked the man and got ready for the evening little realizing that this would be called later the "Upper Room" and would feature strongly in the resurrection appearances of Jesus.

The two disciples departed from the Upper room towards the temple. Jesus had sent them to organise the meal, and so they had to buy ingredients for the Passover meal, chief amongst the ingredients was the lamb which for Passover had to be slaughtered at the temple. The two disciples chose the lamb, bought it and queued up in the temple until it was sacrificed This was not unusual. Many bought the lamb on the Thursday also and had it properly sacrificed at the temple to make certain they had the lamb ready for the meal on Friday evening. Thousands were at the Passover and there were only so many sacrifices that could be accomplished on the preparation day which by the time it started on Thursday evening was too dark to get a lamb and would finish on 6pm the following day when the Passover meal would be served. The two disciples hurried back to the upper room, so they were able to start to cook the lamb with the herbs they had bought as the Passover prescribed, and prepare the room for Jesus and the rest of the twelve.

The Last Supper—Thursday (The first day of Unleavened Bread 6pm Thursday until 6pm Friday) (Luke 22:1-39)

After Jesus had finished teaching in the temple, Jesus and the rest of the twelve were led to the Upper Room. Peter and John had worked as a team and one had stayed cooking the meal whilst the other had gone to lead the others. They all arrived at the Upper Room whilst itbws still light. This was the first time any had been there. Peter and John had set the table well and had cooked a meal that smelt delicious. They took their seats and started to eat. When the lamb stew pot was empty, Jesus then arose from the table and picked up some water and bowl and began to wash their feet (John 13:2ff). Jesus in this way gave a lesson about serving one another they would never forget, though at the time they had much to learn. Jesus returned to his seat and then said, "one of you will betray me" (Mark 14:17, John13: 18ff). This made them all be sorrowful wondering if they would be the one. Jesus then took the bread and broke it and gave it to them saying this is my body. The disciples took their bread and reached forward to the pot which had been full of meat and vegetables an hour before, to take any remnants of the meal by putting their bread into it. Whilst they were finishing the contents of the dish between them, the disciples were still thinking about who would betray Jesus for he had said it would be one of them. This soon degenerated into an argument as to who would be the greatest. (Luke 22:24). Jesus reiterated his teaching about serving as the mark of greatness. The stew pot was now nearly wiped clean. Jesus took the last piece of bread and put it in the dish quoting a verse about the one who eats bread with me has lifted up his heel against me " (John 13:18) Peter signalled to John who was sitting next to Jesus to ask him who it was who would betray him, Jesus said to John it was he who he handed the last piece of bread to. Jesus wiped the bread round the dish and then handed it to Judas. Jesus then said to Judas to go, and he left. The disciples were not concerned about this. Judas often had been given tasks to do they knew nothing about because he was the treasurer. They did not see the connection between betrayal and Judas' departure. Jesus then taught about his departure and the coming of the Holy Spirit (John 14-16). He then prayed a spontaneous prayer and they sang a hymn together and then left the city.

Chapter 64

The arrest of Jesus Thursday (Luke 22:39-53)

When Judas left it was already dark, and it was an hour or so later that Jesus and the eleven made their way from the house onto the street below to make their way in the darkness through the water gate towards the Kidron Valley. They walked north parallel to the Kidron valley past the simple rock hewn tombs of the rich marked out with their elaborate monuments. They climbed up the mount of Olives. Every day they had done this but seldom at night. They stumbled as they climbed the steep hill in the dark and Jesus said to them all that they would stumble and run away because of him (Mark 14:26,27). They all were askance, denying this would happen. Peter said even if everyone else did so, he would not. Jesus turned to him saying he would deny him that night even before the cock could crow three times to herald the dawn. Peter spoke even more his determination not to deny him as did the other disciples. They soon came to the flatter terraced ground which defined the "garden" of Gethsemane and went to their familiar place amongst the olive trees. When they got there, they began to get ready to sleep. Jesus said he was troubled. He knew within the hour he would be arrested (Matthew 26:40,45)and his suffering the Father had foretold would start. Jesus requested instead of them sleeping they should watch and pray. He took the three Peter James and John and went a short distance from them.(Matthew 26:36) They could see Jesus was greatly distressed. His prayer was urgent and deep. In the moonlight, they saw sweat dropping off him like drops of blood. The sorrow of Jesus transferred as a burden to the disciples who could not stay awake. (Luke 22:45). Jesus tried to wake them up. They awoke just to hear him pray "Father take this cup from me but not my will but yours be done" (Matthew 26:42) before falling back into sleep. Jesus came to the disciples again and though some stirred it was obvious that they were asleep. This time he left them to pray the same prayers he had prayed before as he waited for the betrayer to come.

It was with surprise that a few hours later they were awoken by Jesus who warned them of the oncoming soldiers to arrest him. The "soldiers" were not professional Roman soldiers. They were personal security for the high priest – more a vigilante group in the eyes of the Roman military. Their duties ranged from civic duties to debt collection; from carrying out the will of the Sanhedrin to ensuring the safety of the high priest and his family. At the front of the group was Judas who identified Jesus by a kiss and Jesus was quickly seized, bound and held tight. The disciples fled in to the darkness. Peter and John hid and watched as they took Jesus away, and followed quietly at a distance. All sleep had now gone.

The group of soldiers returned fairly satisfied with the outcome of their arrest. Jesus had come without a fight though one of the disciples had tried to put up a fight cutting off the ear of one of the group with a sword – Malchus was his name. Jesus had intervened. The fight stopped as soon as it started and Malchus had had his ear restored. They went now went through the dark streets to go to the house of Annas and Caiaphas (John 18:13, Matthew 26:57) which lay on the west side of the temple mount[187]near the old Hasmonean palace where the high priest used to live in the times of the Maccabees but now only carried out business transactions from there. There were records of debts owed and property owned kept there. Annas' family had continued in the office of High Priest since his deposition in 16AD and so had maintained his seat of power. First his son Eleazar took the office and then Caiaphas in 18AD a year or so after he had married his daughter. Caiaphas

---

[187] Josephus says the High Priest's house near the old Hasmonean palace in mid-1st century. It is probable that this is the same place as the house of Caiaphas in 33AD (Josephus wars 2.17.6

remained High Priest until the Romans again decided to appoint another (which would be not until 36AD when Pilate also would be called back by Caesar).

Trial before the chief priests Friday (Mark 14:53-15:20,John 18-19:13, Luke 22:1-23:25, Mattthew 27:1-31)

They went through the strong outer gates of the large building and ascended the stairs which led into an open courtyard. His guards took Jesus through into the house so that Annas could question him about his disciples and doctrine whilst the witnesses were assembling. This was normal procedure. At the start of any trial they needed the facts of the case. The meeting with Annas was a preliminary stage before the public trial allowing all accusations and witnesses to be heard. Scribes and the Chief priests who would eventually pronounce judgement gathered in the adjoining hall for the trial. It was the largest house in Jerusalem except for the palaces. [188]The spies that the chief priest had placed amongst the crowd when Jesus taught in the temple with other witnesses were quickly brought from their homes into the courtyard. Jesus was led bound under guard and placed in full view some distance from the High Priest. Witnessed shouted from the crowd as the judges sat on the platform above them.

Peter and John had been able to mingle with the servants of the high priest and officers as they followed the captors with their prisoner. Peter wanted to see the outcome for himself (Matthew 26:58) though he had no expectation of anything good coming from it.

There had been many men sent to ensure Jesus' arrest. Jesus was seldom alone. As it happened the arrest had been straight forward, and they had returned without trouble. Apart from the arrest of Jesus,

---

[188] For further details see https://www.thegospelcoalition.org/blogs/justin-taylor/is-this-the-high-priestly-palace-where-jesus-stood-trial/

Malchus' loss of his ear and remarkable healing was gossiped amongst the servants as they walked and afterwards when they met their wives and girlfriends.

The fortified door to the street was opened by one of the servant girls (John18:17). No-one was allowed in without permission. Even at night there could be those homeless or fanatics who would seek to sponge off or threaten the family, so there was always someone on the gate.

Peter was refused entry and had to stay outside. He was not allowed but John could go in – he was known to the high priest (John 18:16). John saw that Peter had been stopped at the gate. John now on the inside was able to have a word with the servant girl in charge of the gate and got Peter in as far as the courtyard. John went on ahead to get a closer view of proceedings, but Peter knew he had to stay where he was towards the back of the courtyard. Meanwhile in the courtyard some of his servants went to one of the storage sheds in the courtyard to get dry wood to make a fire. It was cold and they all knew this could be a while. Some servants had already gone out to summon those they thought would testify against Jesus. They also went out to members of the council and leaders of the synagogues to come at first light in the morning, so they could pass on the news of the successful arrest of Jesus and ask them to convene an official legal gathering, so they could pass Jesus onto to the Roman authorities for trial and execution.

The fire was lit in the centre of the courtyard and once the wood was well alight coals were placed on it to increase and maintain the warmth. Beyond it Peter could see the backs of many enemies of Jesus some who would stand up and testify against Him. As the fire grew, and he felt the cold more, he gathered like many others towards the fire. Round the fire mixing with the servants who were making sure the business of the high priest could continue even at night, were some of the witnesses at the trial as well as soldiers of the high priest. They were used to the courtyard becoming the public gallery of the court of the high priest when crimes linked to the temple or the breaking of religious laws were to be judged, but this happened at night only in exceptional circumstances.

Peter had to be on his guard at this place, but he was pleased to be able to get this far wondering how the events of the night would turn out. His earlier sleep in Gethsemane had gone. Adrenalin and anxiety filled his heart. He was wide awake. The events in the court were on a raised area which formed part of the house of Annas, so Peter could look up and see the proceedings. The courtyard was an open space in the centre of the building complex. Ahead of them on a raised-up level was a luxurious reception space which meant the trial was witnessed. Peter stood at first towards the back of the courtyard. The chief priests from the temple, the elders of the synagogues of Jerusalem (Matthew 26:59) took their places alongside many of the council and scribes in the make shift courtroom – the great and good had been assembled for this and there were a lot of them. Their role was to pronounce judgement based on the evidence presented by public witness. This would then be presented to the full council meeting in the morning. Jesus stood before them bound with guards near at hand. From the public courtyard stood up witness after witness but none could agree. Peter knew Jesus was innocent and hoped that justice would prevail.

Outside in the courtyard the woman who had been watching the gate looked closely at him. She had now locked the outer gate come into the courtyard passing the place where Peter was sitting (Matthew 26:69) When Peter had come in she had thought she had seen him with Jesus in the last few days. There was something about his face which had caught her attention then. She saw that same face now, but it was dark, and she could be mistaken. Peter just said firmly "Woman I am not "and she kept her peace. After all it would be unlikely that a follower of Jesus would gain access to the house of Annas. Those around the fire heard

Peter speak and recognized he spoke with a Galilean accent, and so accused him of being a follower of Jesus but by his denials he was able to convince them otherwise.

It was clear that Annas was getting exasperated. It was nearly dawn and so far, they could not get any testimony to ensure Jesus' guilt which would mean he could legitimately pass Jesus onto the full council to be tried and handed over to the Romans. They needed two people to give the same testimony for an accusation to be legally valid to be tried by the religious court which would convene later. The only testimony that seemed to have some credibility was that Jesus had said he would destroy the temple and rebuild it in three days" but even here they disagreed about him saying his aim was to destroy the temple. (see John 2:19). It would not be easy to take even this testimony and make a case for the execution of Jesus. Finally, he had a break. Jesus said something "hereafter you shall see the Son of man sitting at the right hand of power and coming to the clouds of heaven". Now they could charge Jesus with blasphemy. Up to now Jesus had said nothing – for he had not been asked and Jesus only said what the Father told him to say (John 12:49) This was the only sentence he had been told to say. The council gave their verdict "He is deserving of death" and began to rise from their seats to go. The guards stood with Jesus as the dignitaries left and then slapped him saying prophesy.

Peter saw this and was horrified to see Jesus so treated, but he could do nothing. At this very moment a man directly challenged him as being a disciple of Jesus. This is over an hour since he had previously dealt with this. The servant girl at the gate who first had questioned him had been still troubled – whether she should have let Peter in or not. When she met one of the male servants who was a relative of Malchus and heard about the fight at Gethsemane, she disclosed her concern. For all she knew, this could be a terrorist secretly entered to attack someone in the house. The relative resolved to try to resolve this by asking Peter directly (John 18:26.) So, the servant girl was able to point him out by the light of the fire and the relative of Malchus approached Peter and asked him face to face. He again denied it in such a way that there was no doubt that they had got this wrong. Peter had to use expletives to give the impression that he was offended at the question. He had to do this, and it worked. But then a cock crowed at the first sign of dawn and Jesus turned amidst the insults and abuse to look at Peter. Only Peter knew the significance of the moment. He remembered what Jesus had said the night before about his denial and what he had said – how he would never deny Him. The horror of what he had now done swept over him. Self-accusing thoughts which would continue to afflict him in the hours ahead began to unsettle him. He had to get away. He left the court turning his back as Jesus was led away into the house and down through corridors for trial. Peter went out quickly through the streets. Tears rolled down his cheeks as he wept bitterly with a deep hollowness and despair he had not known before – a brokenness that affected him for the rest of his life.

One of the rooms in the house of Caiaphas was lit. Access to Caiaphas was straightforward and the council members had travelled the route many times. The family of Annas all lived near each other. Jesus was firmly bound so there was no possibility of escape and taken to a secure place where he was held until a decision was reached (John18:24). The day was now dawning as already a cockcrow had heralded, so time was of an essence. This spurred Caiaphas on. The full council were assembled to authorize the next step, and he needed a quick decision. Jesus was held in an antechamber guarded and bound whilst the council held their meeting. The chief priests wanted this to go to Pilate immediately before any supporters of Jesus could react. With the public meeting In Annas house over, decisions could be implemented swiftly. The purpose before Caiaphas and the Council was how to change an agreed decision of Jesus being guilty of blasphemy into an accusation which would make the Romans put Jesus to death. Blasphemy had to be phrased in some way as an affront against the Roman Empire rather than just an affront to their religious laws before the Romans would act. The charge they came up with was that Jesus claimed to be The King of the Jews thus setting himself up as another Caesar and so deserved execution. Messengers were urgently sent to the palace to prepare Pilate for the important trial and Jesus was taken from Caiaphas' house through the narrow streets that characterized the upper city until they reached the Upper Market place and then beyond to the fortress in which was the royal palace where Pilate lived at the western edge of walled Jerusalem.

Chapter 65

The end of Judas—Friday (Matthew 27 :3-10)

It was not long before Judas knew the fate of Jesus. He felt guilty about the betrayal because he did not envisage Jesus being bound and taken to Pilate with the intention of execution. Murder of Jesus was never what he had intended. He wished he could be back in the earlier days of Jesus' ministry before everything got so complicated for him, but he knew there was no going back. Full of remorse he brought back the thirty silver pieces to the temple to acknowledge it was for the betrayal of innocent blood. No-one cared. He could see the chief priests were satisfied with how everything was proceeding, and they were not going to change course. Judas threw the money down on the floor of the temple and stormed out determining to hang himself. He walked northwards out of the city. After two or three miles he saw a suitable tree in a field just away from passersby. There he stood on a wall. Having secured the rope around the tree he put the cord over the tree branch nearby and the noose he had made he placed firmly around his neck and jumped. Death was rapid. [189]

It was later that day when Judas' body was discovered. By then it had fallen to the ground facing downwards. The rope had gradually frayed against the bark in the wind and broken under the weight of Judas' dead body. When his body was lifted from the ground, it was discovered that in the fall it had split open in the middle with his entrails gushing out (Acts 1:18). There was the question of his burial. It needed to be done immediately because the Passover was imminent, and so the religious authorities were informed. They recognized the man found dead in the field as the same man who had betrayed Jesus.

---

[189] This could be Jeremiahs field at Anathoth (Jeremiah 32:7ff) which was three miles north of Jerusalem

The solution was to buy the field with the money he had handed back and bury him in it. The field was large enough and well positioned away from the inhabitants of Jerusalem for the burial of strangers and so was designated for those who had no relatives, and unknown in Jerusalem. It seemed a perfect solution. The city had thousands of visitors a year and there would be other burials needed in the future.

The trial before Pilate Friday April 3rd (John 18:28-9:16; Matthew 27:11-31; Mark 15:2-20; Luke 23:1-25)

This was Pilate's seventh year in office, and he was already used to responding to sudden requests from the religious leaders of Judaea. He had been told by the guard at the front gates of the fortress that the High Priest was bringing a criminal for trial to him. One of his servants came to see him as he waited for their arrival in the main hall of the palace. He was told everyone had arrived and requested his audience to be held outside the palace. The religious leaders were refusing to come into the palace because they would be religiously defiled preventing them taking part in the Passover which started at the end of the day. After all Jerusalem was full of people who had arrived a week early, so they could go through the various ceremonies required to deal with defilements to take part in the Passover. They needed to be able to take part. In addition, the chief priests there had responsibilities during the feast. Pilate knew this and went out to see them. He stood in front of the main entrance to the palace Caiaphas and others whom he knew approached him up the impressive stairs at the front of the palace with the prisoner. Pilate knew nothing about Jesus but was not at all keen to respond to their request for him to judge him. He felt at root that this was a dispute arising from internal religious jealousies (Mark 15:10) and had no wish to get involved. At this some of the crowd -for there were many with Caiaphas and the chief priests- accused Jesus of being a rebel forbidding taxes to be paid and saying he is the Christ a king. They also said it had to be the death sentence (John 18:31)

So, Pilate brought Jesus into the palace – the same place wise men from the east had come at Jesus' birth. It was called the praetorium whilst the Roman military commander was there. It was the name given to the headquarters of a Roman leader wherever he was – whether in a house or on the battle field. Jesus was led into the palace for questioning by one of the Roman guards (John 18:33), so Pilate could pronounce his verdict. This was normal practice for criminals. What was unusual was the absence of his accusers who would normally be part of this process bringing their accusations which the defendant would answer but as they had refused to come in, Pilate had to begin the interview himself. He asked, "Are you the king of the Jews?" (John 18:33, Luke 23:3, Mark 15:2, Matthew27:11) -a phrase which Herod the Great had taken to himself and a title which Pilate's rival Herod Antipas wished he could have (his actual title was tetrarch - a title given to a vassal king). Jesus replied his kingdom was not of this world (John 18:16) Leaving Jesus under guard where he was, Pilate went out to see the chief priests to find out more. He was still not convinced over any guilt Jesus might bear even when they said he stirred up the people. In this context they mentioned Galilee, so Pilate asked if he was a Galilean (He knew so little of Jesus he did not even know where he was from). When he found out he was from Galilee, he sent him bound to Herod who was staying in another part of the palace. It had a north and a south wing each with banqueting halls baths and accommodation for hundreds of guests, and was surrounded by groves of trees, canals and ponds with bronze sculptures and fountains. Pilate occupied one wing and Herod the other one. Though they lived at the palaces at Caesarea and at Jerusalem, they normally avoided each other preferring to stay in the palace when unoccupied by the other. The Passover had brought Herod into Jerusalem (Luke 22:7) at the same time when Pilate was staying there. Jesus was taken away through the open centre court from Pilate to Herod.

Jesus stood bound before the murderer of John the Baptist. Herod Antipas was pleased to meet Jesus and chose to meet him privately first. Herod talked a lot (Luke 23:9) hoping to enter similar dialogue as he had done with John the Baptist, but Jesus did not say a word to him. In the back of his mind he hoped Jesus would do some miracle like he had heard he had done all over Galilee, but Jesus did nothing either. The chief priests with their legal counsel (the scribes) were finally let in and they vehemently spoke against Jesus with such power that Herod as well as his soldiers began to treat Jesus with contempt. Herod provided a purple robe. They engaged in the mockery of the emperor by dressing Jesus in a purple robe and sending him so attired back to Pilate for him to pass judgement.

Pilate meanwhile had heard that Herod had not passed judgement on him, so he ordered him to be brought out before the crowd, so he could say he agreed with Herod. The crowd shouted out that Jesus should die. Pilate heard why they wanted Jesus dead was he had claimed to be the Son of God. This made him even more afraid, so Jesus was brought back into the Praetorium for a second interrogation. This time still in the purple robe Jesus answered nothing. Finally, when Pilate said he had the power to crucify or release him, Jesus reminded Pilate his power was from above. This unexpected comment made Pilate determined to release him. He had a plan. Pilate had come up with a possible way to avoid condemning Jesus to crucifixion and hoping to make all sides content. He sat on the judgement seat sited on the pavement outside the palace [190]. It was an imposing picture. The large paved area was elevated about 15 feet above ground set on colonnades which sheltered those who walked near the buildings. The crowd gathered before two flights of marble stairs guarded by soldiers. The stairs ascended to a mezzanine terrace before joining in one wide staircase up to the

---

[190] Josephus wars 5:11:4. Ibid 2.14.8

pavement where Pilate was seated. There were soldiers stationed behind the governor.

Pilate called the chief priests, the rulers of the synagogues and the people to gather on the court below so he could present his verdict in as wide a context as he could (Luke 23:13) to minimize any unhelpful responses. Pilate started well. He made out the charge was all about "Jesus misleading the people" in the hope that the people present would want to state they were not misled. He added to this he found no fault in him and mentioned Herod reaching the same conclusion. So, he went on to say his solution. Jesus deserved a beating for creating upset amongst the authorities, but he would let him go which Jesus' accusers could save face about because they could say it was part of the normal pardon of an accused which happened during Passover. (Luke 23:16,17). The flaw in the plan was that the release of a prisoner was not his choice to make. It required the people to choose. So, they were given some minutes to discuss this idea. During this time where he was waiting for them to return, Pilate's wife came into the room and went up to where Pilate was sitting and whispered in his ear. She had got out of bed after being woken by a dream. She had hastily got dressed and made her way to where Pilate was. She had no time to tell the dream just the fact it was not pleasant, and it was all about Jesus. She told him to have nothing to do with him. (Matthew 27:19) The situation however was out of his hands. He was waiting for the people's decision. The chief priests meanwhile used their influence and position to convince, threaten and manipulate the people to ask for Barabbas. Pilate stood up and asked Which of the two do you want me to release to you"?" They all shouted "Barabbas" (Matthew 27:21). This was a blow to Pilate's hopes. He took Jesus and ordered him to be beaten though he had not yet given Jesus the death sentence. The beating was in public and there were a set number of stripes with the leather thong with bits of bone which cut into his flesh. Although it would often be the precursor to execution, Pilate hoped that going this far might placate the crowd from demanding his death. This was a vain hope. The Roman soldiers unbound Jesus from the post and saw his outer garments which had been discarded for the beating. They did not give him back the purple robe but told him to put on his normal robe. Jesus was taken into the barracks which was a large military camp built within the fortifications of the palace[191] to accommodate many hundreds of soldiers. It was not long before the purple robe and accusation of Jesus as the king of the Jews produced an idea. They gathered the whole garrison (Matthew 27:27) made up of soldiers from different parts of the empire. They stripped him and put on the purple robe again to dress the condemned prisoner up as an emperor or king. The atmosphere in the barracks was a heady mix of cruelty, bravado and violence in the name of a bit of excitement or protest some of the hardships they had known. One of the men got some thorns and twisted them to make a crown and rammed it on his head. The blood flowed. They laughed. They put a stick of authority in his hand. And came before him and knelt as if he were a king mocking him as they addressed him as king of the Jews. They laughed at the comic walks and rude expressions the soldiers made as they approached Jesus in mock servitude. Some decided the anger within them demanded more of a statement and so they rose from kneeling in front of Jesus, spat on him, took the staff out of his hand and beat him with it continuously around his head and body. Time alone brought this ordeal to an end. Pilate asked for him to be brought out again for sentencing. Jesus came out from the barracks dressed in the purple robe with the crown of thorns on his head. Pilate pointed at him and said to the crowd, "Behold the Man". Pilate said to them "What shall I do with Jesus who is called the Christ?" Without any indecision, the loud answer came "Let him be crucified ". Pilate asked, "what evil he

---

[191] The barracks was near the palace not adjacent to the tower of Antonio (see Josephus Wars 2.15.5)

has done" but the question just provoked more cried of "let him be crucified" and there were the possibilities of a riot occurring. If things got out of hand, and he sent in the soldiers to restore order and the reasons for such a riot was his refusal to execute a rebel whose crime was he claimed to be a king. Pilate knew that this would look bad in Rome. There would be an enquiry and Pilate could easily have lost his job and career if not his life at the hands of the emperor. He also heard some shouting from the crowd "if you let this man go you are not Caesar's friend". That did it.

Pilate decided he had to act quickly. In front of the palace was an extended pavement which then went down several steps to street level. Pilate sat on the throne that was placed there whenever the area in front of the palace was transformed into a tribunal[192]. As he sat down he could be seen by everyone in the crowd. The crowd hushed waiting for his verdict. Pilate asked for a bowl to be brought with a flagon of water. He took the water and poured it into the bowl before them all. Pilate said, " I am innocent of this man's blood". He then sent for Barabbas and released him to the crowd whilst Jesus was handed over to the soldiers. Pilate went into his palace for breakfast reflecting how it had been a difficult morning.

The soldiers took Jesus to the cells. They took the purple robe off him and put his own clothes back on him. Jesus was weak, perhaps unable to dress himself even if he had wanted to. But any help Jesus had was done without sympathy, compassion or thought. It was just to get the job done. They then took him out with fellow conspirators of Barabbas to be crucified.

[192] Josephus wars 2.15.8

SECTION 11

The Death and Resurrection of Jesus

Chapter 66

Crucifixion—Friday April 3rd(Matthew 27: 33-50 Mark 15:21-41 John 19:23-30 Luke 23:32-48)

They took Jesus into the courtyard of the barracks and put on his back the cross beam which he would carry. The two other prisoners were there also (Luke 23:32). They were all led out carrying their cross beams. Guards were surrounding each prisoner as they set off in the midst of a military unit escorting them through the military gate of the barracks complex to Golgotha. The rising sun cast its early morning light as he stumbled through the narrow streets struggling with the weight he carried. Behind him were the curious adding to the crowd who followed. Jesus' disciples were there watching too. The military guards with their prisoners walked out of the city northwards towards the hill of Golgotha. Jesus as he left the city (Matthew 27:32a) weakened by the beating he had received and loss of blood, collapsed under the weight of the cross. He had not the energy to carry the cross any further. The beatings and torment he had suffered that night had taken its toll. Ahead was the steep slope to the execution site. A man coming into the city, a black North African Jew called Simon, was commandeered by the soldiers to pick up the cross Jesus was unable to carry. Simon had no choice. He picked it up, walking behind the prisoner. It was all Jesus could do to walk unaided up the final ascent. towards a hill called Golgotha which because of its shape the hill resembled a skull. It was a part limestone quarry, part tombs of the dead. It was a fitting backdrop for execution.

The crowd dropped back as they came to Golgotha. The Romans had the site well organized and grieving relatives or friends of the condemned were kept at a distance to allow the execution to be performed decisively. The cross beam was taken from Simon of Cyrene without ceremony and placed on the ground above the wooden beam which was ready to be lifted into ready-made sockets in the ground next to it. The cross beam was nailed in position and then Jesus was taken by his guards. There was a team of four soldiers assigned to each prisoner for crucifixion (John 19:23) under the authority of a centurion who was responsible for the execution. They picked up their prisoner, cut his cords and his clothes removed before picking their prisoner up – two soldiers by his shoulders and two shoulders by his feet. Some victims screamed or tried to escape but to no avail as the soldiers held them down to the cross whilst nails were driven through hands and feet. Jesus however did not resist. All he said was "Father forgive them. They do not know what they are doing ". One soldier gave him wine mingled with myrrh, but he refused the drug. Jesus needed to be alert even amidst the pain. The accusation "This is the King of the Jews" was nailed above his head. With a soldier at each point of the cross, one soldier guided the cross into the socket whilst the other three burly soldiers lifted the cross, so it glided into the socket where it stayed. The soldiers then picked up cross and lowered it into the prepared socket in the earth. Jesus experienced further excruciating pain as his body hung and pushed down on the nails as he struggled to breathe.

Jesus was crucified between two others who had the same done to them. The four soldiers in charge of Jesus' execution had finished their first task. Before they settled down, they divided Jesus' last possessions into four parts between them. It was one of the perks of the job. The outer garment of Jesus however could not be divided. To tear it would have ruined it and it would have been no benefit to anyone, so they cast lots to see who of them would have it, and the winner picked it up and put it under his arm as they went to sit down to wait for Jesus to die. The centurion in charge and the twelve soldiers (four assigned to each prisoner) had to wait until it was all over so they stood or sat down not far away (Matthew 27:36) taking it in turns to be on guard at the cross. The rest of the soldiers departed, leaving behind a small token force who continued to ensure the crowd who watched could not get too close. As most of the soldiers departed back to their barracks, the crowd were able to inch their way slightly forward but most chose to remain at a distance. They wanted no misunderstanding or complications with the Romans. Amongst the crowd were the religious leaders who said, "he saved others himself he cannot save". Others shouted out of the crowd to Jesus to come down from the cross to prove who he was. Some shouted abuse at Jesus echoing witnesses from the public trial "Aha you would destroy the temple and build it in three days". His friends were silent, devastated and horrified in equal measure. The reviling of his enemies continued around them. Jesus did nothing except move up and down on the cross struggling for breath. Each move to breathe bringing further pain. The soldiers would get up and offer sour wine which Jesus constantly refused. The soldiers also joined in saying why not come down from the cross (Luke 23:37) The criminals suffering the same punishment as Jesus on either side of him joined in telling Jesus to save himself and them as well until one of them told the other to stop it and asked Jesus to remember him when he came in his kingly power. Jesus who said nothing to those who insulted him, broke his silence for this criminal and said, "today you will be with me in paradise" (Luke 23:43)

By the time noon arrived, it was getting darker and darker. Far off, behind the bystanders who mocked or hoped for something spectacular, was Mary his mother, Salome his sister, with Mary Magdalene and Mary the wife of Clopas. Each one broken at the sight, but for Mary she felt a sword going right through her (Luke 2:35). She wanted to approach her dying son, and John went with her for support pushing through the crowd to the front. Jesus saw his mother and John standing next to her. Those ahead of them were no longer shouting like they had been. Many had already left to prepare for the Passover meal they would have with their families that evening, but Jesus continued to writhe grotesquely on the cross as he struggled for breath. Everything

336

was more obscure as the darkness grew, but Jesus recognised his mother as she came closer. He said "Woman behold your son" as he looked towards John who was standing next to her. He then said to John "Behold your mother". Jesus in these words handed the care of his mother over to John (not to James his older brother). Mary would not return to Nazareth. From now on wherever John went she was there also (John 19:27). Her family now was to be the church of God for yet none of her children were believers[193]. Faith had birthed in her sister Salome and her children so there was still a blood family connection to her new world as it emerged. All that was for the future. For now, grief overwhelmed her.

For over two hours the pain of crucifixion continued as the victims fought to breathe. Jesus then broke the silence in his native tongue "Eloi Eloi lama sabacthani" – the opening verse of Psalm 22 "My God My God why have you forsaken me". Jesus knew it was finished and wanted to be able to shout the victory shout, but his tongue stuck to his mouth (see Psalm 22:15). So Jesus said, "I thirst" (John 19:28) One of the soldiers hearing the cry got up from where he had been sitting, and began to immerse a cloth in some sour wine and put it on pole to bring it to Jesus' mouth." People in the crowd shouted "stop don't do it. Let us see if Elijah comes". They had misheard " Eloi ,Eloi" and thought Jesus was calling Elijah. They ,even now, still hoped for something spectacular. They had not given up on the unexpected with a man who had worked so many miracles. But Jesus did not come down from the cross nor did Elijah come to save him. The Roman soldiers ignored the crowd's cries and offered Jesus the sour wine which he received (John 19:30). It gave him the moisture he needed. Immediately he shouted a triumphant cry "It is finished". Sin's price was paid! Satan' accusations

---

[193] Her sons James and Jude did believe after Jesus' resurrection. James became leader of the church and wrote the epistle of James in the New Testament and Jude wrote the epistle of Jude

emptied of power! The Kingdom of God could come to mankind! Jesus then spoke a prayer he had said many times before but now with the greatest of meanings "Father into your hands I commend my spirit" and then bowed his head as he died.

At the same time as this there was a minor tremor -a shaking which most felt just for a moment but was an echo of the seismic shock in the unseen dimensions of creation. A sinless man entered the world of the dead. The light of the world pierced the darkness and death could not master him. There was a removal at a stroke of all the sins of the world stacked up against mankind to be used against it legally by the evil one. His power base had been vapourised and creation was beginning to change from its beginning to a new place. The Lordship of Jesus was known in the place of the dead, and the old enemy of man was defeated.

The centurion in charge of the execution had watched closely as Jesus was dying. He had heard the insults and seen his reaction. The coinciding events which surrounded his death emphasized to this man what he already believed: that Jesus must have been a righteous man (Matthew 27:54 Luke23:47) The actual words he used however had a deeper significance though he did not realise it at the time. He said, "Surely this man was the son of God" (Mark 15:39). The centurion then turned away. He still had a job to do, and with his soldiers they turned their attention to the thieves on either side who were still to die.

The crowd beat their breasts as a sign of respect at the passing of another and many turned away to go to their homes. There was no point delaying any longer. Some had stayed hoping against hope that Jesus would not die, others because they could not bear to be anywhere else even though they did not want to be there. This was the day when they prepare the Passover meal (John 20:31) and the Sabbath which was also the Passover itself that year would start at 6pm. For most in Jerusalem there was much to do , though for Jesus' disciples , the

Passover would never again would it have the same feeling for them as it did in the past.

Chapter 67

Jesus' body taken down from the cross (Matthew27:57-61)

Only the Romans and a few bystanders remained. Some were the relatives of the other thieves, John and Mary Jesus' mother stood with the other women from Galilee (Luke 24:49). They were unable to leave Jesus even though they knew he was dead. They also needed to know what the authorities would do with his body. There was a tangible quietness in the air interrupted only by the thieves who were still alive on the crosses nearby. As the unusual darkness of the day lifted, Mary remained standing at a distance. The Roman guards made sure everyone kept their distance as was usual in every execution.

Behind the scenes , unknown to everyone, Joseph, a wealthy disciple who was well connected in the city, and a prominent member of the Sanhedrin had managed to approach Pilate and ask for permission to take the body of Jesus away for burial. Joseph had moved into Jerusalem some time ago from Arimathea and had purchased a plot in the cliffs near the crucifixion site ready for him or his family when the time came. He had arranged for the first cave to be cut out for no-one knew when death might strike. The tomb had taken several days to cut into the limestone and prepare. It seemed to Joseph that this cut tomb would be the right place for Jesus' body to be laid. Pilate was surprised Jesus was already dead and so sent a slave to summon the centurion to attend. The bystanders noticed the servant come, talk with the centurion who then went up the steep path back into the city. The rest of the soldiers remained as before. The centurion arrived to see Pilate waiting for him with Joseph standing nearby. He confirmed that Jesus was dead and so Pilate gave Joseph permission. Joseph went with the centurion to take Jesus' body down from the cross. No-one was allowed near. The soldiers were making sure there was no possibility of disturbance.

It was usual for the crucified to be left hanging on the cross as a grim reminder to remain loyal to Rome, but relatives might be given permission to take their bodies. It was by no means certain that permission would be given. Now that Joseph had authority to remove Jesus, permission was extended at the request of the religious authorities to ensure the quick removal of all those crucified before the Passover began. (Mark 15:44; John 19:31.). The thieves were still alive. The soldiers came and broke the legs of the thieves to end their misery. Unable to press up to breathe they suffocated. In this context it was an act of mercy. Their pain was over. They saw Jesus was already dead and Mary and John ventured closer. Before the body of Jesus could be taken down they also needed to make sure he was dead. It was a long time since he had died. The soldiers had to be sure. One of the soldiers reached a spear and pushed it into Jesus side up to his heart. Blood flowed but death had already caused the blood to break down – "out flowed blood and water"(John 19:34).

Joseph returned to Golgotha with the centurion who knew his orders to let Joseph take Jesus' body. Joseph came with Nicodemus and together they took Jesus body and laid it on a cloth which would become his shroud. The body was wrapped in strips of cloth quickly by Nicodemus and Joseph with a mixture of myrrh and aloes placed between the folds as they did so, masking the smell of death a then the shroud was pulled up around the body, lifted up, carried and placed in the empty rock tomb.

This all took time and there was some urgency to finish this before the Sabbath began (Luke 23:54). The women wanted to stay to see where they were taking the body. They had to balance this with their duties of preparing the meals where they were staying. Some went whilst Jesus' mother and Mary Magdalene stayed (Mark 15:47; Luke 23:54).They noted both where they laid the body and how it was laid.

The burial on Friday was a hasty affair. The stone which had been hewn from the rock to make the tomb had been done in one piece, so it was relatively simple with some hard effort to push the stone into position (Matt 27:60) There was no time now to allow the family to complete the anointing of the body after the Sabbath. Mary, his mother wanted to anoint the body and the other women would help her after the Sabbath. Or at least that was the plan. In the moments before the Sabbath began; before they rested according to the Jewish law, they prepared spices and fragrant oils for anointing Jesus' body. The Sabbath ended at 6pm on Saturday evening, but by the time they would be able to get to the tomb it would be too dark to see anything and so they decided to get up at first light on Sunday morning to complete the task.

Meanwhile the Jews met at their synagogue at the end of that day (Matthew 27:62). The day of preparation was over and the Passover was beginning. They talked about the events of the day and discovered that one of his disciples had already taken Jesus' body for burial. They knew Joseph of Arimathea and also the tomb. It occurred to the Pharisees that Jesus' disciples might try to pretend Jesus was raised from the dead by taking his body (Matthew 27:62ff) so they went to Pilate and got permission to seal the tomb and extend the guard on it for three days to prevent any such action. The Roman guards unaffected by the Sabbath or the Passover were sent from the barracks (notice Matthew 28:14 they were under Pilate's authority) and they found the tomb hewn out of the rock still in position. The Romans had a guard on the execution site whilst everything was cleared up. (Matthew 27:65a, 27:54). They secured the tomb, sealing the stone with wax and stood guard so there could be no interference.

Chapter 68

The Resurrection of Jesus Sunday April 5th 33AD
(Matthew 28, Mark 16, Luke 24, John 20)

The women were unable to sleep waiting for the dawn. They were eager to complete the task that the Sabbath had interrupted, and so even before it was light, got ready and set out in the twilight just after 5a.m. carrying the ointments they had prepared. The women included Mary the mother of Jesus with her sister Salome helped by Mary Magdalene They were known as the women from Galilee (Luke 23:55) and were staying together. With them were one or two of their friends or relatives (Luke 24:1).[194] They left Peter and John [195]who were asleep upstairs. John had brought Peter to stay there after the trial for his safety and recovery. The disciples were afraid in case they would also target Jesus' followers now Jesus was dead.

The women went out of the house making their way to the north gate of the city which they had followed Jesus as he went to his execution. It would take nearly an hour to go through the gate and then onwards down the steep slope to the tomb in the dark. All the time the twilight was changing to the light of dawn. They got to the tomb just after 6am just as the sun had risen(Mark 16:2). They could see as they approached there was a large stone there which had not been there when they had left the tomb. They had no other choice but to keep going thinking amongst themselves who they could ask to move it. They

---

[194] There are "certain other women" as well as "the women from Galilee". Joanna is mentioned in Luke 24:10. It could be she owned the house in Jerusalem. She was wealthy and as the wife of Herod's steward is likely to have had a town house large enough to house many guests.

[195] Possibly James and John were intended to be staying with Salome at the house but after the events at the trial James stayed elsewhere whilst Peter came for support with John.

knew nothing of the guards and the decree that had been made overnight.

Before they arrived, there was a great earthquake (Matthew 28:2); a greater tremor than had happened when Jesus died. To many at the time it would seem that the tremor experienced on the Friday was a precursor to the main event on the Sunday morning. It was however much less and more localized than the greatest earthquake in two thousand years which had struck sixty years before destroying many buildings in its epicentre of Jericho. So the inhabitants of Jerusalem might have thought, but for guards by the tomb they understood the earthquake differently. At the same time as the earthquake, an angel of the Lord came and rolled back the stone. He appeared like lightening and the guards were overcome by the supernatural presence and looked as if they were dead. In the darkness to the women it looked like the earthquake had moved the stone away the entrance. The women found it was possible to enter the tomb. Not everyone saw the angel still sitting on the stone by the entrance to the tomb or even heard his voice to take in all he said. All they knew that they could go into the tomb. This is why they had come and so they did so without question. Their focus was elsewhere. Just as it is possible to see and not perceive or hear and not understand so it is common for mortals to not see the supernatural.

They had passed the guards also without a thought, whether they were dead or alive, now was not the time to find out. They had more a more pressing task. They took the ointments, went past the stone and stepped into the tomb. To their surprise and alarm, they saw a young man in a white robe sitting on the right of the tomb. He said to them "Do not be alarmed! You are seeking Jesus of Nazareth who was crucified" – reassuring them that the two Marys had led them all to the right tomb. They had no time to think for the young man (who was actually an angel (Matthew 28:5) continued "He is risen! He is not here. See the place where they laid him". They turned to look and sure enough there was no body – just the shroud on the place where Mary had seen it placed. He said, "Go and tell His disciples – and Peter (Mark 16:7) (for after his denial he regarded himself as no longer a disciple and this was immediately known in the supernatural world) -that He is going before you into Galilee, there you will see him as he said to you". They turned and went. Uncertain what to do or say so they said nothing at that time (Mark 16:8). The only one to say anything was Mary Magdalene who went to John and Peter and just told them the fact that there was no body to anoint. Only later in the day would the women recount the full story. they ran to the tomb. Mary went with them to show them where it was. They all went at speed. Mary pointed out where it was, and Peter and John sprinted ahead of her. John was faster than Peter. He went around the stone and looked inside. The sun was shining into the tomb making every detail clear. He did not go in. He saw the shroud undisturbed sunken as nobody was now in it and the bandages Joseph and Nicodemus had placed around the head still in place as if the head was still there, but it was just air. He knew this is no robbery of a body. Something else had happened and he believed what he had heard the report Mary had brought. Peter however went straight in

Mary could not bring herself to leave with the others. There was something deeply unjust that they had been prevented from doing this last act for Jesus. As she wept, the Risen Jesus came. Her first encounter was not with Jesus but with two angels in the tomb, one at the head and one at the foot of where Jesus body had been. They had been there all the time unseen by the two disciples but not to her. She only knew they were there when she decided to put her head into the tomb to look. They asked her why she was crying. She was too upset to rationalize all this. She just blurted out why she was crying – "Because they have taken away my Lord and I do not know where they have laid him". She withdrew her head from the tomb and turned around and saw Jesus standing there. She thought at first, he was the keeper of the garden, but recognized him as he called her name. Her whole life changed direction from despair to hope, and from sorrow to joy. Jesus then underlined the message they had already heard as he turned and left her. Mary went back to the upper room where by now all the disciples had gathered as they had arranged. They were uncertain about the future. The front door was locked, and they were on major security alert. When Mary knocked the servant opened the small window at eye level. Mary was well known and the door was quickly opened. She was led up the stairs into the upper room where the eleven and others were mourning and weeping. It was for many the start of the shiva. Mary told her story to them (Mark 16:10) which encouraged the other women to tell their story also. It seemed like foolishness to those who heard it (Luke 24:11). The eleven spent the morning together before some went to the temple as the feast of unleavened bread continued during the week. Thomas left for the temple with some of the others. Peter went away to process all that had happened. [196] Mary (another Mary who had the same name as the mother of Jesus and the woman from Magdala)who had been with the women at the cross and her husband Clopas set off for Emmaus where they lived – a journey of about seven miles (Luke 24:13). The rest of the eleven remained together. Peter joined them again in the evening having encountered Jesus that afternoon and told his story. There was a knock at the door and an excited Cleopas and his wife Mary came in. They had walked back from Emmaus much quicker than then they had gone. Their excitement and joy were evident to all. They had walked on the Roman road from Jerusalem through the mountain pass named Nahal Lian and during their journey a fellow

---

[196] Jesus appeared to Peter (Luke 24:34) which had the effect of reinstating him with the disciples and appeared to James so Paul states in I Cor 15:7. Peter did develop close links with James as he and John led the Jerusalem church (Galatians 2:9). We know Jesus appeared to both Peter and James. It is likely to be at the same time and would explain why the appearance to James is not mentioned in the gospels.

traveller had joined them and walked with them. It was not until they invited him into their home once they had reached Emmaus that they recognized it was Jesus. During their journey he spoke from the scriptures about the death and resurrection of the Messiah. As they shared their encounter with Jesus and what he had said, Jesus appeared to them and showed them his hands and side. He then commissioned them. He breathed on them and then said "Receive the holy Spirit. As the Father sent me even so send I you". This word would be demonstrably fulfilled at Pentecost not just for those there but for all the disciples gathered together that day.

Thomas was not with them. It was not until the next day when they gathered together again in the upper room when he found out what had happened. Thomas heard what they said about the wounds they had seen. Thomas said, "Unless I out my hands in the nail prints and also into his side I will not believe". For the moment they continued to attend the festival of unleavened bread. It lasted eight days. After this was over, they were still all together and the following day they were leaving Jerusalem and going back to Galilee as they had been told by the risen Jesus. Thomas still had no answers. It was on this last evening that Jesus came. Now they all knew Jesus was alive. They went to Galilee light of heart and a deep joy within them. They went back to Magdala

Magdala (John 21:1ff)

Peter and John with James and Nathaniel from nearby Cana and Thomas (who was not going to be absent again) (John 21:2) made their way from Jerusalem back to Galilee. They went to Magdala region possibly staying with Mary (John 21) or someone she arranged for them. Since they had been on the road full-time, Magdala had replaced Capernaum as a base for the ministry. It was here by the part of the sea near Tiberius (John 21:1) where Jesus would appear to them by the shore.

When they arrived at the designated place Jesus was not there. They waited all that day until as evening came Peter said he was going fishing and the others with nothing better to do said they would join him. They got into a boat and were there all night without success. In the morning Jesus was on the shore. It was not unusual to see people on the shore and they were too far away to tell who it was.

The man on the shore told them to cast their net on the right side of the boat and when they did the catch was unusually large- too large for the fish to be put in the boat (John 21:8) John remembered this had happened before with Jesus, and then he recognised Jesus. He exclaimed "It is the Lord". Peter who had been the first out of the boat to see Jesus when he might have been a ghost, was also now the first one out of the boat swimming and wading through the waters to see if it was really Jesus. The parallels with the day when Simon Peter had renewed his call as a disciple (see Luke 5) was not lost on him. Peter as he was still on his journey back from his denial.

The other disciples stayed in the boat rowing the two hundred cubits to land with the fish caught in their nets behind them. When they got to shore they got the boat onto land and got out quickly to meet Jesus who was standing next to Peter. They came leaving the fish still in the sea with the fish still in the net. Jesus said bring some of the fish and so Simon always strong went and pulled the net out of the sea (John 21:11). They were overjoyed to be joining Jesus for breakfast. It did not take long because Jesus had already got a fire going with some fish, but there was not enough for everyone. Some fish they had just caught needed to be added, whilst some cooked, others counted the fish. When they all sat to eat they were amazed to hear they had caught 153 and that the net was unbroken. This was a precious time and before the wider group of disciples came to hear from Jesus for the last time whilst on earth. Jesus spoke about meeting the many disciples so that it was not just the eleven who saw Jesus raised from the dead. They fixed the time and place where the gathering would be held and knew who they should tell so the news could travel quickly to every part of Israel. Jesus got up and, leaving the others by the fire, walked with Peter along the beach (John 21:20). John decided to get up and follow. He heard Jesus reinstating Peter telling him to "Feed my sheep". After breakfast the five disciples went back to join the others and prepared for the gathering.

Chapter 69

Meeting in Galilee at Mount Tabor

As during his earthly ministry, Jesus had gathered his followers to teach them so now after his resurrection he gave a similar invitation to what many would have received during his earthly life. The gathering was accessible from the Sea of Tiberias. It was to be a teaching gathering of disciples like they used to have. (Matthew 28:16-17) It was to be on a mountain in Galilee[197], not too far away.

Many who had come to the past gatherings did not come for this one. There were just five hundred there (1 Corinthians 15:6) instead of the thousands in the gatherings in Galilee and elsewhere. It was more like the earliest days of his ministry. Jesus appeared and taught them instructing them about the kingdom (Acts 1:3b) commissioning them to go to all the world. He told them first to stay in Jerusalem. Jesus dismissed the crowd in a similar way as he had done so many times before and they all departed. Only one hundred and twenty disciples obeyed Jesus and went to Jerusalem. Of the rest some did not believe it was really Jesus and others did not see why they should go to Jerusalem.

The Ascension

After the mountain gathering Jesus appeared at other times to his disciples when they were assembled together (Acts 1:4,6). The last time was to the eleven and those disciples with them when they had gone back to Jerusalem as he had instructed them. He met them in the upper room (see Acts 1:13a) and led them out to Bethany (Luke 24:50). They

---

[197] The actual venue is unknown. The narrative assumes it is Mount Tabor. 11 miles west of the Sea of Galilee centrally sited not far from Nazareth, and accessible from the west. It is also had easy access eastwards to the Jordan rift valley. Its shape makes it distinctive to see and find. It was an ideal location to meet his disciples.

350

walked past the garden of Gethsemane up to the ridge at the top which led to Bethphage and then took another ridge down towards Bethany where he taught them before walking back up the hill towards the city. Jesus led them away from the road up to one of the three uppermost points of the Mount of Olives. Jesus continued to teach whilst they walked. When they reached the top, Jesus stopped talking, and suddenly he ascended from the earth before their eyes. All they could do was watch until a cloud obscured their view. (Acts 1:9). They heard a voice next to them and turned to see two men in white standing with them telling them that Jesus would come back in a similar way to the way they had seen him go. They accepted what was said and turned to obey what Jesus had told them. Without further delay they made their way down the track into the city to the Upper room where they were staying, and they continued to meet together there until Pentecost[198].

[198] Pentecost was on Sunday May 24th in 33AD

APPENDIX

THE BIRTH OF JESUS

The census happened when Joazar was High Priest but continued until Quirinius (Luke 2:1) arrived in 6AD It started therefore in the reign of Herod the Great.

Joazar was made High Priest by Herod the Great. "Herod deprived Matthias of the high priesthood and made Joazar who was Matthias' wife's brother high priest in his stead...and that very night (that he deprived Matthias of the high priesthood and burnt the other Matthias who had raised the sedition alive) there was an eclipse of the moon" (Antiquities 17:6.4.) which was in March 4BC

Josephus writes "because the Jews although at the beginning they took the report of a taxation heinously, yet did they leave off any further opposition to it by the persuasion of Joazar who was the son of Boethus and high priest. So they being over-persuaded by Joazar's words gave an account of their estates without any dispute about it" Josephus Antiquities 18. 1.1. an account of their estates "refers to the census. See also The census happened through the efforts of Quirinius (Luke 2:1). Antiquities 20.5.2 "Judas who caused the people to revolt when Cyrenius (Quirinius) came to take account of the estates of the Jews".

The census was to do with property ownership not numbers of people

"to take account of the estates of the Jews". (see above)

This means Joseph had lands in Bethlehem or he would not have had any need to go.

The census was not completed until 6AD after which Caesar's tax was introduced into Judea.

"Cyrenius (Quirinius) came himself into Judea which was now added to the province of Syria to take account of their substance and to dispose of Archelaus' money" Josephus Antiquities 18.1.1.

"When Cyrenius had now disposed of Archelaus' money and when the taxings were come to a conclusion (which were made in the thirty seventh year of Caesar's victory over Anthony in Actium) he deprived Joazar of the high priesthood which dignity had been conferred on him by the multitude (in the deposing of Archelaus the Jews had tried to reappoint Joazar) and he appointed Ananus the son of Sethto be High priest while Herod and Philip had each of them received their own tetrarchy and settled the affairs thereof" (Antiquities 18.2.1.)

The battle of Actium was in 31BC 37 years after this makes 6AD

IN CONCLUSION
Herod the Great and the birth of Jesus
Matthew records that the birth of Jesus happened when Herod the Great was still alive and able to function as leader in Jerusalem. He was ill (Josephus Wars 1.33.1) but still active until March 4BC after which he became suddenly worse and lived at Jericho. Archelaus acted as regent. The removal of the eagle from the temple gate happened in that year and Archelaus was making decisions causing the perpetrators to be arrested, but Herod came from his sick bed to pronounce judgement upon them (Wars 1.23.4). He then called the powerful people to Jericho (Antiquities 17.6.3) for implementation of his judgment and Josephus states at that time he was too weak to stand. (Antiquities 17.6.3.)

The start of his rapid decline happened near the time of an eclipse dated to March 13th 4BC (Josephus Antiquities 17.6.4) when he appointed Joazar High priest and "burnt the Matthias who had raised the sedition with his companions alive". (Antiquities 17.6.5))

The wise men by contrast find Herod well enough to convene chief priests and scribes when they arrive in Jerusalem. They must have arrived at the end of 5BC or the beginning of 4BC at the latest.

The census and birth of Jesus

The birth of Jesus must have been in 5BC Luke records it happened at the time of the census. This was finally completed in 6AD (the thirty seventh year of Caesars victory over Anthony at Actium (Josephus ant. 18.2.1.) i1.e. 6AD). It cannot have started in 6AD. Josephus writes "because the Jews although at the beginning they took the report of a taxation heinously, yet did they leave off any further opposition to it by the persuasion of Joazar who was the son of Boethus and high priest. So they being over-persuaded by Joazar's words gave an account of their estates without any dispute about it" Josephus Antiquities 18. 1.1. The census was in process before Joazar came to office. The officials taking the census travelled from place to place. The opposition to the census grew to a point where the High priest had to intervene. This would have taken some weeks if not months. When Simon was deposed as High Priest and replaced by Joazar, it would be reasonable to assume that Herod gave him the task to facilitate the census. If this is so, it is probable that the census was introduced in 5BC (Joazar was replaced by Eleazar – see below)

EVENTS AFTER THE BIRTH OF JESUS

Archelaus was one year as regent after Herod's death

Eleazar was appointed in 2BC before Archelaus had been ratified as king

"In the first and principle place Archelaus would deprive that high priest which Herod had made (Joazar) and would choose one more agreeable to the law and of greater purity to officiate as high priest (Eleazar). This was granted by Archelaus although he was mightily offended at their importunity because he proposed himself to go to Rome to look after Caesar's determination about him" (Ant 17.9.1).

Joazar served whilst Herod the Great alive (4BC). He was deposed by Archelaus immediately before going to Rome to find out Caesar's decision about the will of Herod. This means the decree of Joazar about the census was in 4BC Joazar was also appointed High priest at the people's request when Archelaus was exiled (antiquities 18. 2.1 but was removed from office in favour of Ananus (bible Annas) before Cyrenius started the final phase of the census.

Quirinius the legate governor of the Roman province of Syria. He is a known historical figure who indeed was a Roman senator who was in Syria (the Roman province of which Judea and Galilee were a part). It became fully integrated within the province in 6AD after the Romans removed Archelaus from his rule. During Archelaus' rule objections to the introduction of Caesar's tax which had escalated into violent revolt.

Judas the Galilean had broken into the military store at Sepphoris and had had some military success in 4BC Varus the Roman general of Syria at that time defeated them and he stepped down from office after 4BC Archelaus was exiled. Judea was annexed into the Roman province of Syria. Coponius was appointed procurator under Cyrenius the governor of Syria.

Caesar may have had views on the removal of the Boethus family from office.

Herod Philip the son of Herod the Great and Mariamne II the daughter of Simon Boethus was excluded from any position of power in Israel at Augustus' decision. When the will was disputed , he was a possible successor to his father. Herod Philip was the first husband of Herodias and lived at Rome.

Jesus returned from Egypt three years (5BC to 2BC) after his birth

Joseph chose to go to Nazareth rather than Bethlehem (Matthew 2:21)as it was outside Archelaus' jurisdiction. He only knew this after the decision Caesar made.

Joseph Mary & Jesus returned before 6AD It was likely to be in 2BC because

1. Joseph came because Herod was dead (died in 4BC
2. He knew Archelaus needed to be avoided because he had already had a fierce reputation for cruelty from when he was regent.
3. He arrived when Archelaus was king not regent. This could have been in late 3BC but it is unlikely as Archelaus was still regent having to go to Rome on the Passover after his father's death (presumably 3BC) when as regent at that Passover he harshly treated those who mourned those who had been executed by Herod the Great because of the removal of the golden eagle from the temple. Kings and other officals were appointed at that time of year meaning Archelaus would have become king near Passover 2BC

The revolt of Judas the Galilean and others against the census delayed the introduction of the tax until 6AD

Judea annexed to Syria in order to get the tax sorted (Josephus Antiquities 18.1.) was not the start but the end of the policy implementation

The Roman general had defeated Judas in 4BC and had destroyed his base at Sepphoris in Galilee. Judas the Galilean though still continues to be trouble. It is unlikely that there were two Judas linked to Galilee involved in revolt over the census. He is only finally defeated in 6AD

Josephus mentions Judas the Galilean as founding a school whose teaching grew in popularity bringing about eventually the Jewish revolt. (see Ant. 18.1.2-6)He itemizes Pharisees, Sadducees, Essenes and those of Judas the Galilean and Sadduc. Judas the Galilean was a Rabbi Josephus describes their teaching in the same terms as the teaching of Rabbi Judas son of Sepphoris and Rabbi Mathias who had stirred up the crowd to first damaging and then removing the eagle from the temple gate. Herod decided to put them both to death (Wars 1.23.2-4.), but therewas some ill will on the part of the leaders at Herod's decsiuon so he convened a meeting at Jericho where some leniency was shown. Judas the son of Sepphoris might have been pardoned. If so Judas son of Sepphoris is the Judas the Galilean who was defeated in 4BC by Varus (The Roman legate governor of Syria until 4BC) when Sepphoris was burnt down and its inhabitants sold into slavery. This same Judas further revolted when Quirinius was legate governor of Syria in 6AD (Antiquities 20.5.2 "Judas who caused the people to revolt when Cyrenius (Quirinius) came to take account of the estates of the Jews".

Dates of the Ministry of Jesus Christ

The date when John the Baptist ministry starts is 29BC and Jesus was crucified in 33AD

Luke 3:1 says that the ministry of Jesus started with his baptism by John the Baptists who started his ministry in the fifteenth year of Tiberius. (Augustus died September 14AD making the fifteenth year of Tiberius started September 29AD)

Jesus was crucified on the day of preparation (John 19:31) when the Passover started in the evening of that day (John 18:28) which was also a Sabbath day (Friday evening to Saturday evening) (Mark 15:42, Luke 23:54. The only possible years for this are 30AD (too early) and 33AD

Dates used in the book

http://www.cgsf.org/dbeattie/calendar

The dates used in this book are from the calendars by M.J. Beattie published at *cgsf.org*. They are the calendars of the Western world and of the mainstream Jews. M.J.Beattie writes about them:

Roman Years

The Roman calendar is the calendar in common usage in the Western world today. It is a solar calendar with no correlation to the movements of the moon; it is based on the calendar established by Julius Caesar in 46 BC. Augustus Caesar later borrowed a day from the month of February to make the month named after him just as long as the one named after Julius. He also rearranged the lengths of the three months after August. With these slight modifications by Augustus Caesar, the 365¼-day Julian calendar continued in use without further modifications until the time of Pope Gregory XIII. The Gregorian calendar, established by Pope Gregory in October 1582, adjusted the calendar to stabilize the dates of the equinoxes and solstices, and to compensate for the 10-day drift of the vernal equinox away from the date on which it had occurred in the year of the Nicene Council (325 AD). Gregory's revised calendar was readily accepted by the Catholic European nations but was met with resistance elsewhere. The Germanic states finally accepted it in 1700. It was adopted by the English in 1752, by the Russians in 1918, by the Greek Orthodox Church in 1923, and by the Turks in 1928.

The Roman calendar on this web site is the Gregorian calendar from 1582 to the present and beyond. Prior to 1582, it is the Augustan version of the Julian calendar. In other words, it is *not* accurate for dates in Protestant countries from 1582 until they changed to Gregorian counting. Nor is it accurate for any time before the reign of Augustus Caesar (r.27BC–14AD). (The calendar of Julius Caesar was only slightly different than what you will find here. Prior to that the Roman calendar varied greatly, and any "Roman" dates illustrated for such years are purely hypothetical.)

Hebrew Years

The "Hebrew" years shown on this web site match the Rabbinic calendar which has been in use by the majority of the Jews at least since the writing of Maimonides' *Mishneh Torah* (1170-1180 AD). (See http://en.wikipedia.org/wiki/Hebrew_calendar and related articles). This is a calculated calendar, with the beginnings of months and years established by Rabbinic rules for computation and "postponements" of new moons. The calculations result in months and years that approximate, but are *not* in complete harmony with the natural lunar and solar cycles

Bibliography

The Complete works of Josephus Translated by Wm. Whiston/ Foreword by Wm, S. Lasor ISBN 0-8254-292-8 Kregel publications 2000

Biblical Archaeological Review Nov/Dec 2015 vol 41

Shimon Gibson *The Final days of Jesus* ©2009 Lion Hudson

Harold W. Hoehner *Herod Antipas* 1972 Cambridge University Press

Karl Ritter *The Comparative Geography of Palestine and the Sinaitic Peninsula* Vol 1 1866 digitalised 2006 by Google

Web Sources accessed February 2018 (unless otherwise stated)

The Calendars of the Western World and of the Mainstream Jews Synchronized: M.J. Beattie *Calendars* published at *cgsf.org*